MW00478961

Ralph Cushman

JESSE CHISHOLM

Russell Cushman

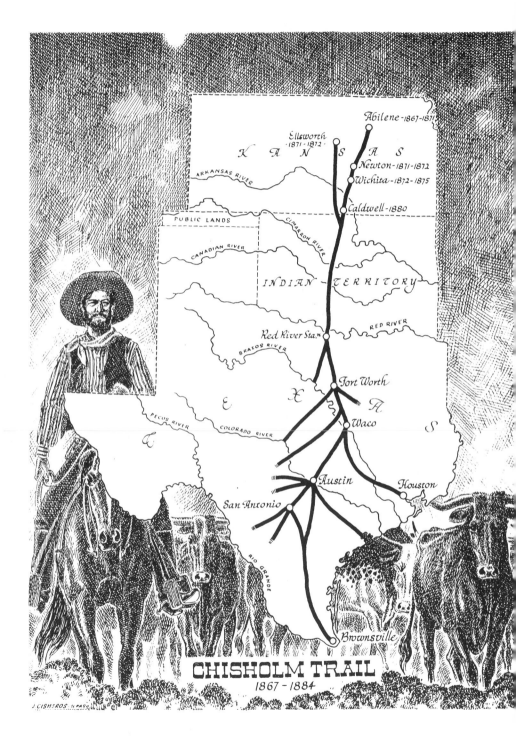

Abilene -1867-1871
Ellsworth -1871-1872-
K A N S A S
ARKANSAS RIVER
Newton-1871-1872
Wichita-1872-1875
Caldwell-1880
PUBLIC LANDS
CIMARRON RIVER
CANADIAN RIVER
INDIAN - TERRITORY
RED RIVER
Red River Sta.
BRAZOS RIVER
Fort Worth
T E X A S
PECOS RIVER
COLORADO RIVER
Waco
Austin
Houston
San Antonio
RIO GRANDE
Brownsville

CHISHOLM TRAIL
1867 - 1884

J. CISNEROS EL PASO

JESSE CHISHOLM

Texas Trail Blazer and
Sam Houston's Trouble-shooter

By Ralph B. Cushman

EAKIN PRESS   ★   Austin, Texas

FIRST EDITION

Copyright © 1992
By Ralph B. Cushman

Published in the United States of America
By Eakin Press
An Imprint of Sunbelt Media, Inc.
P.O. Box 90159, Austin, TX 78709-0159

ISBN 0-89015-826-6

Library of Congress Cataloging-in-Publication Data

Cushman, Ralph B.
    Jesse Chisholm : Texas trail blazer and Sam Houston's trouble-shooter / by Ralph B. Cushman.
        p.   cm.
    Includes bibliographical references and index.
    ISBN 0-89015-826-6 : $22.95
    1. Chisholm, Jesse. 2. Pioneers — Texas — Biography. 3. Frontier and pioneer life — Texas.
4. Texas — History — to 1846. 5. Texas — History — 1846–1950. 6. Houston, Sam, 1793–
1863. 7. Chisholm Trail. I. Title.
F391.C49C87   1991
976.4'0099--dc20
[B]   91-18318
                                                                                    CIP

To the
Milby High
connection:

Bess W. Scott,
my patient mentor;

W. G. (Bill) Roberts, Jr.,
who taught me to
polish the gem;

and

Margaret Spraggins Cushman;

and also to
my wife,
Mildred Cushman,
and son,
Russell Clark Cushman.

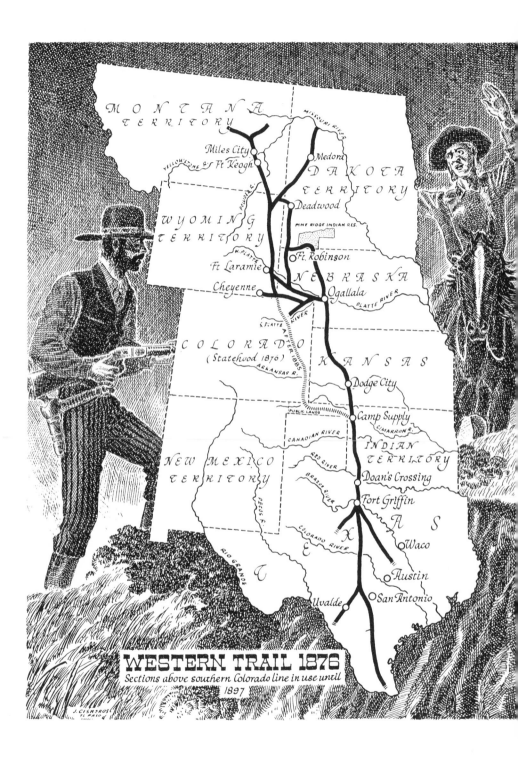

WESTERN TRAIL 1876

Sections above southern Colorado line in use until 1897

J. CISNEROS
EL PASO

Contents

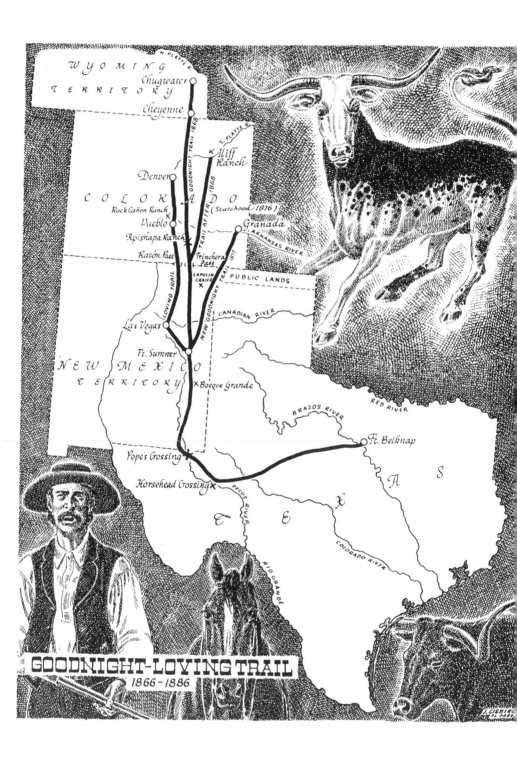

GOODNIGHT-LOVING TRAIL
1866-1886

Preface

At about eight years old I was exposed to Texas' pioneer giants, those legendary men who kindled my boyhood dreams. My maternal grandmother, Virginia (Ginny) Durant McDougald, first introduced me to those earthy characters.

Ginny was an eyewitness to the founding of Alvin, Texas, in the 1870s by her father, Maj. George William Durant, a repatriated Confederate soldier. As a teenager, she spent many hours listening to her maternal grandfather, John Wesley Durant, recount his life during Texas' early years as a republic. John W. had represented Horry County in the 32nd General Assembly of the South Carolina legislature during 1836 and 1837. He also had served a hitch as captain in the South Carolina Militia during the Florida War in 1837.

John W. Durant, a lawyer by profession, arrived in Texas in the spring of 1839 and settled at Washington-on-the-Brazos. There, John W. renewed his acquaintance with Sam Houston and developed a lifelong friendship with him.

The U.S. Census Report of 1850 shows that John W. settled at Centerville and was practicing law in newly formed Leon County, Texas. By 1854 he formed a law partnership with Judge William D. Wood, who also was editor and publisher of the *Leon Pioneer,* the local newspaper.

An outspoken secessionist, John W. was elected senator of the 18th District, comprising Leon, Madison, Robertson, Brazos, and Burleson counties in Texas' Ninth Legislature in 1861. He served under Governor Francis R. Lubbock, who had been elected to that office when Sam Houston was impeached. John W. also served as senator in the Tenth Legislature under Governor Pendleton Murrah through 1864.

My grandmother, Ginny, found her grandfather's third profession more impressive than his political career. He was a circuit-riding Methodist preacher and remained active as a preacher until shortly before his death in 1889 at Alvin, Texas. She said John W. was probably heard by more people than any other man in Central Texas. He exposed his listeners to seven days of hell's fire and brimstone, readily expressing his views on theology, current events, politics, and economics.

John W.'s daughter, Emma Sherrod Durant, married a cousin from North Carolina, George William Durant, in 1865 after the Civil War ended. George surveyed and then settled on the site of what is presently Alvin, Texas, where the Durants' only child, Ginny, was reared.

Ginny remembered her grandfather John W. saying that he occasionally disagreed with his friend Sam Houston. They were estranged for a short time because of their differences about secession. John W. expressed great satisfaction that he and Houston had reconciled before Houston's death in 1863. When Houston died, Durant hurried to Huntsville to offer his support to Houston's widow. He continued this support after Houston's widow moved to Independence, Texas. It was during this period that John W. established a close friendship with Andrew Jackson Houston, the last surviving son of Sam Houston.

I spent the summer of 1935 with my Aunt Mattie and Uncle Henry Jonas at their home in LaPorte, Texas, and there I met Col. Andrew Jackson Houston. He and his two daughters, Margaret and Ariadne (Ari), regularly walked single-file along the shell-topped road fronting the Jonas home en route to and from church services about a quarter of a mile away, near Sylvan Beach. The old gentleman wore a heavy black wool suit even during the torrid July heat. His weather-beaten, black felt hat was pulled down to his eyebrows, except when he carried it, thereby exposing his partially bald head and a few stringy gray hairs. His salt-and-pepper mustache was full and neatly trimmed.

The two Houston daughters, both "old maids," always dressed as if they were going to a costume ball. Margaret and Ari were past fifty years old. Their antique clothes were a sight to behold. Margaret wore a great plumed hat with a snap brim, while Ari let her tightly curled red hair blow unrestrained.

From the time I learned the identity of Colonel Houston, I wanted to meet him. Like most young Texans I was thrilled about Texas' history, and I put steady pressure on Aunt Mattie to introduce me to this vital link with the state's past. The great moment came one July afternoon in 1935. Aunt Mattie had taken me to hear Professor

Brown, a local astronomer, who was exhibiting his latest invention for predicting weather. On that day, two big fans produced most of the weather as we sat with Judge A. Muldoon, the local justice of the peace, in the steamy LaPorte School Auditorium. Colonel Houston came in view. As Judge Muldoon stood up to greet the colonel, I found myself between the two old men. Colonel Houston spoke to Aunt Mattie, and she introduced "my nephew, Ralph Cushman, Jr." I silently marveled at his fragile hand, seemingly void of muscle.

Aunt Mattie did not share my ecstasy for the Houston family. Inhibited by pride and some prejudice, she felt the Houstons were not her peers. She had succumbed to false gossip that Sam Houston had been a traitor to the South. For Mattie Cushman Jonas, daughter of Basic C. Cushman, a repatriated Confederate officer, Houston's alleged breach of loyalty was irreconcilable. But B. C. Cushman, my great-grandfather and retired treasurer of the Southern Pacific Railway, lived in peace and harmony with Colonel Houston, his LaPorte neighbor, for nearly ten years. Aunt Mattie's allegations seemed to lack substance. I recall that Uncle Henry F. Jonas, a nationally renowned design engineer who designed the old Galveston Causeway (still in use), was silent about this misunderstanding, even in his own home. He knew his wife's prejudices and never openly questioned her opinion.

Nevertheless, I presented myself at Colonel Houston's home for a visit the following morning. Margaret announced me. The Houston home was very simple — no frills. The family obviously did not expect company on that day.

When Colonel Houston saw me, his eyes showed the surprise he felt. With obvious reticence but compelling good manners, he welcomed me to sit on his stoop for our first visit. My poor manners eventually drove him to the cooler shade of his living room chair with me on his heels.

During our first visit, I was eagerly trying to gain his confidence. I blurted out, "My great-grandfather, John Wesley Durant, was a friend of your father." To my surprise, Colonel Houston said, "He was also a good friend of mine." He then recalled several yarns about my kin that put me at ease.

Aunt Mattie disapproved, but I continued to visit Colonel Houston almost daily. We often would stroll leisurely along the bayshore as the colonel fielded the torrent of questions I posed. He was past eighty years and did not have much stamina, but he was in good health. Once he began to feel his subject, he became engrossed with the story he was telling. The old gentleman saw my unabashed idolatry for his father, Sam Houston, and therefore carefully nurtured my sentiments. After our third or fourth visit, he began to let me see his father through a son's eyes.

Suddenly, after two weeks of jawing, Colonel Houston abruptly became very reluctant to talk further about his father. About the same time, his tales about J. W. Durant seemed to be exhausted. He was bent on telling me about his personal hero, Jesse Chisholm.

"Jesse who?" I asked. I thought Colonel Houston had tired of my presence and was using some mythical character to get rid of me.

Colonel Houston's first effort to hook my interest in Jesse Chisholm was a failure. Initially, I believed he was trying to "pull my leg." Then I found I had no interest in the fact that Chisholm took food and supplies to his widowed mother at Independence, Texas. It was only after the old gentleman began to bare his soul to me on subjects he seemed to know intimately — public scorn, dire poverty, and social rejection — that I began to understand my host. Through him, I was introduced to the "cold, hard facts of life."

Colonel Houston vividly recalled the hate and spite that a large segment of Texans heaped upon the Houston family as the result of Governor Houston's stand against the secession of Texas from the Union. It had been seventy years since that episode of A. J. Houston's life, but he flinched when he told it. The hurt had not gone away. Sam Houston's tarnished image in Texas did nothing to make young Andrew's life pleasant nor the lives of his brothers and sisters, who also endured the taunts of their schoolmates. "Hadn't Sam Houston been kicked out as governor of Texas and branded a traitor?" they would hear.

The wounds inflicted on the Houston children left pock marks on Andrew's heart. He carried them to his grave. But out of this personal pyre, Andrew J. Houston had found one true, lasting, understanding friend — Jesse Chisholm. The more time I spent with Colonel Houston over the years, the better I knew his friend Jesse Chisholm. In fact, I know Chisholm as few can — through first-hand stories from a loyal friend.

Colonel Houston told of the dire poverty the Houston family suffered after his father's death. He acknowledged that poverty in Texas was fairly general after the Civil War, but he squirmed as he recalled the criticism he received because he was a Houston. Some family members believed they were victims of Sam Houston's poor business sense and were suffering for his sins. Colonel Houston was still groping for answers the last time we talked.

It had been nearly twenty years since Andrew Jackson Houston had settled in the relatively obscure backwaters of Trinity Bay near LaPorte, seeking peace and quiet. Unlike his famous father, Colonel Houston abhorred the limelight. Upon Texas' hundredth anniversary in 1936, he knew his family would be drawn into the centennial celebration, but he didn't look forward to the role he would be asked to play in those ceremonies.

After nearly two decades as neighbors to the Beasley, Bradley, Cushman, Jonas, and other families, he doubted any of them liked him. There had been little communication. Neither faction tried to get to know the other.

Houston told me he had lived his life doubting his own ability. He had received an appointment to West Point followed by a string of state and federal job appointments, but he held deep resentment for his lot in life. He showed me a collection of letters from people he called "vultures, trying to capitalize on the good Houston name."

Even his oil paintings and whittling drew unwarranted attention, according to Houston. He admitted that he had toiled long and diligently on his various literary works, but he said each work had been done with the help of others. He knew other writers received help, but he wondered if the public would forgive him for accepting assistance as he edited his works for publication.

Probably his greatest anguish came from criticism he got from his family for joining the Republican Party. He conceded that being a Republican in predominantly Democratic Texas was indeed to wave the red flag at the bull. With his lack of conformity he drew heavy attention, not all of it favorable, and he opined that "the Republican Party used him too."

All the time Colonel Houston was airing his thoughts I was totally unaware of his motivation for telling me all this "boring stuff." Try as I would to steer him back to yarns about his father or even his friend, Jesse Chisholm, he continued to analyze his own station. As I came to know him better, to know him as a sensitive, shy, honest and intelligent man, I began to understand his oft-repeated phrase, "I've never been seen as anything but 'Old Sam's daft son.' " I argued with him but with no success. He was sure he would die without knowing his own ability or the depth of commitment of his friends.

In 1938 my English teacher, Miss Martha Dobie, read one of my poorly composed but uniquely different themes, and she questioned me about my subject, Jesse Chisholm. Sensing that I had stumbled onto an unexplored crevice of history, she encouraged me to write more of my personal experiences with Colonel Houston and his stories of Jesse Chisholm. Since it didn't require any outside reading, I jumped at her suggestion.

Miss Dobie told me later that her brother, J. Frank Dobie, had expressed a desire to meet my friend Colonel Houston and wondered if I could arrange a meeting during the Christmas holidays. Dobie was an English professor at the University of Texas and had already written several books. I eagerly agreed to set up the meeting.

Using the school's telephone, I tried to place a call to Colonel Houston but learned to my surprise he had no telephone service in his home. This embarrassed me because I sensed Miss Dobie now had some doubts about my ability to produce the meeting. Before she had time to react, I placed a call to Aunt Mattie and asked her to go get Colonel Houston and bring him to her phone. She was less than enthusiastic but finally agreed to try to get him to her phone. To add to Aunt Mattie's anxiety, she had to wait for not only Colonel Houston but both of his daughters, who insisted on accompanying their father to hear him make "phone talk."

The "phone talk" revealed a side of Colonel Houston I'd never seen. He was flustered, maybe even awed, by my telephone call. He couldn't understand why I would need to make an appointment with him, after years of just popping into his living room. I explained I was calling for another man who wanted to meet him. He asked why this man didn't call himself. It was a frustrating conversation that ended with me telling Colonel Houston I would visit him the next Monday morning and would bring Mr. Dobie with me. His response was non-committal and caused me to be qualmish. I worried over what I had gotten myself into by pushing for this meeting.

En route to LaPorte, I discussed with Mr. Dobie the colonel's re-action to my call. The great Texas writer said he would understand if the meeting didn't go well and that we would simply excuse ourselves and leave if Colonel Houston didn't feel comfortable with us. My worries left me when Houston invited us into his home. The meeting was a success from my viewpoint, primarily because Mr. Dobie was relaxed and patient, even though Colonel Houston was still bemused about Dobie's reason for seeking him out. Even my high-pressure efforts to get Colonel Houston to talk did not dampen Dobie's composure. After nearly two hours of mostly grunts and wheezes, Dobie observed casually, "Jesse Chisholm's story should be told to all people."

Like lightning illuminates the night, Dobie's words lighted Houston's eyes and melted his reticence. Four hours later, Dobie reluctantly took his leave. He had a new cache of Chisholm lore.

I knew Dobie was an author as well as a college professor, so it occurred to me that he might write a book about Jesse Chisholm. I asked him if he had given the idea any consideration and assured him that Colonel Houston had many more yarns he didn't have time to tell during our visit. I also told Dobie that Houston had told me about his frustrations with his father and the anguish he suffered as Sam Houston's son.

"Maybe this is your story," Dobie observed. I rejected the idea, but to my discomfort, Dobie persisted. He reasoned that some of the confidence Houston shared with me, his friend, he might not share with any other person. He implored me to write down everything Houston told me and to question him more fully about Jesse Chisholm. Dobie said that I conceivably, in Colonel Houston, had the one living link with Jesse Chisholm, who had then been dead for seventy years.

Ironically, Andrew J. Houston, just a teenager when Chisholm died, was passing the Chisholm legend onto another teenager in the twilight of his own life. He seemed intent to accomplish his mission through me.

In 1939, Dobie introduced me to Dean T. U. Taylor, head of the University of Texas Engineering School. The dean was an authority on Chisholm history and lore. Dobie also introduced me to J. Marvin Hunter, publisher of the *Frontier Times* at Bandera, Texas, and the source of a great archive of Chisholm history. Because of their great admiration for Jesse Chisholm, both Taylor and Hunter treated me with far more courtesy than I deserved, using two days of their time to expose me to their personal files on Jesse Chisholm. Even with such help and encouragement from these three avowed Chisholm boosters, I failed to grasp the impact of what a bonanza I had fallen heir to in the Jesse Chisholm story. My reaction to this good fortune was terrible. I was so little impressed by it all that I did nothing more until I enrolled in the university in 1941, largely through J. Frank Dobie's influence and help, and began studying in the School of Journalism.

World War II interrupted my college career after one semester. During that semester, Professor Dobie had tried again to inspire me to record the Chisholm story. He introduced me to a number of his friends and associates, in each case explaining that I was doing research for a book on Jesse Chisholm. These colleagues included Eugene C. Barker, Roy Bedichek, Walter P. Webb, C. Alton Wiley, DeWitt Reddick, Robert Montgomery, and several others, all of whom were authors who had some interest or information about my quarry, Jesse Chisholm.

Reflecting on the boundless help and opportunities afforded me, I should have been overwhelmed. In truth, I was. I found myself awed by the job I was being encouraged to undertake. I was afraid I would not meet the expectations of these prominent men, and so I did nothing.

At the end of World War II, I resumed my studies at the university. Dobie asked me what progress I had made on the Chisholm story. I sputtered that Colonel Houston was dead and so was Dean Taylor, and therefore I guessed I would be unable to do the book. Dobie glared at me. Then he exploded in an angry spate of biting sarcasm, amply spiced with ribald references to my character or lack of same. In short, he questioned my honor, integrity, loyalty, and every other decent precept by which men are judged. To stem Dobie's ever increasing tirade, I pledged to renew my effort and with his help would get the Chisholm story told. Dobie told me he would be too busy to help much because he was working to get Homer Rainey elected governor of Texas. He asked me to check with him after the election. Rather than excite Professor Dobie further, I avoided him.

But it is with a sense of pride that I did press on with the Chisholm story, if belatedly, and I readily acknowledge the encouragement — if not literal prodding — I got from J. Frank Dobie.

Introduction

Hundreds of ornately festooned Comanches from the Staked Plains raced in a giant circle over the sun-parched Kansas prairie, putting on a fierce, world-famous show for their sworn enemies, the blue-jacketed troops of the United States Cavalry. Under mustard gray clouds their mustangs surrounded smaller circles of wild Comanches, each ring of warriors and horses racing in opposite directions, like a giant kaleidoscope gone mad. It was a performance intended to intimidate.

The elite troops of the U.S. Seventh Cavalry, impeccable in dress blues, were transfixed by a spectacular exhibition of horsemanship seldom witnessed by white men. The mustangs were caparisoned in barbaric trappings surpassed only by the striking attire of their riders. Man and beast seemed blended, like some colorful prehistoric beast. Each tried to outperform the other.

The very nature of this spectacle apparently stimulated superlative individual performances. Pride in their horsemanship pushed the Comanches to awesome feats of derring-do.

Washington Irving, the great American writer, had seen a similarly glorious Comanche performance some thirty-five years earlier. He had written in his *A Tour of the American Prairies* that these fierce Indians were the greatest horsemen in the world.[1] The Comanches, chil-

1

dren of the wind, did nothing on this day in 1867 to tarnish Irving's accolade.

The importance of this event was so great, President Andrew Johnson and Congress, in a rare truce, had stopped feuding long enough to initiate an all-out effort to secure peace with the Indians. Congress appropriated $150,000 for President Johnson to set peace machinery in motion.[2] Now the unprecedented peace feelers were revealing themselves. Optimists believed victory through peace was within the grasp of a war-weary American populace.

The primitive ritual was unfolding on ancient wilderness hunting grounds of hostile Indians. Soon leaders of the enemies, the United States and the Indians, would begin their difficult search for peaceful solutions to complex problems. The council site was Medicine Lodge, long the ancestral home of untamed Kiowa and Cheyenne Indians, deep in unsettled Kansas.

A month earlier, the idea that the United States and defiant "Redmen" could mingle — even hesitantly — would have been hooted down by Congress and army groups wanting to perpetuate their dreams of conquest. Most experts said the hostility was too deep, that it could not be changed. Indians did not want peace; they wanted war. Yet, as so often happens in great moments in history, the experts had been wrong. Here the enemies were face to face and ready to begin peace negotiations.

This impressive prairie pageant would enter history books as the Medicine Lodge Treaty Council.[3] Many men had worked to bring it about. But it was happening primarily because of two grizzled veterans of many treaty sessions, weather-beaten and hardened by the plains, now squatting on the rim of this show unfolding before them. Ten Bears, head chief of the Yamparika Comanches, and Jesse Chisholm,[4] trader, trailblazer, and interpreter of Indian dialects, had brought off the impossible. The magnitude of their deeds defied oddsmakers.

Various accounts estimated between 1,400 and 1,800 United States soldiers were on hand — an unusually large contingent.[5] They were wary as they mingled with 4,000 painted faces. Tension was palpable. The truce was delicate. A single spark could set off a wild fight and indescribable carnage. Heat steamed off the scorched Kiowa ceremonial ground. Peacemakers hoped tempers would remain cooler.

Many attempts to end hostilities had been exhausted before Jesse Chisholm had been virtually commanded by the U.S. government to bring Indians in for peace talks.[6] Jesse was the Indians' final, last best hope. He had been reluctant. Getting the old frontiersman to accept this responsibility was almost as difficult as getting the Indians to listen to new proposals. Jesse insisted on certain ground rules before he finally accepted the assignment. He persuaded Gen. Wm. S. Harney and the commission members to make these concessions.

Unwarranted attacks on Cheyennes in Kansas and Colorado and Comanches in Texas had made all the tribes uneasy.[7] The Kiowas and Comanches were particularly edgy and ready for instant war when large bodies of U.S. troops were around their lands. To convince the Indians of good faith on the part of U.S. negotiators, Jesse told General Harney to bring only such troops necessary for pomp and ceremony. He told him and the commissioners that the Comanches would be suspect of any large buildup of soldiers, and that a large cadre of troops would set off a deadly response. Jesse also requested food and favors for all who attended. And he warned commissioners to be ready to answer some ugly questions. Indians were angry and would ask point-blank why railroads had encroached on their lands and why the white man was slaughtering their buffalo for hides, leaving the Indians' life-sustaining supply of meat to rot on the prairie.

His requests were agreed to by the commission. Jesse's promise that these agreements had been made had induced Indians to come in for a peace parley. They trusted Jesse.

What he spotted on the dusty horizon surprised Jesse and left him frustrated and angry when he first approached Medicine Lodge. He saw a "sea of blue" — the Seventh Cavalry. Hurrying to confront the commission, he was not surprised that the military would renege on promises when it suited their purpose.

Some of the officers that Jesse knew capable of changing the rules while the game was in progress included William T. Sherman, Phil Sheridan, John M. Chivington, William S. Hancock, Kit Carson, Phil Crook, and George Custer. He had watched them do it in the past. They were filled with ill-will for the Indians, and some with justifiable hatred, because Indians regularly killed and maimed soldiers who challenged them. These men heaped abuse on any person, white or red, who proposed leniency for Native Americans.

When they were "in the field," as service in the West was called, Sheridan, Chivington, Custer, and others made law and meted out justice on the spot. Indians answered with swift and deadly action, sometimes in a crazed and depraved manner. Cruel and inhuman acts were common to each side.

Jesse had lived with and worked with both the military and Indians since about 1820.[8] He knew both Indians and soldiers from top to bottom ranks. The soldiers were courageous men, fully convinced of the superiority of their arms over any on earth. They gambled on anything: cock fighting, cards, dice, and races. Horse racing was the most popular. They drank hard, fought recklessly, and played with enthusiastic abandon.[9] These men were contemptuous of Indians and considered them worse than predatory animals. It was not surprising that Indians resented this abuse and retaliated with cruel assaults on hapless frontiersmen and their families. An unmarked grave would be the fate of an Indian killed by U.S. troops — unless the Indian got off the first shot. Then a white scalp would make a necklace for the warrior.

The presence of U.S. troops at Medicine Lodge once again threatened a chance for a peace treaty. Jesse angrily confronted General Harney. He charged breach of faith and demanded that troops be withdrawn or he would tell the Indians to return home to their regular pursuits.

He was not conscious of his effrontery to the general's dignity, but it worked. An embarrassed General Harney tried to explain that the unusually heavy concentration of troops was necessary because so many newsmen, government personnel, foreign dignitaries, writers, artists, and thrill-seekers had been allowed to attend.[10] They needed a large force to control the United States' own mob. The general offered to talk to the commission and withdraw troops if he thought their presence would make the Indians afraid to continue the conference. Jesse showed he was a canny trader.

"Fear" was the word he emphasized when he interpreted General Harney's remarks to Chief Ten Bears and Kiowa Chief Satanta.[11] The fearless old warriors replied as Jesse expected: "Let the troops stay — but out of our way."

Jesse's technique was so graceful that most present looked on it as a minor point, and few appreciated the ease with which he had averted a dangerous crisis. Bloodshed had been spared by his skillful use of the word "fear." The two Indians he confronted didn't acknowledge even the possibility that they could fear any man or beast.

Jesse had ridden more than 1,500 grueling miles tracking down the nomadic Indians in order to try to persuade them to come talk peace. He had found the Yamparika, biggest and most dominant tribe of Comanches, encamped near Wichita Falls, Texas.[12]

Bone-tired and worn out from his trip, when he faced Chief Ten

Bears he was troubled and surly, and in no mood to quibble. He told his courageous friend and ally of forty years that the Indians' free life was over. Ten Bears had to make peace with the white men, he said, or be destroyed. If there was no peace, the Indians would be wiped out. They must coexist or cease to exist.

The straight talk made Ten Bears angry. He went into a fit of rage, boasting that his warriors could kill many whites before they were destroyed. Jesse readily agreed. But after awhile, he bluntly interrupted Ten Bears' tirade to ask if the chief would reconsider. If not, Jesse would go on his way. The threat on Jesse's part to wash his hands of the problem perplexed Ten Bears. After thinking a minute, Ten Bears somberly said he would call a council of his tribe and his neighboring tribes.

The old chief cagily agreed to let Jesse explain to the assembled Indians that their freedom to roam as they pleased had expired. To add to Jesse's task, Ten Bears would let him tell the assembled tribes that they would be bound by new restraints of movement.

The Comanches listened as Jesse spelled out their options. The drama lasted ten days. He watched calmly as Indians vented their rage with violent rhetoric. They seemed determined to resist to the last man. Indian cynics demanded proof of good faith on the white man's part. Old wounds were reopened. It was an angry din.

Then Ten Bears rose with dignity to make his declaration. He would accompany Jesse to the peace council alone if he must. He would go to listen only. It was a face-saving solution.

Chief Ten Bears had given other tribal leaders of Comanches and Kiowas a way to participate if they chose — only to listen. The Comanches agreed to attend under those terms, and in short order the Kiowas agreed to accompany their fighting allies to the conference.

Jesse had wanted to inspire an eagerness for peace in the Indians, but U.S. authorities were elated just to get these elusive savages to listen to peace talk. In 1867, all America grasped at any chance of ending the bloodshed of decades.

Experienced observers saw few signs that Indians at Medicine Lodge would submit. They were flaunting their guns and horses, displaying their power. The Indians had acquired many guns during the Civil War from both the North and South.[13] Each side had hoped to win the Indians' support. Jesse had warned Northern and Southern agents against arming Indians. He predicted these same guns would be turned on the donors.

The exhausting horsemanship performance had served its purpose and proved to be just that — a ceremony, an exercise. The Indians now were ready to relax.

The potentially volatile ceremonial began winding down as Jesse watched. His script was being acted out. Thus far, his plans had succeeded. It was then that a newsman covering the famed treaty council posed a question that has been asked countless times in the hundred-plus years since that day: "Who is Jesse Chisholm?"

He had a mystique which set him apart from every other leader of his era. As a humanitarian, he had no equal. But Jesse Chisholm has remained a mystery man, despite his link with posterity by having the famous "Chisholm Trail" bear his name for all eras.

His life spanned one of the most chaotic and convulsive periods of our history. He was a bigger-than-life figure wherever he moved, though he held no official title. During the latter part of his life, he was the most influential man in the territory. He coped with the giant egos that regularly sought his unique services and he handled any opposition he encountered by using his own type of reason, integrity, and love.

He had either of two armies at his disposal; yet, he always went alone to try to settle disputes. His very presence excited men when he moved in response to some urgent situation. His pacific disposition seemed ludicrous in the angry arena he traversed.

He was part Indian and part white, but his life didn't fit into either race, nor has his history been recorded in either Indian or white lore. He was never a soldier, but he was regularly called upon to lead troops. Nor was he a politician, but he was often asked to lend his special talents to the political spectrum. Both the Indian and the white man curried his favor and friendship, with each claiming him as their own. But he lived apart from both and spent his entire life in the narrow gauge, which in reality was a vast chasm that separated the two races.

Historians have dealt kindly with Jesse's friends and contemporaries — great trailblazers and frontiersmen such as Kit Carson, John C. Fremont, Randolph Marcy, B. L. E. Bonneville, Meriwether Lewis, William Clark, Jim Bowie, and Davy Crockett. But they have forgotten the Great Peacemaker, the man some think greatest of them all: Jesse Chisholm.

Early Life

A Texas sun was scorching the earth, as well as the residents around LaPorte, Texas, on this torrid July day in 1936. A bald, wrinkled, and time-worn man rocked gently, while his audience of one swayed ever so slightly, reacting impulsively to every change in the inflection of his raspy and labored speech.

The old storyteller's voice ebbed and flowed with the patently regular cracking response of his squeaky cane-bottomed rocker. The assembly this humid-hot afternoon consisted of Col. Andrew Jackson Houston, eighty-four-year-old son of Texas' immortal Sam Houston, and myself, Ralph Cushman, at that time a red-headed teenager. While I lolled on the wooden sun deck of Houston's LaPorte home, overlooking Trinity Bay, the old man began another story about his special friend, long since deceased, Jesse Chisholm.

"Old Jesse has been dead for nearly seventy years, so I'm probably among the few people living who knew him personally," Houston began. Slowly, even deliberately, Colonel Houston continued his tale about a man he obviously revered greatly. "This man, more than any man I knew, was brilliant in every way. Even when I knew him as an aging giant, he was an awesome physical specimen. He exerted a messianic influence over friends and acquaintances, never turning down anyone in need of help."

He continued, "I remember Jesse Chisholm best for his seemingly limitless compassion for all humans. He was especially sensitive to the needs of children,

9

particularly those orphaned tots held captive by Indians."

Houston seemed to be searching the sky for counsel as he paused. "Jesse had a big family and was a good provider, even in the most primitive region on the Western hemisphere. He loved his family greatly and would drop any task he was doing to come to their aid when trouble loomed. Jesse was justifiably proud of his family's imprint on the frontier — his grandpa, John Chisholm, in particular."

Chisholm was a name well known to both Indians and United States leaders from the nation's beginning in 1789. The personal accomplishments of Jesse's grandfather, John Chisholm, are well documented during those turbulent years prior to George Washington's first election as president.

Chisholm's Tavern, Knoxville's earliest public meeting place, was headquarters for such leaders on the Tennessee frontier as William Blount, Andrew Jackson, John Sevier, William Cocke, and James Robertson.[1] The tavern was built in 1792 by John Chisholm. As Chisholm's prestige and popularity grew, so did demands on his time. His vivacious wife, Patsy,[2] took over the day-to-day operation of the tavern. She was helped by their three children, Elizabeth, John D., and Ignatius. Patsy's reputation as a good cook made business boom, and her clean and comfortable accommodations were welcomed by travelers in this wilderness settlement.[3]

John Chisholm, soldier of fortune from Drum, Scotland, was red-haired and pugnacious. He had been a justice in Washington County, once a part of North Carolina, as early as 1778. He was politically active in Tennessee from the time it was called the "State of Franklin," later to be separated into a province. He held elective and appointive jobs for twenty years.[4] This educated Scotsman's prestige cast a wide shadow across the territory. His reputation as a leader reached as far as the seat of government of the Thirteen States at Philadelphia.

Chisholm got a chance to measure his power against John Sevier, the most powerful man in the province. Although Chisholm failed, his actions made him a friend of Indians forever — and later proved invaluable to his new country, the United States. A group of Cherokee, Shawnee, and Chickasaw Indian leaders called on John Chisholm to help them stop abuses and wanton killings of Indians by General Sevier's troops. Sevier's reputation as an Indian fighter had grown to legendary proportions since his earlier rescue of young Katie Merrill from the savages. He had married the grateful young woman.[5] Sevier devoted his time and his troops to killing Indians — any and all Indians. Few dared challenge the powerful old warrior.

Chisholm, although Sevier's longtime friend, finally could no longer tolerate the suffering of the friendly Indians. He first wrote Sevier, imploring his help in easing the Indians' burden. Sevier thought the request ridiculous and ignored Chisholm's plea. Rebuffed, Chisholm joined the chiefs of these tribes and made the long journey to Philadelphia to call on President George Washington.[6]

The president gave Chisholm and the Indians courteous attention and said he would do what he could. But President Washington reminded Chisholm that Sevier was beyond his jurisdiction, not to mention his official influence. As an old friend of Sevier's, however, the president promised Chisholm he would try his personal influence on the proud old campaigner, even though Washington felt certain he would have little impact on the doughty Indian fighter.

Washington's efforts, in fact, did not blunt Sevier's onslaught. But from that moment in 1795, John Chisholm's name was irrevocably recognized as an ally of Indians in American history. Ironically, his close relationship with Indians wrecked Chisholm's life. Senator William Blount was impeached on the U.S. Senate floor on charges of trying to incite the Indians to insurrection against the U.S. Aaron Burr faced similar charges in the Senate. Also accused, along with Blount, was John Chisholm and his son Ignatius.[7] The Chisholms stoutly denied charges of collusion with Blount or of any wrongdoing. They were never brought to trial, but the stigma of the charges so angered John Chisholm that he retired into seclusion. Angry and disappointed, he sailed for England in 1797, disappearing forever from history.[8]

Ignatius also smarted from the unwarranted attack on his honor. He moved into a Cherokee settlement near Kingston, Tennessee, in the Southwest. At Kingston, Ignatius met Capt. John Rogers' beautiful daughter Martha and married her in 1803.[9] When Ignatius married Martha, they were social equals, but their financial levels were far apart. Martha was obliged to leave her father's baronial manor for Ignatius Chisholm's crude cabin. John Rogers, Martha's father, was a wealthy Scottish trader and merchant, highly educated and politically active. Rogers had married Jeannie Dew, sister of Cherokee chiefs Tahlonteskee and Oolooteka (who became known as John Jolly), and they had reared a large family.[10]

The union of Ignatius and Martha brought a son, Jesse Chisholm, born in 1805 or possibly 1806.[11] He was one-quarter Cherokee.

The same year Jesse Chisholm was born, his uncle John D. Chisholm made an agreement ceding Cherokee land at Tellico to the United States.[12] President Thomas Jefferson's agent was Return Jonathan Meigs. Daniel Smith and John D. Chisholm represented the Cherokees. It was one more milestone in the systematic confiscation of Indian lands.

Less than three months later, Chisholm was in Washington for a treaty ceding the old Cherokee treaty ground "Great Island" on Holston River to the United States.[13] Chief Doublehead was executed by Cherokee tribal authorities for his part in the "treaty signing." [14]

Thus began a traumatic life for the Cherokees. Purely and simply, all Cherokees were banished from their century-old homelands east of the Mississippi River. Some Cherokees voluntarily began moving to Arkansas Territory as early as 1809.[15] At the time, this event did not suggest the powerful impact it would have on history.

A young Sam Houston ran away from home in 1809 and went into an Indian settlement to hide from his family and friends. That same year many of Houston's new friends would leave for Arkansas.[16] Sam was large for his sixteen years. His physical prowess and friendliness impressed the Indians. He won instant approval. Chief John Jolly, especially, was fond of Houston and adopted the lad as his son.[17]

Houston's older brothers found him in less than a year and took him back to his grieving mother. But before another year had passed, Sam Houston persuaded his mother to let him return to his Indian friends. He stayed with the Cherokees until 1812, when he reluctantly left the "good life" to "pay the fiddler." [18]

Houston learned to think like an Indian while he sojourned with the highly civilized Cherokees. He lived in Chief John Jolly's home, where he developed a life-long friendship with John Rogers, the oldest son of John and Jeannie Rogers who would later become a chief. John's sister Tiana became Houston's second wife. Another of his sisters, Martha, was the mother of Jesse Chisholm,[19] a child of seven when Houston went back to civilization.

Young Jesse Chisholm, like all Indian youths, grew up fast. The only other options for the young in Indian society were illness, crippling injury, or premature death. He played the Indian games deemed necessary to develop a young man's mind and body: stick ball, hoop and pole games, and the green corn dance. This dance embodied the theology and mythology of the Cherokees.[20] Chisholm excelled in every undertaking. His early exposure to the forces of the elements and other ordeals made him mentally alert and as physically tough as the rawhide that covered his powerful body. Although his exterior was tough, his nature was sensitive and he had a feeling of compassion for all mankind.

Jesse was forced to mature rapidly. He was ten when his father moved the family to Spadra Bluff in Johnson County, Arkansas,[21] an area unspoiled by humans. Jesse learned from his father how to survive. After his father went hunting in 1817 and never returned, his uncle John Rogers helped round out his wilderness education.

Young Jesse mastered essential survival techniques as a youth. He learned how varied forage could indicate the nearness of water, in relation to both direction and distance. He studied the movement and behavior of animals, birds, and even insects to find signs of water. He noted that horses, cattle, and deer moved in a line toward water but meandered and grazed after drinking their fill. Some birds such as sparrows and wrens held their beaks open en route to water, but they carried something in their mouths flying back to their nests. Doves and pigeons flew to water holes in large coveys at dusk.[22]

In this most primitive area, young Jesse developed and honed his great "homing instinct" — his God-given talent for knowing where he was heading at all times and under all conditions. His associates over a lifetime marveled at his ability to stay on course during snow storms, dust storms, or pitch black nights.[23] Chisholm's super-sensitive "homing ability" was so renowned that he became a most sought after guide on the frontier.

On the Southwestern frontier, Chisholm's new world, his ability to find water, preferably good drinking water, added to his fame as a guide. His peers said Chisholm moved out when others sought refuge. Some of his "tools" could be learned by others, but his innate skill of homing or trailing was nontransferable. Chisholm's instincts reached farther, and those with him survived.

Stories of Kit Carson, Daniel Boone, Gen. John Fremont, or Jesse Chisholm do not truly convey the gut-wrenching pain caused by alkaline water, the blinding agony of blowing dust, the excruciating torture of freezing sleet on a bare face — all common perils on the frontier. Travelers also faced exhausting heat on unshaded deserts, flies in killing numbers, diseases such as cholera, smallpox, typhoid and "lock jaw," the hazards of snake bites and personal injuries from falls, not to mention Indian attacks or sneak attacks by vagrants infesting the frontier. Even the adventurer who sufficiently insulated himself from these dangers might suddenly find himself fleeing before a hell-like inferno prairie fire, whipped up to seventy miles per hour by the racing wind. These fires made ashes of every living thing in their paths. They sometimes burned on for 300 miles or more; thirty miles was a short race for a prairie fire. The fire consumed the oxygen, and victims were asphyxiated when they sought refuge in caves, creeks, or ditches.

For more than fifty years, Chisholm was able to square with his image — competent, fearless, successful. He had developed his reputation during his fatherless youth in the most untamed wilderness on the North American continent. And despite his rustic roots, he could relate to people in all walks of life. Some became great national heroes — Sam Houston,[24] Gen. Zachary Taylor[25] (later President Taylor), Gen. Christopher "Kit" Carson,[26] Gen. John Fremont,[27] Josiah Gregg,[28] George Catlin,[29] Washington Irving,[30] Jefferson Davis (the future president of Confederate States of America),[31] Col. Randolph B. Marcy,[32] Robert E. Lee,[33] to mention a few.

Jesse's instinct for moving through the wilderness first surfaced in 1817, when he struck out alone for Tennessee to find his kin and old friends in the Cherokee Nation. He arrived in late August. His Rogers cousins greeted him warmly. While Chisholm was "home" he learned that two of his uncles, John D. Chisholm and James Rogers,[34] and eight minor Cherokee chiefs, acting without tribal approval, had ceded another parcel of Indian homeland — more than one million acres — to the United States. The Treaty of July 8, 1817, was helped along by bribes to the Indian signers from Andrew Jackson's personal agents, Gen. David Merriwether and Tennessee governor Joseph McMinn.[35] Cherokees are still indignant about these infamous acts.

Indians who "bartered away their heritage" rationalized their actions. They argued it was better to get something than nothing. They reasoned, probably correctly, that they would lose their land by force if they didn't sell. Other Indian leaders felt they could defend their homes — they had done so in the past. Divided within, overpowered without, Indians ultimately lost their land, their liberty, and for many, their very lives.

Largely through Andrew Jackson's influence, President James Monroe appointed Sam Houston as agent for Cherokees of Tennessee in October 1817.[36] Houston was always loyal and trustworthy in his relations with his Cherokee "brothers," but nevertheless he counseled Chief John Jolly to move his tribe to Arkansas lands designated as its new home. Capt. John Rogers agreed to take his family and slaves and head for Arkansas.

Jesse watched the charismatic giant, Houston, as he wheedled, cajoled, and coaxed Cherokee leaders to voluntarily lead their followers to the territory. Houston did not deceive his friends in promoting his argument for removal. He spelled out their options graphically — and they were not pleasant.[37] The Indians grudgingly admitted their desperation and their limited options. They hoped only to buy time to prepare for an ultimate showdown. Experts later could find no other reason for Indians to succumb in peace.

Chisholm, then twelve years old, never forgot Houston's reasoned oratory during these negotiations. With this model, Chisholm became an equally effective peacemaker during his era, sometimes outstripping his mentor, Houston, in overall effectiveness. He used reason and logic as his principal weapons — never arms.

Along with his lesson in the art of negotiation, Jesse received his ultimate acceptance to manhood in late 1817, when his grandfather, Capt. John Rogers, asked Jesse if he could guide them back to his home in Arkansas. This was no ordinary feat.

The calm, almost indifferent manner in which Jesse accepted his role of leadership gave one the impression he was in his natural element. He led his three-wagon caravan into Knoxville. There they boarded keelboats and rode the Tennessee River to its rendezvous with the mighty Mississippi River at Memphis.[38] After several days on the "Big River," Chisholm abruptly headed west on the roaring Arkansas River. Jesse landed on the south bank at Dardenelle, Arkansas, after an arduous week. His first mission as guide was a complete success.

His return trip took thirty-three days by water and by land. The old Scotsman, Capt. John Rogers, beamed as he told his daughter, Martha Chisholm, about the prowess of her spectacularly gifted son, Jesse.

Serene home life soon made Jesse itch. He felt a great personal loss because of his father's disappearance. In a few weeks he told his mother he must get out again to find his father.

He carried only his basic survival equipment, a knapsack containing his "fire" (steel, flint, and cotton stuffed in a reed tube), a leather thong, a leather jacket, and salt in a leather pouch. With only this equipment and a prized gift from his grandfather, a knife — his reward for leading the family home to Arkansas — Jesse Chisholm was off to search for his father.

His first goal was New Orleans. Along the route he inquired for his father at each sizable borough and settlement. These included Hot Springs and Little Rock (Arkansas), Greenville, Vicksburg, and Natchez (Mississippi) and Francisville, Donaldsonville, and New Orleans (Louisiana).[39] He found no leads. Setting out across Louisiana on foot from the junction of Red River and the mighty Mississippi, he followed the Ouachita River, then Saline River near Crossett, Arkansas, to a site west of Little Rock. There he cut across for home, a wiser young frontiersman but weary and frustrated. He had not found a single clue to his father's fate.

It was early spring in 1818 when he arrived "home," but after only a week's rest, the urge hit him again "to look for Pa." He traveled "where the itch was," crossing the Tennessee River for Nashville, and met up with Chief John Jolly and his party of 300 followers. They were meandering in the general direction of the "territory."

Jesse fell in with Jolly's entourage. It was convenient and the Indians had good food. He quickly realized the Indians were off the beaten path — lost, in fact — and he was needed as guide by Chief Jolly. Jesse was the only one who had scouted the route the Indians were trying to find. No one had made the trip before, save Chisholm. Suddenly, he was furnishing directions, leading the party. He led his friends to Memphis[40] and there asked to be free to continue his search for his father. Reluctantly, Chief Jolly gave him his leave and they parted company. Jesse took the north fork of the trail leading to St. Louis.[41]

In St. Louis, the inland mecca of fur trading, the fourteen-year-old adventurer "heard his call." The misty Creole scent was everywhere. While some dugouts and pirogues still moved over the mighty Mississippi River like a swatch of water bugs, bigger and more seaworthy keelboats now clogged the piers. More than a decade would pass before steamboats took over the duties of these smaller vessels.

This was St. Louis, "Gateway to the Great American Desert." Even the spine-tingling lingo, which he found out was French or some corrupted facsimile thereof, excited young Jesse. The highly expressive modes and expressions of the natives made him feel warmth if not pleasure to be among these exuberant people.

Never in his short life had Jesse seen anything to rival the magnitude of animal hides assembled on the docks of the city founded by the French brothers Chouteau.[42] There were furs of contrast — some small, some large, varying in color and coming from a great variety of animals. Some he had never heard of or seen, but all had one thing in common: an unforgettable scent.

As he watched the volatile Creole traders swap gold coins for bundles of hides, his mind fixed on events taking place before him. If money could be made gathering hides, he felt he was on the road to a fortune in gold. And what was even better, he knew where he could get all the hides he needed.

The same day Jesse arrived, he signed on to help a Creole family unload their hides. For his effort he was given the "worst meal of my life." Jesse thought the spicy food laced with hot peppers was an effort on their part to kill him. After he watched them eat the same fare, he decided they had a taste for roughness. Following the evening meal, the music commenced and the carefree laborers started dancing. When Jesse finally dozed off to sleep, the cock had already ushered in the new day. It seemed like minutes later that his employer roused him for breakfast, the last respite before a long day of moving smelly hides. Jesse admitted he worked in a daze, while the other all-night revelers seemed to be none the worse for wear.

Chisholm developed a genuine affection for these high-spirited, high-living, French-speaking merchants. He did learn to tolerate their food, but not without some bad side effects. The monumental work Jesse performed endeared him to his host.

The few Indians he observed peddled their hides from the floor of their dugouts but did not venture onto the docks. Many seemed wary, even intimidated by the Creole buyers. Physically, these Indians didn't seem to be any different from the Creole people except in dress and language, but there was a gulf between the two. It was during this period of Chisholm's life that he saw the difference first-hand, which was manifested by the utter contempt, bordering on hatred, that whites had toward Indians.

Although Jesse was part Cherokee, he didn't inherit the physical characteristics of his Indian relatives. Jesse had never been more acutely aware of that difference until he watched in stunned disbelief the abuses being heaped upon the Indian traders. Throughout his life he would be spared similar abuses only because he didn't look like an Indian. But this day, on his maiden voyage into St. Louis, he discovered the vast chasm existing between his kin, Indian and white, while he perched perilously between the two adversaries. For this day at least, his reddish-brown hair, which partially shielded his freckled face, would deliver him from the wrath of Indian abusers.

The confrontation he witnessed between Indians and whites on the docks in St. Louis had a profound effect on Chisholm's future behavior. It was at this interval that he opted to travel the narrow-gauge track dividing the two races. Most mixed-blood Indian-whites who tried to straddle this neutral zone in order to co-exist in both worlds found their position untenable.

Even those few linguists, like Chisholm, who spoke English fluently and several different Indian dialects with equal proficiency found that acceptance in either society didn't come easily. Indians didn't trust white men and were equally wary of those of their own who tried to curry favor with whites. On the other hand, whites deemed themselves vastly superior to the "children of nature" and treated them like they were animals from the forest. Jesse rejected both views and set about quietly to breach the barrier of difference which separated his two racial families.

2

Chance

S everal times I tried to get the old man to reminisce about his famous father, Sam Houston, on this cloudy and humid morning. But the colonel
was in no mood for idle conversation. He was intent on getting into one of his
favorite stories about his special friend, Jesse Chisholm.

He started off by saying that just as Jesse had exerted a great and lasting
influence on his own life, so did the man he would tell about today influence
young Jesse Chisholm's thinking and behavior for the rest of his life. Only on
rare occasions did Houston demand my full attention to details. This was one
of those special instances when he had some jewel of lore he felt compelled to
share. He began.

"Chance," patron saint of the Scots, smiled on Jesse in his fif-
teenth year. Back home with his mother after two years of unsuccessful
searches for his father, he rested at his Spadra Bluff home. Here
"chance" loomed bigger than life for Jesse. Martha Chisholm had a
new boarder, an old man, Mathew Lyon.[1]

Lyon was not a household word in the world, but he was a man by
which to measure men. Jesse was instantly drawn to Lyon, and Lyon
saw something special in this young frontiersman.

Lyon had been appointed by his friend President James Monroe to
be agent or factor to Cherokees in Arkansas in 1820.[2] The appointment

came after his retirement and followed an eventful career, now in its twilight. He thus began adding to a storied career which started when he was fifteen years old and was emigrated from Ireland to the U.S. and sold into slavery as an indentured servant.³ He had bought his freedom in six years — in time to fight for his adopted country against the British in 1776.

Jesse listened and questioned the old warrior. Lyon delved into Chisholm's lore about the wilderness and its inhabitants. Each was rewarded for time they spent together, while Lyon was being introduced to his charges, the Cherokees.

Chisholm became so enraptured as he listened to Lyon's story he could think of little else. For starters, Lyon had served as a congressman from Vermont in 1796 and was reelected in 1798 — while he was in prison!⁴

When Congress passed President John Adams' "Alien and Sedition Law," Lyon virtually stood alone in opposition. The bill in effect outlawed freedom of the press, one of America's most sacred freedoms. The nation, instead of becoming indignant, was indifferent.

Mathew Lyon, an immigrant, war weary but freedom loving, heard the clarion call to fight this usurpation of "his" rights. He would fight alone if need be. Initially, he acted because he was piqued with President Adams. But as the issue raged he became obsessed with his cause, and he got the crowds' attention quickly.

Lyon paid for and personally distributed a scathing attack on President Adams,⁵ principal architect of "this vile bill." He told the crowds the bill did away with freedom of the press, guaranteed by the Bill of Rights, which had been added to the national constitution only a few years earlier. For his effort, Congressman Lyon was arrested and jailed without a hearing.⁶

No patriot ever received a ruder trial and conviction. Lyon faced a kangaroo court. He was sentenced before his defense could be mounted, and was jailed under deplorable conditions. It was harsher treatment than a U.S. congressman should expect.

Ethan Allen, leader of the Green Mountain Boys and one of the country's greatest heroes, secured Lyon's release.⁷ Allen helped Lyon win reelection to Congress even as he languished in jail. Lyon's fight against the Alien and Sedition Act was the first of many to protect freedom of the press.

Lyon retired after his second term, in 1800,⁸ to try to recoup his business losses. He moved to Kentucky and was elected to Congress in

1803, where he served as Kentucky's representative for four consecutive terms. Lyon retired again to commence his personal business affairs.

In two years, after moving to Arkansas, Lyon once again was elected to Congress — but the vote count was contested. He was never seated. The old warrior died before the challenge could be resolved. Had Lyon been seated from Arkansas, he would have served in Congress from three different states.

Lyon's personal magnetism was clearly manifested. Like cream, he came to the top wherever he moved. His experience was not lost on young Jesse, his eager listener. Jesse relived the Battle of Ticondaroga with Allen's Green Mountain Boys through Lyon's vivid retelling of his spectacular life story. Chisholm quoted the old warrior throughout his life and tried to emulate Lyon's ideals in his own life.

Lyon commissioned one of Chisholm's earliest trips into the territory west of Arkansas. Lyon needed a guide to lead him to Col. A. P. Chouteau's trading post on Verdigris River, near the future site of Fort Gibson.[9] Chouteau had moved 2,000 Osage Indians, more than half of the tribe, to this site years before to help build his empire.[10]

Chisholm and Lyon were shocked at what they found when they reached Chouteau. He was living like a king, with the Osages his willing subjects. Chouteau had selected an area unsettled by whites. He and his family lived with all luxuries one would find in St. Louis, without the demands of civilization.

Whites were few in the wilderness. There were only three known settlements in Texas, none in Oklahoma, and fewer than 3,000 whites in Arkansas. Chouteau's palatial manor stood out like a mirage on the desert.[11] Jesse busied himself taking in the opulence of Chouteau's empire. He learned later that his visit was more substantive than he could have imagined.

This scion of wealth and power, rooted in St. Louis' Chouteau clan, was the single most powerful influence west of the Mississippi. Auguste Pierre Chouteau, a close friend of Andrew Jackson, was a man worth being allied with in any undertaking.[12]

This first meeting with Chouteau was perfunctory and not earth-shaking, but Jesse made such a profound impression on his host that he was invited back. In years to come, Chisholm valued this man as one of his closest friends, one whose counsel he sought. In turn, Chouteau had found a young ally he could trust to carry his most sensitive messages.

Throughout his life, Jesse heard others go to excesses when describing some of his epic feats where physical strength and stamina were involved. Inevitably, he recalled the herculean efforts of his friend Lyon and delighted in telling about the experiences with Lyon which impressed him. He recalled one episode when Lyon, then about seventy-four years old, asked him, a big, strong lad of sixteen, to get a balky mule on board his keelboat. The two travelers were returning from Fort Smith, Arkansas, where they had obtained supplies, when their boat became snagged as it was being pulled in the shallows by a mule. The mule couldn't or wouldn't push through the heavy underbrush, so Lyon reasoned the mule should be put on board and they would pole the craft past the obstruction.

Jesse failed to budge the mule. The fiery Lyon jumped into the water, grabbed the mule by the halter, and tried to drag him aboard. Failing at this, the old man moved to the other side of the balky beast and proceeded to lift the animal off its feet, and with a mighty sideward movement, he thrust the mule over the deck of his boat. The mule was scrambling wildly, trying to regain his feet, while his adversary was trying desperately to keep him down. Lyon shouted to Jesse to get on board and take charge of the mule. Once Lyon released his hold, the mule jumped to his feet and seemed content to stand on the deck.

After a brief respite, Lyon was back in the water, trying to rock the land-locked boat out of the sand. A steady flow of grunts, sighs, and curses broke the wilderness quiet for fully five minutes. In a heavy, gasping voice the old toiler finally said, "Boy, let's even the fight a little. I can't move the boat, the mule and YOU! Get down here and help me."

On another occasion, Jesse was with his idol, Lyon, when he was campaigning for a seat in Congress. As was the custom in this environment, Lyon was atop the bar of a saloon in Fort Smith delivering a speech. He had already bought drinks for the house, the price candidates paid for the privilege of addressing such an august body of citizens. Two men in his audience posed a question about his age: "How could an old man like you stand the trip to Washington City?" Lyon either didn't hear the question or chose to ignore it, and he continued his speech. In short order, he was interrupted again by his tormentors. This time their rebukes were more ribald than reasoned. He leaped onto his hecklers and proceeded to club them senseless with his pistol. Next, he moved for their unfinished jug of "confined lightning" and said, "You didn't pay for it." The old warrior explained his action had nothing to do with trying to suppress free speech, but was brought on by their breach of promise. "They promised to listen if I bought the drinks," he said.

Jesse recalled that his friend, well on in years during their association, had muscles in his arms that stood out "like a grapevine covers a tree." He also developed a real concern for Lyon's well-being, because the old man seemed to become more bellicose with each new challenge. It wasn't any concern about who stood up to Lyon, but the apprehension that some foe might ambush him. The feisty Irish refugee, who gave so much to a fledgling United States, never quite found a comfortable station to enjoy the fruits of his labor. He remained a rebel to the end.

Chisholm's name first appeared in recorded lore of Arkansas Territory in 1821, in Thomas Nuttall's *A Journal of Travels into the Arkansas Territory*. Nuttall recorded that Chisholm reported "the Cherokees, now forgetting the claims of civilization, fell upon the destroyed 90 persons," referring to Cherokee retaliation to an attack by Osages in which several Cherokee families were killed.[13] Jesse's grandfather John Rogers said Nuttall also wrote about the Cherokee penalty for stealing: "eyes cut out with a knife." [14]

That same year Chisholm first saw Sequoyah's (George Gist) newly published syllabus. When he was a child Jesse had been sent to Sequoyah's home to learn his rote. Sequoyah, the crippled scholar, didn't learn to read or write until 1809, when he was nearly fifty, but he soon was passing his knowledge on to others. Now this legendary figure in Cherokee lore had given every Cherokee child a syllabus to help them break education barriers which bound them in ignorance. The young Indians could master Sequoyah's syllabus in weeks.[15]

For the next twenty years, Chisholm, once Sequoyah's student, was his protector. The old man was given to monumental drunken binges,[16] and this, added to his violent temper, often thrust Sequoyah into "hot water." The Cherokee Nation recognized Chisholm as Sequoyah's close friend and in 1843 commissioned Jesse to go to Mexico' and find Sequoyah.[17] The old Cherokee leader, already a living legend, had disappeared a year earlier, causing his family and friends great concern. (This adventure will be told later in this story.)

The biggest news in Arkansas in 1821 was Texas. Stephen F. Austin had advertised in broadsides and newspapers for 300 families to go with him to settle land granted by the Mexican government in their "Province of Tejas." A rash of prospects hurried to Arkansas, the jumping-off place to Texas. Fort Smith, built in late 1817, was primarily a cluster of log enclosures. It was not well planned or well built.[18]

Now Fort Smith was dealing with a sudden rush of immigrants bound for a chance at land in Texas. The settlement became a scene of unusual and sometimes unpleasant activity, much of it criminal. This pitiful military post was overtaxed with troops who had no uniforms or guns. Sometimes the troops went hungry. President James Madison had ordered the fort built to serve as a buffer zone between Chouteau's savage Osages and the migrating civilized Cherokees in Arkansas.[19] Somewhere in the transfer of power from Madison to President Monroe, Fort Smith was forgotten, lost "in the shuffle."[20]

Jesse, now sixteen, began bringing in a few hides to trade in the tempest that was Fort Smith. Old John Rogers was in the right place at the right time with the right product — whiskey.[21] As the small settlement grew, so did demands for Rogers' whiskey. And so did Rogers' profit. He was selling whiskey for two to three dollars per gallon when the crush started, and the price was quickly hiked to six dollars per gallon.

Once again the enterprising Rogers family prospered. Liquor traffic in the territory was frowned on — some believed it was illegal — but there was no law against Indians making their own whiskey. Charles Rogers, a chip off the old block of John Rogers, remembered the still his father had abandoned in 1817 when they left Tennessee to move to Arkansas. He asked the government to indemnify their loss by replacing the abandoned still. The government paid him his loss, and he started making his own whiskey.[22]

Chisholm watched the whiskey trade and decided the business wasn't worth the trouble. It was not a moralistic decision; he had nothing against whiskey. He even helped the Rogers family run their whiskey for a while. But he abhorred the wild behavior of both white and Indian when they "let their finger ride their thumb too long."

Unscrupulous white traders were blamed for bilking mentally "poor" Indians. Indeed, some of this was going on. But a coin has two sides, and on the other side of the coin Jesse saw Indians plying exactly the same game — whiskey — to outsmart fellow Indians.[23] Chisholm watched the unequal struggle between two different social strata fight for existence in an atmosphere totally new to both factions. It was a case of trying to stop suicide, when white or Indian was bent on self-destruction through whiskey. There was no apparent power in man's hand to alter this desire.

Stealing was a fact of life for some Indians in spite of the heavy penalties if caught.[24] There were no excuses — just punishment. On the other side, white men deplored stealing but thought nothing of using trickery, sham, ruse, and deceit in their dealings, particularly with Indians. Whites felt they were exempt from scrutiny. Let the buyer beware; or, more exactly, let the public be damned.

Chisholm decided he would not use liquor as a vehicle for reaching financial success.

Lessons Jesse learned around Fort Smith in this turbulent era indelibly marked his way of thinking out problems for the remainder of his life. He disavowed intemperate approaches. He measured men with one yard stick, against one set of rules.

Slavery was a way of life in the United States, and Jesse had mixed emotions about it.[25] He saw it when Jim Bowie and his brother Rezin arrived at Fort Smith with a number of slaves for sale.[26] Jim's fame as a fighter and fun-lover was established, and he seemed at ease with his image. As usual, the boisterous Bowie brothers attracted a host of followers bent on action. After the sale, the crowd followed the Bowie brothers to John Rogers' tavern, where serious drinking and gaming was the order of the day.

Jesse had met Jim Bowie in 1818 in Marksville, Louisiana, when he was looking for his father. This brief encounter with the legendary Bowie gave tone to Jesse's report to Sam Houston about Bowie: "If I was in a fight, I would want him on my side!"

His reputation always seemed to precede the swaggering, brawling Bowie. Jesse, as did everyone else, took note of Bowie, but he was not awed. He treated Bowie as he did all others: with a reasonable respect, but no awe. Jesse would be "happening upon" Jim Bowie for the next fifteen years. Chisholm accepted him, without approval, because Bowie's ways were set. He made no effort to revise, repair, or remake this famous man of knife-wielding legend.

By 1821, Mexico, as well as nations north of Mexico, shaped the scene for an inevitable showdown between Mexico and those colonists north of the Nueces River. Spanish rule had been overthrown and a new dictator now ruled Mexico. Antonio López de Santa Anna[27] was running Mexico, working behind the scenes in the beginning.

Augustin Iturbide was named first emperor of Mexico in 1821 largely through efforts of Santa Anna. A year later, Iturbide was overthrown and the country was ruled by a military junta. A special election was called by Santa Anna in March 1823. Santa Anna was elected president without opposition.[28] (Such an election system was still being practiced in the 1990s — one nominee, no opponent.)

Santa Anna, born February 21, 1795, was two years younger than Houston. Santa Anna imagined himself "the Napoleon of the West" and, as he said to Houston after the battle at San Jacinto, "a man born to no common destiny." [29] Affairs and actions in Mexico were so linked with those of Texas and neighboring Arkansas and Oklahoma territories that it was an invisible government.

"Chance" would link Chisholm with Santa Anna. He never imagined he was doing more than running an errand when he first encountered the little Mexican dictator. Jesse's infrequent but significant meetings with this little monarch would make him a vital link of communication between Mexico and the Cherokees, and later for Sam Houston.

Chisholm met Santa Anna first in 1822, when he traveled to Mexico City[30] with Chief Bowles and several other Cherokees to apply for a permanent land grant. It began a long-standing relationship with Santa Anna that became widely known. The link was of significant help to Stephen F. Austin when he, too, called on Santa Anna seeking a land grant. Jesse not only advised Austin about the best travel route through hostile Indian country to Mexico City, but gave Austin his impressions from face-to-face talks with the proud dictator.

Andrew Jackson was elected to the United States Senate from Tennessee in 1823. His protegé, Sam Houston, was elected to Congress — without opposition.[31] Other news revealed the death of R. J. Meigs,[32] longtime agent for Cherokees in the East. William Carroll was governor of Tennessee,[33] so the state seemed safely in Jackson's control. This was bad news for all Indians, especially in Tennessee and Georgia.

Hot quests for power were erupting on all sides. The continent's temper was reflected in the mood of its leaders. Chisholm the Peacemaker was as popular as a wet blanket in a blizzard. He sensed this lust for blood and exiled himself with Indians settling at "Three Forks," near Chouteau's empire.

Chouteau selected one of his lackeys among the Osages, Big Track, to be head chief[34] of the 2,000 Osages he had persuaded to leave Spanish territory and set up their own domain under his authority. The Chouteau operation was unique in its influence on the frontier.

Under Chouteau's direction, the Osages were docile and friendly. But left to their own leadership they were as vicious and as feared as any tribe on the frontier. They were especially feared by other Indians. The Osage people were loners. They seldom were asked or expected to attend peace parleys. They roused great passion in others with their "Chouteau air" and unpredictable behavior. There could be no common rallying of all tribes because Indians did not trust the Osage tribe. Chisholm had no difficulty moving freely among the Osage, but he never understood their position. Nor did they understand his.

Jesse was working for Chouteau in 1823,[35] placing and running traps for hides and bargaining with Plains Indians for buffalo robes. He was learning the trading business from one of the most successful merchants on the frontier, and he earned Chouteau's respect in the process.

It now seemed to Jesse that this great crush of men, red and white, was threatening his longing for serenity. No sooner had he settled in his fur trading business with Chouteau than Col. Matthew Arbuckle arrived from Fort Smith to establish a frontier military post at Three Forks. A new post under Arbuckle's command was completed in April 1824. It was called Cantonment Gibson and consisted of five companies of the U.S. 7th Infantry.[36]

Fort Gibson was a bustling area of the Indian Territory, located at the head of navigation of the Arkansas River. The post was "situated only a short distance southeast of the Creek and Osage agencies, which together with its own military activities, made it the center of much of the official and social life in the Indian country in the early days." [37]

The rush was on. A month after Cantonment Gibson was opened, a smaller fortification was established to the south, on Texas Road near its junction with Red River.[38] It was called Fort Towson. Completion of these two forts caused a mass exodus from Fort Smith of merchants and other interests who had been relying on troops for their existence. Fort Smith became a virtual ghost town with little activity to sustain diehards who chose to stay.

Jesse now lived with the Cherokees under the rule of Chief Jolly. The atmosphere had become so violent that there was only small safety even with large numbers, and almost no safety for persons who traveled alone or in small parties. The services of a peacemaker like Chisholm were not needed by the violent majority of men who dominated the territory. Jesse watched the ugly confrontations between soldiers and Indians, soldiers and white settlers, and Indians and white settlers. Life was a scene of constant dispute.

The sign of the times was there for all to see. A sixty-ton, steam-driven sidewheeler, *Florence,* traversed the erratic Arkansas River from Fort Smith to Fort Gibson carrying Colonel Arbuckle and 100 members of his new command.[39] This was an auspicious event. It meant the new fort would be amply supplied and reinforced by a major water carrier.

On another front far away, Andrew Jackson suffered his first major defeat when John Quincy Adams beat him in his bid for the presidency in 1824.[40] This setback gave those who hated Jackson a four-year reprieve before he would be back again.

In Texas, Stephen Austin endeavored to get his colony settled in spite of unstable reactions from his Mexican rulers. One day he was told to proceed, but the next day he was told to wait a few days. Austin's patience merited recognition. By 1825, he had the "go" signal for 500[41] additional families to supplement his original 300; by 1828, he had settled 1,200 families in the Mexican province.[42] At the same time, the Mexican government gave DeWitt Green permission to settle 400 families next to Austin's Colony.[43]

If the frontier didn't have enough problems already, colonization of Texas set off a violent chain reaction. The impact was felt all over the world, with France, Spain, and England most affected.

Colonists drew their own boundary lines. These vaguely defined lines often overlapped land claimed by their neighbors. Sometimes disputes arose because ownership could not be established in the confusion over which was valid, the Mexican or Spanish title,[44] and violent fights erupted.

Indians still claimed Texas as their own homeland. They had lived on the land long before there were Mexicans or before Columbus "discovered" the New World for Queen Isabella. Their persistence produced more troubles for authorities. Comanche, Kiowa, Delaware, Caddo, Apache, Tonkawa, Chickasaw, and other tribes had never been conquered and did not intend to cede their land to Mexico or anyone else without a fight.

With all of these factors combined, a minor spark could set off a conflagration in the territory. As it happened, the spark came from a different source — squatters, unauthorized and ungoverned. The squatters provoked Mexico, rankled Texas authorities, and interfered with the well-organized colonists. Indians' rights and their land were trespassed regularly by the uncontrolled squatters. War was raging out of control by the time Jesse became a major communication link on the Texas Plains.

Chisholm, not wanting to participate in war, studied his options. Capt. B. L. E. Bonneville, a new friend, furnished one solution. Bonneville left Fort Gibson in May 1825 to escort the respected Marquis de Lafayette home to France.[45] It was a signal honor for the ambitious Bonneville. He enjoyed the assignment so much, it took him a year and a half to get back to his base at Fort Gibson. This long absence did not enhance his standing with Colonel Arbuckle, his commander, nor the troops at this frontier compound.

Events were popping, especially in the Creek Nation in Georgia. A group of Creek chiefs headed by William McIntosh ceded large tracts of Creek land at Indian Springs, Georgia, to the United States.[46] Not all Creeks went along with this deal.

Opothleyohola, chief of Upper Creeks, flatly repudiated the transaction by the Lower Creeks and took off for Washington. He met with Secretary of War James Barbour to plead his case.[47] He was an able and reasonable negotiator. Secretary Barbour had the "McIntosh treaty" abrogated and made a new one with Opothleyohola. The new treaty in substance gave up the Creeks' claim to Georgia land but allowed them to stay in Alabama. It was a victory in principle more than in substance, but it did enhance Opothleyohola's immaculate record for integrity.

When Opothleyohola arrived at his home in the territory, Jesse attached himself to this great old statesman of the Creeks. He remained his close associate for the remainder of his life. Two Indians of this era stand out head and shoulders above all others: John Ross, venerable and indomitable Cherokee chief, and Opothleyohola, the Creek chief. The wisdom and devotion of these two leaders saved their tribes from total obliteration and earned the respect of freedom-loving frontiersmen.

Jesse, by now, had married a Cherokee woman, but in short time the couple chose to "split their blanket."[48] Chisholm, like Sam Houston in a similar situation, never discussed this misadventure which resulted in divorce.

He was now twenty-one, a man. His experience over those twenty-one years was greater than most men get in a lifetime. His destiny seemed apparent to those who knew him: He would be the peacemaker, a man around whom all men could rally with confidence. This friendly giant, more ponderous than pretty, moved with ease and freedom in the white man's world and could instantly move into the Indians' world "assuming their customs, mannerisms and tongue so naturally that he became one of them." [49] Jesse began to exert his compelling charisma and native ability. [50] His fame as a trailblazer as well as an envoy to Plains Indians put him in a position of respect, far sooner than a younger man could expect.

In a distant arena, Indians were making new moves. The Cherokee Nation, in session at its capital, New Echota, Georgia, in July 1827 approved a significant new constitution patterned after the U.S. Constitution. This singular act, if nothing else, established these intellectual Cherokees as prime allies with their North American neighbors.

Two years prior to this move, Cherokee legislators passed a law declaring brass, copper, lead, gold, and silver found in the Cherokee Nation to be public property of the nation. One of the metals cited, in particular, raised eyebrows: gold.

The facade was now public. The main reason Indian lands were to be confiscated was to satisfy man's lust for gold. Two years earlier, in October 1823, the United States had tried to sneak up on the Cherokees' blind side by sending Creek Chief William McIntosh with a $12,000 bribe[51] to John Ross, Charles Hicks, and Alexander McCoy in exchange for Cherokee land cessions to the U.S. The three angrily rejected McIntosh's overture.

At every gathering of civilized Indians, discussions of their troubles always surfaced. Jesse listened intently as Rogers, Jolly, Sequoyah, Brown, and other Cherokee leaders lamented internal decay that was weakening the Indians' position. They regularly discussed the need to unite all Indians into one body to keep from being overrun by white poachers. Each agreed their only hope was unity.

Trouble was, Indians could never agree among themselves, nor could they get unification under way. Sequoyah maintained that the best course was to unite by agreement and then argue — just like white men did. [52] His wisdom was great, but his ability to sell his idea failed. With this failure went the hope of Indian unity. It would have been an amazing achievement if they could only get along with other Indians in the immediate surroundings.

Jesse kept quiet and listened as these Indian chiefs talked. One time, his opinion was asked. He told his elders they would draw more flies with honey than with salt. "First draw them in. Then salt them," he said.

He reminded his civilized brothers that almost every time they were attacked by their wild brothers, the civilized Indians reverted to old ways: they stripped their bodies, applied war paint, and met the wild redmen as wild redmen themselves. Jesse was right, but this taunt usually caused the meeting to erupt in angry words, not so much at him but at their seemingly insurmountable problems.

Early in 1826, Cherokee chiefs from the Texas group, Bowles, Hunter and Fields,[53] had met with chiefs in the territory to seek land from Mexico on which they could build an Indian empire. They came to no agreement, so the Texas group left to call on Santa Anna in Mexico City.[54] Chisholm went along.

Colonel Chouteau had recently entertained a group of Indians interested in forming an all-inclusive body of Indians under his rule.[55] The idea was "talked to death," Chisholm said, "and we went our own ways." This meeting was recalled in 1865 by William Bent and Jesse during a "jawing" break at a treaty session on Little Arkansas River. General Harney, Kit Carson, and others sat around a campfire and listened as old-timers Bent and Chisholm spun tales and told of the parley in 1826 at Chouteau's trading post.[56] All present agreed that Indians were always vulnerable due to their inability to unite into one formidable force.

A flood on the Arkansas River in 1826 wiped out encampments along its banks.[57] Hardest hit financially was Chouteau's trading post. Water came into Fort Gibson and did little damage, but south of the fort there was great damage and a heavy toll of lives. Jesse's hides and corn stored with Chouteau — everything he owned — washed away. Years later he laughingly remembered his first major disaster, comparing his own loss with Chouteau's. "We were both swept clean," he said, "but Chouteau salvaged his 'letter of credit.' "

Jesse borrowed his Uncle John Rogers' Pittsburg wagon, loaded it with a salt consignment, and set out to repair his damaged finances.[58] He followed the north bank of the Arkansas River, trading with Creeks and Cherokees along the way. He was a shrewd trader and made more than $200 profit on this trip.[59] Now he was set for bigger ventures with the money. He spent almost half of it for corn, which he doled out to associates to be planted "on halves." From his corn-growing venture he made nearly $400 profit for his half of the operation.

Jesse was beginning to show his head for business. He was breaking new ground for his business ventures, bartering horses and cows. But cows were too plentiful to be profitable at that point in time. Those same wild cows which roamed the Southwest, we know now, were destined to alter the way of life in this area some thirty years later.

3

Indian Woes

A *swarm of bees made its presence known by a steady, electric-sounding drone. Colonel Houston's probing stare acknowledged the noisy horde, as his voice trailed off. His old black hat was pulled down nearly over his eyes. Then he took up just where he was interrupted.*

"As you know, I was named for President Andrew Jackson." He paused while I tried to assimilate this statement and guess who President Jackson was. Sensing my bewilderment, Andrew Jackson's namesake beckoned me into the living room and pointed to a large framed likeness of a man, who was obviously important enough to share wall space in the same room with his mother and father.

"There's President Jackson," he said. With the formal introduction to President Jackson behind us, we returned to the porch, and Col. Andrew Jackson Houston commenced establishing President Jackson's role in the upcoming story.

Bored by the routine of big-city life, reckless thrill-seekers headed for America's unsullied frontier. The turbulent Indian wars and occasional skirmishes with diehard British troops from 1812 to 1820 were followed by a decade of tranquility. Those ten years, 1820 to 1830, were almost idyllic by comparison with previous decades.

Immigrants began pouring into New York from Europe.[1] They

34

were looking for arable land and took any means to get to the free country west of the Mississippi, especially to romantic Texas.[2]

All pretense of dealing fairly with Indians ended when Andrew Jackson was elected to the presidency in 1828.[3] Sam Houston, a protector of Indian rights, was governor of Tennessee,[4] but his power was limited to the boundaries of that state and his tenure there was short-lived. On the other side of the state line, Georgia Governor John Forsyth hated Indians.[5] His election, brought off by dedicated "crackers," gave him a mandate for complete expulsion of Georgia Indian tribes.

President Jackson, the South's "Robin Hood in Buckskin," relentlessly pursued a national policy which created havoc out of prosperity. Jackson used the naked power of the presidency with an ease that made him the mòst feared man ever to occupy the nation's highest office. His lasting contribution to the country's political system was his perfection of the "spoils system." [6]

The Jackson spoils system bode evil for all Indians. At first that system meant "to the victor belongs the spoils," but there were not enough spoils to satisfy the greed of Jackson's followers. So he created enough spoils to go around. During every presidential administration except George Washington's, the United States had systematically acquired Indian lands under the guise of making new treaties.[7]

Serious doubts arose about Jackson's integrity, particularly in Cherokee circles, highlighted by his relations with his former friends and allies. The friendly and intelligent Cherokees had readily answered Jackson's summons when he was in desperate need of help. As a youth, Jesse Chisholm recalled his family discussing this conflict and the heroic role of his kinsmen.

Seven hundred Cherokee warriors, led by Lt. Sam Houston, had spearheaded Jackson's assault on Creek Indians at Horseshoe Bend less than fifteen years earlier.[8] Eighteen Cherokees died and thirty-six were seriously wounded. Houston received wounds which still drained nearly fifty years later on his deathbed.

Jesse had known Jackson as long as he could remember. He was impressed by the tall, ribald frontier-soldier who had regularly visited his Grandfather Chisholm's tavern at Knoxville. Young Jesse recalled the hero adulation most Tennesseans felt for Jackson after his spectacular victories at Horseshoe Bend, Alabama, and later against the British at New Orleans. First news of Jackson's betrayal of the Cherokees was too incredible for young Jesse to comprehend.

It was his surprising victory over the Creeks at Horseshoe Bend that catapulted Jackson to national attention. Without the Cherokees, Jackson probably would have lost the battle. His white soldiers, including himself, were physically depleted from dysentery.

Hopes for victory were slim until Cherokee warriors,[9] including Sequoyah, Boudinot, and John Ross,[10] and other prominent tribal leaders came to his aid. Ross was elected head of the Cherokee Nation a month before Jackson became president, and these two former comrades in arms were soon locked in deadly conflict.

Jesse watched in amazement at what appeared to be the complete metamorphosis of Andrew Jackson, a man he had trusted and respected. He couldn't account for the change in his former idol. Some former friends reasoned Jackson was "bitten by the greed bug."

Discovery of gold in Georgia in 1828[11] was a death knell for the Cherokees' hopes of keeping their land. Georgia's legislature quickly confiscated all Indian-held land. The U.S. Supreme Court, under a respected and honorable chief justice, John Marshall, ruled the Georgia act unconstitutional.[12] Jackson replied, "Let him [Marshall] enforce it [his ruling]."[13]

Houston remained sympathetic to the cause of his Cherokee friends. His stand created many enemies among Jackson's henchmen, including ex-Governor William Carroll. Carroll announced he would oppose Houston's election to a second term as governor in 1829.[14]

Houston opted not to seek reelection after his marriage with Eliza Allen failed. He resigned as governor and left Tennessee under a cloud of rumors just before the election was held.[15] Houston's move was a grave blow to Indian hopes. With Houston gone, along with his power base, there was no effective challenge to the rush for total Indian removal from the precious gold lands. Their expulsion was mandated.

Jesse in many ways respected President Jackson, his fellow Tennessean, but he was not prepared for the barbaric treatment his family and friends in the Cherokee nation would receive. His protest to Jackson was drowned by "Old Hickory's" cheering followers, who stood to reap the most from Indian removal, already under way.

U.S. Army forces herded Creek Indians like cattle into the remote wilderness near Fort Gibson in Indian Territory. In 1828, 780 Creeks were transported by a steamship towing a keelboat to Fort Gibson.[16] They occupied the trading post sold to the U.S. a year earlier by Col. A. P. Chouteau, who relocated further west on Grand Saline River.[17]

A calm that had settled on the territory was now shattered by the influx of unhappy, sick, and hungry Indians. There was no advance preparation; indeed, it would have been impossible to accommodate this sudden mass exodus of more than 100,000 human beings.[18]

This ruthless scene would be repeated regularly for the next eight years, until all Indians were uprooted and moved. Those who resisted were killed. In light of history, the government's handling of Indian removal ranks infamously with the Bataan "Death March" that American servicemen were subjected to in World War II.

As Jesse watched these events unfold, he quietly resolved to help Indians all he could. But at the same time he felt he could be more effective if he maintained a friendly rapport with their enforcers. He could be of significant service if he remained alive, which he would not be if he opposed the various governmental agencies carrying out the Indian removal edicts. Feeding as many hungry Indians as he could was Jesse's response to the challenge he confronted.

A group of Cherokees made the scene at New Echota, Georgia, site of the Cherokee capital, more difficult to comprehend by starting their own newspaper in 1828.[19] It was a singular achievement, requiring will and resources. Elias Boudinot established the best and in some instances the only recorded history of events occurring in the Cherokee eastern capital. The *Phoenix* (the name chosen for the newspaper) allowed Cherokees to stay abreast of current news, in both Sequoyah's Cherokee language and in English.[20]

Refugee Indians weren't the only new arrivals in the territory. Jesse, Chief Jolly, and the Rogers family greeted Sam Houston when the steamboat *Facility* arrived at Webber's Falls[21] near Fort Gibson in May 1829. Houston had attracted a crowd wherever he went most of his life, and this visit was no exception.

Word of Houston's troubles in Tennessee preceded his arrival, but the Cherokees wondered what had brought Houston to one of the Western Hemisphere's most remote outposts.[22] Jesse had heard the story being bandied around among troops at Fort Gibson that Houston had boasted of forming his own nation in Texas and planned to use Indian soldiers to oust Mexico.[23]

Houston came down the gangplank wobbling and unsteady. He seemed weary and dissipated, but his spirits rallied as he joined a festive torchlight party. It was soon obvious that Houston was stone drunk, sodden — but not as a result of the celebrations. He seemed to be trying to drown himself in whiskey. His monumental binge had begun weeks before.

The Cherokees' moving and tender welcome to "Coloneh," their adopted brother, left a lasting impression on Jesse, who was part of the welcoming party. Years later, he told Houston he had never seen any white man before or since paid such respect as he had by these Cherokees who welcomed him "home" in 1829.[24] Ironically, Winfield Scott,[25] the blimp-sized commanding general of U.S. forces, landed on the same spot some two months earlier. Despite his title and size, General Scott hardly made a ripple in Fort Gibson's routine business.

Houston regained some sobriety that year and made himself available to lead a group of Cherokees on a peace mission to Washington.[26] He would personally plead the Cherokees' case to the "Great White Father" (President Jackson).

Jesse took care of Houston's trading post during his absence, from December 1829 until his return in April 1830. Houston found his business booming when he returned to take over management of his trading post.

Wigwam Neosho, a modest wooden structure, attracted visitors like a funeral parlor. Houston had a number of business associates, but in his absence, Jesse handled the day-to-day operation of the trading post. Two associates, Peter Harper and Benjamin Hawkins, were generally present but did little other than visit with guests.

Years later, Jesse recalled the Wigwam Neosho connection in Texas. Besides Houston's associates, many of his guests followed him to Texas. Both Harper, who was with Houston at the battle at San Jacinto, and Hawkins, the Creek part-breed who helped Houston with Indian relations, were important allies in Texas.

Dr. John W. Baylor, a regular visitor at Houston's trading post, sent three of his sons, John, Henry, and George, to Texas. Col. Hugh Love, a former competitor and foe of Houston, had his own trading post at Three Forks but was recruited at Neosho and ended up on Houston's Texas team.

Houston's presence in Washington immediately drew a horde of curious people looking for excitement. Predictably, he didn't let them down. Houston attacked Indian Affairs leaders, citing them for "gross ineptness," and he specifically accused Sergeant Hamtramack of stealing from the Osage Indians he had been assigned to protect.[27]

This was strong medicine, to use an Indian term. But Houston had proof, furnished by Col. A. P. Chouteau, and he had the ear of a man who could and would respond to his accusations — President Jackson. The president turned the matter over to Secretary of War John Eaton for prompt action.[28]

The territory got more national attention from the charismatic Houston's visit to Washington than from any subsequent Indian apostle. He created excitement everywhere he moved in Washington circles while clad in his colorful frontier dress.

Attracted by the excitement, visitors hurried to see the wild frontier outpost. In 1832 Washington Irving and his guests, Charles Joseph Latrobe of London and Count Albert de Portales of Geneva, were Houston's guests. Colonel Chouteau also hosted this important group before it joined Capt. Jesse Bean for a twelve-day ride into "real" Indian territory.[29]

Upon his return to the territory, Houston married Tiana Rogers Gentry, Jesse's aunt, in May 1830. That summer Houston set his wife up as manager of Neosho, a log building south of Fort Gibson on the Texas Road.[30] He had other logs to roll and fish to fry.

The first reference to Jesse in U.S. Army records showed up in this same time frame. "In 1830, when bids for supplying corn to the garrison were made, the low bidder was Cherokee Jesse Chisholm, who offered to supply it at 27 cents per bushel," according to records at Fort Gibson.[31] Jesse, in addition to his other activities, continued to work for Houston at the Neosho trading post.

No record is available of Houston's financial success during this period, but there was regular traffic to his modest trading post. Army officers, government agents, Indian chiefs of many tribes, and visitors to the territory kept a path well worn to Houston's place.[32] Jesse met and came to know many of the prominent callers at Houston's Neosho.

The territory was shocked and saddened when news filtered down with the report of President Jackson's latest Cherokee land grab. Congress had passed an Indian removal bill in May 1830,[33] only six weeks after Houston's personal plea to Jackson on behalf of the Cherokees. He had asked for the government's compassion and patience in dealings with his adopted Cherokee family. Jackson's agents bribed some minor chiefs to sign over Cherokee land in Georgia, Tennessee, and North Carolina. This new "treaty" agreement was hastily acted upon by Congress in its plan to speed removal of all Indians from those states.[34]

Jesse watched Houston, the master politician, as he encouraged and advised his Cherokee friends, while at the same time artfully dodged efforts to link him with anti-Jackson factions. Jesse adopted a similar posture in his relations with both white and Indian friends. That Houston had Jesse's mutual respect and rapport is history, so it was natural that Jesse would follow Houston's example. Later, after

Houston reached Texas, he often called on Jesse to act as his personal emissary, sometimes covertly.[35] Just as Jackson used Chouteau as his personal contact and advisor on Indian affairs, so likewise did Houston use Jesse.

The full weight of Jacksonian power was now being felt throughout all Indian nations. In 1831 the Supreme Court ruled that Cherokees were a "domestic dependent Nation" [36] and therefore were not allowed to initiate any court action. In November of that year, the Arkansas legislature passed a despicable bill that forbade any person with as little as one-quarter Indian blood to file either criminal or civil suits against a white man.[37] Jesse, who was one-quarter Cherokee, fell into this suppressed category.

Nearly 20,000 immigrants had poured into Texas, the Indians' last remaining haven. Now anti-Indian sentiment was deeply entrenched and was spreading faster than a wild prairie fire.

In less than a year, Houston left the territory again for Washington on Indian business, leaving his new wife Tiana and Jesse to run his trading post.[38] Before Houston left, Jesse had seen his Uncle Sam attack his friend and benefactor, Chief John Jolly — and live to talk about it.[39]

At the time it occurred, Jesse reasoned that Houston probably didn't understand the Indians' thought processes as fully as he believed. Upon applying for and being accepted as a citizen of the Cherokee Nation, Houston had promptly offered himself a candidate for their national council. He was soundly defeated. Jesse attributed his defeat to excessive drink and poor timing. Houston had moved too quickly in the simple Indian culture. In his hurt and anger, Houston sought refuge in the whiskey barrel. Then, in a drunken tirade, he accused his foster father and great benefactor, Chief Jolly, of betraying him.

Chief Jolly tried to placate Houston's hurt but was struck by his foster son. A wild melee followed. Houston's drunken condition and his high standing with Chief Jolly were factors that caused his life to be spared. In all probability, another man would have been destroyed.

As a redemptive measure to his sagging fortunes, Houston took off again on Cherokee business. Now news came that Houston had been arrested for attacking Congressman William Stanbery on Pennsylvania Avenue in Washington.[40] This distressing news about Houston caused the Cherokees much concern. Jesse joined other Cherokees who were openly musing the possibility that Houston's thirst for hard whiskey would destroy a man who seemed invincible to his other enemies. As it turned out, whiskey was not Houston's problem in this incident.

Some of Houston's associates expressed concern for his welfare in Washington. His friends apparently had forgotten about President Jackson's power and his love for Houston. It took several months, but the president's friends finally got Houston released with a token fine, which Jackson probated.[41] It was a perfunctory "wrist slap" for his mischief.

During Houston's absence, Jesse was asked by Colonel Arbuckle to guide a group of explorers to the Wichita Mountain range in search of gold.[42] Jesse thought the trip absurd and tried mightily to get out of the assignment, but the colonel turned down his pleas. After six weeks of cold, hunger, and most debilitating circumstances, Jesse returned with a sad but wiser party of gold-seekers — sans gold. Aunt "Diane" (Tiana Houston) welcomed his return and his help in running Neosho.

Tranquility in the Indian Territory was sorely affected by events transpiring in Washington, Tennessee, Georgia, and Texas. Even foreign powers such as Mexico, France, and England recognized the stress brought to the Southwest by the United States' mass removal of Indians.

While in Washington in 1832, Houston had agreed to host Washington Irving and other internationally famous authors and artists on a tour into Texas' Indian home grounds. President Jackson conveniently substituted his friend A. P. Chouteau as his proxy host for this notable delegation while Houston was under house arrest in Washington. Colonel Chouteau was in Washington to testify as a character witness for Houston as a favor to President Jackson when he learned of his appointment as host for Washington Irving's visit. Colonel Arbuckle, commandant at Fort Gibson, was also summoned by President Jackson and arrived at Washington City in February 1832 to learn first-hand of Houston's difficulties.[43]

Arbuckle learned from Jackson the role he would play in Irving's tour of the plains.[44] Houston had recommended Jesse to act as guide, so in July, Arbuckle advised Jesse of his newest assignment. All he could get from Chisholm was a promise to escort the party as far as Chouteau's new post on Verdigris River. Jesse had already been hired by Robert Bean to help him lay out a road bed to Fort Towson, a top government priority.[45]

Houston returned home on October 8, one day before Washington Irving arrived. He was in time to accompany Colonel Arbuckle and Irving's party to Chouteau's place. Jesse went to Chouteau's with Hous-

ton then joined Captain Bean's survey party en route to Fort Towson.
Houston met Jesse when their paths crossed on Texas Road in early November, and Jesse learned of his plans to go to Texas. Houston invited Jesse to accompany him, but he declined due to marital problems. Houston understood: He had just "split the blanket" with Tiana, his second wife.[46] The two parted company at Fort Towson, the last outpost on Texas Road before crossing the Red River into Mexican territory and Texas.[47]

In the final analysis, Houston's visits with Jackson did little to alleviate tension which was mounting rapidly around Fort Gibson. The unceremonious uprooting of Cherokees in Georgia and Tennessee, then the dumping of them among peaceful Cherokees who had moved into the territory two decades earlier, caused serious problems. Chief Jolly had less than 3,000 followers. The newcomers, headed by John Ross, numbered nearly 13,000.[48] Each group had its own laws and leaders and neither group was willing to let the other rule.

A general council of all Cherokees was called for July 23, 1832, at Red Clay, Tennessee.[49] The main purpose was to either accept removal or reject same. The latter action was taken. This issue split the once powerful Cherokees. Bad blood which cropped up during this crisis has abated, but even after 150 years it has remained a disruptive influence when discussed in Cherokee circles.

Jesse was drawn into the fight, against his will. His help was sought by all three factions: Jolly's "old settlers"; the Ridge-Boudinot Treaty Party; and Ross' "newcomers," or "Eastern Party." [50] In a manner typical of him, Jesse rejected all of their pleas to take a stand. For assuming a "no stand" position, Jesse was obligated to move out of the Cherokee Nation to avoid controversy. By the time Ross' faction was forcibly removed from Georgia,[51] many divisive acts within the Cherokee body politic had caused hard lines of various opinions to be formed.

To add to the Indians' woes, the big flood in June 1833 left shambles in its wake.[52] The Arkansas River crested ten feet above normal and even higher where sharp bends caused huge backup flooding. Jesse and other residents on nearby rivers and creeks sustained great financial losses. For the second time in his short life he had been wiped out by a flood. This time he promised himself that flood waters would not reach him again. He set out for Bent's Trading Post to see what he might get in the way of goods to trade, or find work to earn money.

While he was at Bent's, a party of Comanches came to trade. Jesse visited with them and learned they held two white children and a black slave.[53] The hostages had been captured during a raid on a west-bound party crossing the Santa Fe Trail. Jesse only had money with which to barter and couldn't strike a deal for the prisoners' release. The Indians wanted guns.

Jesse talked with Ceran St. Vrain,[54] George Bent, and a congregation of mountain men at Bent's. These were robust, sometimes ribald characters, but they were never dull. They held Jesse's attention. He spent several days buying, packing, and loading supplies, and he listened to news about Indians, trapping, bears, fights, women, and other pertinent subjects.

Just before leaving, Jesse told George Bent he needed three good rifles in order to ransom three children who were being held captive by Comanches still camped in the vicinity. Bent chided Jesse because he worried about Indians and proposed a raiding party to get the captives. When told that some 600 Indians were waiting, Bent sensibly dropped the idea and let Jesse have the guns. Jesse struck out alone to bargain with the Comanches for the three captives.

Onlookers unanimously agreed that Jesse's mission of mercy had little chance of success. Indians were fighting among themselves: Comanche and Kiowa against Osage and Pawnee; Cheyenne and Arapaho against Osage and Pawnee. The central reason for this Indian warfare was their quest for food. Whites using the road to Santa Fe unwittingly supplied these tribal wars by losing their goods, guns and lives, in many instances, to raiding Indians. The Santa Fe Trail helped sustain the Indians' war efforts against both white travelers and rival tribes. Most trappers nested together at Bent's place for protection.

Jesse returned with three hungry, dirty, and terrified children, scarcely twenty-four hours since he had set out alone to attempt the hostage exchange.[55] It was a joyous occasion. Even the rough frontiersmen shed their emotional masks and poured out a joyful and affectionate greeting for the children.

Jesse's posture now took on a new, heroic stance. Open respect replaced the doubt which had surrounded him earlier, but he remained a modest giant, barely acknowledging the mountain men's accolades. He planned to embark with his party of four the following day. The entire encampment around Bent's Trading Post would be on hand to wish them well.

Jesse refused an offer for a heavily armed escort. He felt that his methods had carried him thus far and that those same methods offered his best chance of surviving. In his case, even those who would have used other methods agreed with Jesse. One of the men present, J. W. Durant, recalled that none of those mountain men around Jesse that day really understood him or his reasoning. He was a hard man to fathom.

To an observer, Jesse's ethnic origin was questionable. He was not an Indian, and though he had some physical characteristics that "passed him" for white, he did not fit the white mold.[56] His courage, however, was obvious and sometimes fearsome. His steely stare in itself could face down most men — white, red, brown, or black. Durant likened the docile giant to a friendly bear. It was possible to coexist with him, but a maelstrom might erupt if he was riled.

Durant was able to watch Jesse closely for more than two decades. He recalled that Jesse earned respect walking peaceful avenues, defying all manner of ruffians with a brusk but friendly and fearless manner which tended to discourage challenge. He was vulnerable, but for some reason few men ever threatened him or expressed a secret desire to kill him. Jesse was unique in his ability to walk openly among warring Indians or whites with no worry for his personal safety.

Once he returned to Fort Gibson, Jesse asked Indian Commissioner Montfort Stokes to deliver the three children he had ransomed from the Indians to their families. Some days later he was angered to learn that Stokes had given his hostages to local missionaries. Stokes, in turn, was shocked by Jesse's display of disapproval. Whatever his reason, just or unjust, Jesse had always disliked and disapproved of missionaries.[57] James R. Meade, Jesse's friend and business associate, said years later that Jesse told him that he had no use for preachers but readily acknowledged faith in a supreme being, one God.[58]

The Indian situation was worsening, and the government was determined to be rid of it, as evidenced in this report:

> In a letter dated February 16, 1832, accompanying the presentation of a memorial addressed to President Jackson, by the Western Creeks, suggesting the appointment of a commission from the United States to consider their affairs, Secretary of War Lewis Cass took occasion to review the whole situation of administering Indian affairs pointing out the necessity of adjusting the boundary disputes between the Western Cherokees and the Creeks, and of deciding certain questions that had arisen in connection with the removal of approximately 100,000 eastern Indians, then in progress . . . Secretary Cass particularly recommended that the Government's system of general superintendence over the Indians should be centralized in the

hands of a few officials, and that a commission of three men of elevated character and firm principles, should be appointed to examine the country west of Missouri and Arkansas, where it was necessary, to assign reservations, to settle boundary disputes, and to make further treaties with any of the tribes.[59]

Where Cass used the term "boundary disputes," he would have been more accurate using the term "open warfare." The legislation Cass recommended paved the way for President Jackson to take more Indian land.

On July 9, 1832, Congress passed an act creating the office of Commissioner of Indian Affairs, "who should have the direction and management of all Indian affairs and all matters arising out of Indian relations, subject only to the Secretary of War and the President." [60] The last word in this quote is the "catch." The president was essentially given all power since he appointed the secretary of war.

This unreasonable yoke was not removed from the Indians' necks for seventeen years. By congressional act, on March 3, 1849,[61] the newly created Department of Interior took Indian affairs from military and presidential authority and transferred it to civilians answerable to Congress. Such was a step in the right direction for a change, as far as Indians were concerned.

During the president's new campaign for more power, Sam Houston gave up his efforts to reason with his friend Jackson in matters concerning Indian affairs. They simply saw the subject from different viewpoints.

After Houston's departure for Texas, Creeks and Cherokees turned to Jesse for help. His influence among Indians grew steadily. The greater their problems and trials, the bigger Jesse's role became as he sought help for his friends.

Jesse sensed the futility of Indians' struggle for just and decent treatment, and he inwardly wished he could be relieved of his onus. Sometimes he would range far from his base in an effort to escape his destiny as Indian intermediary with whites. To ease his mind, he took a trip to Mexico City. Then he made his maiden voyage to California in 1832, trying to lose his identity or to find an inner peace.[62]

Ironically, when Jesse discovered this West Coast mecca, he was not looking for land but was trying to escape the turmoil in the land he had vacated. What he found were trade opportunities, just waiting to be serviced. Friendly natives impressed him from the outset, and he promised himself he would learn more about California.

Two Titans Square Off

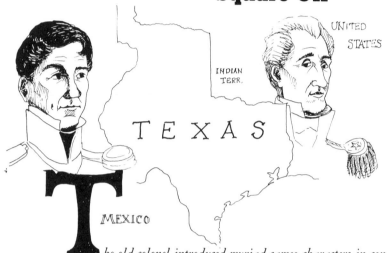

4

The old colonel introduced myriad cameo characters in con-
junction with his giant subject in order to develop appropriate background for
his star. Some players cropped up again and again to shed some light at fit intervals, while the majority of the actors passed like a burning comet across the
wilderness stage, never to be seen or heard from again.

On those instances when Sam Houston was sharing billing with Jesse
Chisholm, Houston's son and the narrator of this epic story treated his father as
casually as any other bit role player. Never once did he let his fabled father, or
any other person for that matter, upstage Jesse Chisholm.

When Colonel Houston introduced me to the conflict between Andrew
Jackson and Cherokee head chief John Ross, he said, "Jesse was close to both
men and respected them highly, but he wouldn't take sides with either faction."

Cherokee Chief John Ross' fervent hopes that Henry Clay would
unseat Andrew Jackson as president were quickly dashed.[1] Jackson
won easily. With the election behind him, Jackson took note of Ross'
financial and vocal support for Clay. The president reacted violently
and began a relentless push for Indian removal to the territory.

The year 1833 was recorded by historians as one of the most
memorable ones in the territory. Those inhabitants who lived out the
experience certainly would never forget it. Pressures continued to

mount from all sides. The trauma surrounding resettlement of some 20,000 emotionally crushed Indian peoples in a hostile environment made the usually calm army post at Fort Gibson bristle with excitement.[2]

Jesse and other leaders in the territory were most concerned about an influx of unsavory confidencemen pouring into the poorly regulated Indian Territory. These shady characters brought with them every conceivable mischief and malice. The United States Army cadre grew in size but was scarcely disciplined. Desertion rates ran high.[3] Officers such as Jefferson Davis[4] and B. L. E. Bonneville[5] were covered when they left their posts without permission or overstayed leaves. A fellow officer merely backdated papers to cover military misconduct by another officer. Enlisted men simply deserted. Usually they went to Texas seeking some of the excitement going on there.

For Jesse, all the news continued to be bad. Cholera struck Fort Gibson; few areas were left unscathed by the violent cholera strain which swept the territory. Some died in three to four hours after contracting the disease. Those who lived were disabled for months. More than 4,000 died.[6]

News from Texas revealed that Santa Anna, the only candidate, was elected president of Mexico. He immediately abrogated all agreements made by previous rulers with settlers in Texas.[7] This action caused great anxiety in Stephen F. Austin's new colony on the Brazos River. Houston and David G. Burnet had become leaders of settlers on the turbulent Texas scene.[8] Jesse got his news about Texas from moccasin media.

While trading with Comanche Chief Buffalo Hump and a group of his followers, he learned how enthusiastic the Indians were about Houston and Burnet's new and influential roles in Texas political circles.[9] In the case of Burnet, who once lived with Comanches in Texas, the Indians learned the hard way that their hopes were placed on unsympathetic shoulders. But, in the inception, Comanches felt Houston and Burnet would be their voice in the ruling Texas forum.

One of the reasons Indians embraced white men like Burnet and Houston was their alternative choice: Mexicans. Indians held the Mexicans in contempt and seldom missed a chance to inflict indignities on them. Mexicans held Indians in equally low esteem. The animosity between Indians and Mexicans spread to colonists, who had begun pouring into Texas. These same savage Comanches, both hated and feared, were Jesse's jovial, intelligent comrades.

Sharp traders, inveterate gamblers, loyal family members,[10] the Comanches were unwilling pawns in games that white adventurers played. In the early stages of white settlement in Texas, Indians only had their scheduled horse races interrupted. But as time wore on, settlers began to interrupt the Indians' lifestyle. Several chiefs of Buffalo Hump's tribe told Jesse tale after tale of treachery inflicted on their peoples by Texas colonists.

Jesse had gone to Bexar, Texas, with Comanches, at their request, in 1832 to hear Houston's offer of peace from the United States government.[11] Acting as interpreter, Jesse introduced Comanches to Houston and Jim Bowie at this meeting. Houston promised fair treatment from the U.S. and another meeting was scheduled for the following April.[12] That meeting never happened. Comanches were given no indication that the government officials would "no show" and hung around several days waiting for white treaty-makers to arrive.

When Jesse approached him about his slight of the Comanches, Houston blamed aggressive acts by Mexicans for his failure to meet with them. He asked Jesse to convey his apology. Houston was lucky to have Jesse available and willing to help him, and it started a pattern of Jesse pulling his chestnuts out of the fire.

Houston's meeting with the Comanches was the first serious act any nation had made toward recognizing the Comanches. But despite this breakthrough, relations with the wily Comanches grew steadily worse, primarily due to abuses heaped upon them by Texas settlers. Jesse reacted with a genuine feeling of empathy for his angry brethren.

For the first time in his life Jesse realized he was hearing the innermost secrets of these powerful lords of the prairie. He was privy to the Comanches' confidence, which no white man could ever attain. He heard their plans for retaliation and when and where strikes would be made. His only purpose in life had been to live and let live while making a living as a trader. Now his role as a trader had put him squarely on the spot.

Buffalo Hump and his warriors wanted to buy guns from Jesse for their war on the white settlers.[13] Indians knew he sold guns and had access to as many guns as his buying power could afford. It was a moral crisis for Jesse. He was dismayed by his options: lose face or lose integrity. He knew his customers could come up with enough barter to order many guns.

His gun sales to Indians in the past had been to help them hunt buffalo, which supplied about eighty percent of their living require-

ments for food, shelter, clothes, fire, implements, and barter materials.[14] Now Jesse sat at their campfire and learned his guns would be
used to kill white men. Why not? Weren't these same whites using
guns to kill and rob Indians of their homelands? Indians were only asking a friend for means to protect themselves, but he knew, in the eyes
of the white world, he would be stigmatized as a "gun runner" or mer-
cenary.

His pulse quickened as he tried to find a way out of his dilemma.
He knew their request was reasonable, but his conscience rebelled at
killing or settling disputes by might, no matter who was right. Chief
Buffalo Hump was sensitive to Jesse's concern. The chief publicly
chided him for his anxiety and frustration. Comanches would get guns
from other sources, the chief said, if Jesse lacked "the stomach" to handle his job.

The old chief's rebuke so stung Jesse that he responded with an
uncharacteristically angry and prophetic warning: If the white men
and Indians didn't learn to live together, the Redman was doomed.[15]
Indians listened in shocked silence to this prophecy from their friend
and ally. Then they turned into an angry, ribald chorus, shouting their
protests.

It remained for Chief Buffalo Hump the dubious job to try to define the Comanches' consensus response to the challenge Jesse had
thrown down. The chief, choosing his words carefully, observed that
Jesse may be right in predicting their certain demise. Looking right at
Jesse, he continued to express his thoughts: "If this is our destiny, we
promise you these grounds will run red with the white man's blood before we are finally done with this life. We will cleanse the white man
of any doubts he may hold about Comanche pride and valor." There remained an electric tension about the assembled warriors as Buffalo
Hump puffed on his pipe.

Before he had fully recovered from this emotional meeting with
the Comanches, Jesse found himself being asked for guns by the Kiowas. The Kiowa head chief, Abate, complained that his tribe was
being attacked because of mischief caused by others. He wanted Jesse
to furnish guns to retaliate against these unjust attacks.[16]

A calmer, somewhat chastened Jesse, still smarting from his encounter with Comanches, held his peace as Chief Abate verbally as-
saulted all "forked tongue whites." The night passed slowly as he
heard the chief's logic and reason. Abate's facts were correct and could
not be disputed.

Later that evening, young Chief Dohasen pressed Jesse to make a stand. Jesse took the position he had taken earlier when he talked to the Comanches, a risky one. Instead of turning wild and angry at Jesse's words, as had the Comanche chief, the reflective Chief Dohasen calmly agreed. He predicted, however, that there would be an interim of hell as Chief Buffalo Hump had promised before Kiowas would be defeated. The chief, resigned and somewhat jovial, told Chisholm not to worry. Kiowas would take care of themselves and get guns elsewhere, he assured.

Jesse knew it would be difficult for him to avoid the conflicting forces, and he found himself battling his own conflict of conscience. His moral struggle became more complex when a large band of Chouteau's Indians, the mighty Osage, set upon the Kiowas' village while its warriors were off hunting.[17] It was the worst carnage Jesse had ever seen. The dead — women, children, old men — were mutilated and beheaded, their heads put into cooking pots. The Osage pillaged and burned the campsite, and took a few young girls home with them. They had carried guns bought from Chouteau.

Returning Kiowa hunters now faced the grisly scene of death and mutilation at their home. They were swallowed by grief. At that moment, Jesse made his decision: He would leave gun running to others. He reasoned the same imbalance of power would exist if Indians had guns and whites had bows and arrows.[18]

It was his nature to live with whatever structure he found. He did not try to force change. And now, Jesse accepted his own limitations, even in the area where peace was his goal.

A messenger from Fort Gibson summoned Jesse from his new home at Edwards Settlement, in the Creek Nation, to meet with Colonel Arbuckle. He responded and met Capt. Nathan Boone, son of the respected and legendary frontiersman Daniel Boone from Kentucky.[19] It was young Boone's assignment to run a survey line, dividing the Creek and Cherokee nations.

Jesse had looked upon Daniel Boone as the country's greatest human treasure. He told close associates that when he met young Nathan, it was like touching the hem of frontiersman Daniel's tassled leather jacket.

Tempers had flared between Creeks and Cherokees over property boundary lines. Neither faction was in a conciliatory mood. When Colonel Arbuckle called Jesse to help Captain Boone, he knew about his strong ties with both tribes.[20] Two years earlier, in 1831, President

Jackson had sent his nephew, John Donelson, and the Reverend Isaac McCoy to do this same job.[21] Their efforts only fanned the angry flames.

Jesse readily accepted the assignment to escort young Boone and to help keep the disputing tribes out of the surveyors' way. When they had idle time, Jesse used it to reminisce with the son about his famous father, Daniel Boone.

Jesse later recalled that when the Creeks and Cherokees learned who the young captain was, they flocked to see and hear young Boone. Their curiosity caused more problems than anything else. Finally, probably out of respect for the name as much as anything, Boone's survey was accepted by all concerned.

The ongoing strife between President Jackson and Cherokee Chief Ross raged on unabated. A "bidding war" had broken out between President Jackson and Chief Ross and was making big news in the Cherokee settlement. Jackson bid $3.5 million for land held in Georgia by Ross' Cherokees.[22] Ross refused the offer. Jackson countered with a million-dollar raise.[23] Ross replied, "No sale!" Jackson's face became as red as his famous mane had once been. He angrily demanded that Ross accept his generous offer or face the certainty of being thrown off the land.

News reached the territory that President Jackson had rejected a treaty negotiated by his representatives, A. P. Chouteau, Montfort Stokes, Colonel Arbuckle, and Maj. F. W. Armstrong, with the Osages, headed by Chief Clermont and his subchiefs. Jackson agreed to postpone action temporarily but did not carry out the agreement.[24] His betrayal negated efforts of his agents at no small cost to taxpayers, not to mention earning more ill-will from the Osage people.

Jesse learned from Colonel Arbuckle that Albert Pike of Arkansas had criticized Sam Houston[25] and predicted in a letter to Secretary of War Cass that Houston would be scalped if he came near the Comanches.[26]

The biggest news of all was the military excursion planned for the next year by the United States.[27] A large body of troops and civilians would seek out wild Indians in their lairs and try to persuade them to sign peace agreements. The whole idea seemed patently absurd to Jesse. When Stokes, the Indian commissioner, and Arbuckle tried to solicit his help, he politely refused.

Jesse was busy stocking his new trading post at Edwards Settlement and had a great urgency to put his own house in order. Stokes called Jesse to try to persuade him to lead the coming expedition. He candidly asked Jesse if he thought the peace treaty plan would succeed. Jesse pondered awhile before he answered Stokes, then responded that the undertaking might succeed if Indians being held hostage by Osages were returned to their own tribal families.

Stokes understood immediately. He commissioned Jesse on the spot to buy as many captives as he could find. Stokes agreed to pay as much as $200 for each captive. Based on this final exchange, Jesse resumed work on his new home in the Creek Nation, determined to "mend his own fences."

He now faced the many problems usually associated with opening a new trading post. Goods ordered to be shipped by boat hadn't arrived from Fort Smith. There were few customers. Worst of all was the utter boredom of workaday life and his surroundings.

A mighty flood had swept over the territory earlier that year, causing a great famine among the civilized tribes. Government aid for starving Indians was slow filtering down to the hungry government charges. The whiskey still owned by Jesse's Uncle Charles Rogers washed away in the flood.[28] Rogers' $3,943 claim was paid, but he was told to stop making whiskey.

Endless problems abounded in the territory in 1833. There was no hope for a quick cure, but any treatment would be welcomed. The bidding war between President Jackson and Cherokee Chief Ross had grown into a bitter feud. Ross had said no to Jackson's latest offer of $7.5 million.[29] Chief Ross raised his asking price for the Cherokee land to one he could accept in behalf of the Cherokees — $20 million.[30] President Jackson's explosion could be heard 2,000 miles away.

Sam Houston passed through Fort Gibson in March, on the way to Washington.[31] He invited Jesse to meet him in June for a peace council with Indians on the Brazos River in Texas. Jesse's job was to get the various tribes to show up. Houston's enthusiasm and excitement impressed Jesse.

His new "calling" as U.S. envoy to Texas seemed to bring out the best in Houston, whose charisma was as magnetic as Jesse had ever seen it. He was sober and jovial, although very upset by Austin's imprisonment in Mexico City.

It was clear to Jesse that Houston was possessed by the events in Texas. Before a year passed, Houston made a second trip to Washington for meetings with Jackson. On that trip Houston learned details of Austin's imprisonment by Santa Anna's vice-president, Gomez Farias, in Mexico City.[32] Jesse first met Austin during Austin's stint as federal district judge[33] in Little Rock a decade earlier, and, like Houston, genuinely admired the handsome and intelligent Missourian.

As they parted, Houston talked about the politics involved in the upcoming U.S. military expedition into Comanche and Kiowa country. Houston believed that bureaucratic upheaval would sink the mission before it crossed the Arkansas River.[34] With this encouraging news, Jesse hurried off to meet with Indian Commissioner Stokes. Houston did not find the opportunity, for some reason, to mention to Jesse that he, Chisholm, had been conscripted to guide this bizarre military expedition.

When Jesse rode into the fort, he sensed a tension unusual for such a seasoned frontier outpost. Uneasiness was so strong that men bristled at each other, and they were turning into unfriendly loners. Each man was acting on his own. There didn't seem to be any leadership, the adhesive needed to hold men in tow.

Jesse learned that the unrest had been caused by the transfer of popular old Colonel Arbuckle. Post personnel seemed to rebel against newly issued orders. He, too, seemed to be affected by Arbuckle's transfer as he headed for his meeting with the crusty and domineering Revolutionary War veteran, Stokes, now seventy years old.[35] The meeting was like most others, when Jesse's help was needed, but this time he found himself being dominated by his host, Stokes.

At Stokes' order, the two mounted horses and started down the Texas Road. When they reached the sandy banks of the swift Arkansas River, Stokes motioned for his guest to behold the view. What Jesse saw was the most motley, ragged, and generally downcast aggregation of men and animals ever assembled. The cold wind was brisk and cut like a razor as they watched the scene below.

This was the famous Dragoon regiment of U.S. Cavalry — the first ever commissioned in U.S. military history. Jesse's emotions flared. Tears of laughter seemed appropriate after watching the scene below.

Stokes, quite casually, told Jesse he wanted to introduce him to the men he would be guiding. He added that Col. Henry Dodge was eager to meet his new guide! Jesse now had the news Houston had not given him.

With the small talk and normal courtesies over, Jesse tried to sort out his emotions. The thought of his plight made his palms damp. These men were foreign to him. Many spoke in dialects he didn't know. Their manhood was obvious, but their experience was suspect.

Years later, Dodge admitted he wasn't impressed by Jesse Chisholm at their initial meeting. Certainly, Dodge didn't demonstrate his leadership qualities to Jesse during this first meeting. Both men hoped, but inwardly doubted, their future meetings would be more meaningful. However, the fated "Dodge Expedition" was now committed to be carried out as scheduled, with Jesse showing the way.

5

Jackson's Extravaganza

ore than a year had passed since Colonel Houston had begun telling his incredible story about Jesse Chisholm. At another story session, I met another visitor, Walter Woodul. Mr. Woodul, lieutenant governor of Texas, had come to invite Colonel Houston to speak at the upcoming groundbreaking ceremonies at San Jacinto Battleground, where a new monument was to be built.

When Governor Woodul learned the reason for my visit, he asked Colonel Houston if he could sit down with us and hear the story for that day. At first the old man shifted around restlessly and tried to play down anything he might relate. The governor, no doubt expecting some rare insight into the immortal Sam Houston's life, opted to "squat" for the session.

Instead of relaying rare Houston family memories, the old storyteller used this occasion to project Jesse Chisholm to epic dimensions, reaching far beyond any area he had led me previously. In this account by Houston's last surviving son, Jesse was depicted as Houston's principal agent for keeping hostile Indians off of the Texas army's flanks while they battled a numerically superior Mexican army. Later that afternoon, when Woodul was taking his leave, he commented, "I'd never heard that version before."

A buckskin-clad, auburn-haired giant slouched over the hitching post in front of Bvt. Gen. Matthew Arbuckle's headquarters, somberly listening to his orders.

The commanding general was trying to impress Jesse with the importance of his role as scout-guide-interpreter for a widely publicized "treaty expedition" into the heart of the savage Indians' lair. For Jesse, the trip would be along his routine trade route. But for a star-studded assemblage of dignitaries, this would be anything but a routine experience.

After months of pressure from President Jackson, the strain was beginning to show on General Arbuckle, who only recently had learned of his demotion to a post command with less exacting duties. Arbuckle had commanded Fort Gibson so long that some residents believed he owned it. In typical military fashion, Arbuckle swallowed his hurt and disappointment and lent his great talent and influence to insure the safe conduct of the expedition.[1]

The impact of the whole affair failed to arouse much emotion in Jesse. He was calm, almost indifferent, this day as the attempt for a highly sensational and controversial peace treaty began to unfold.

When President Jackson sent a special courier to Fort Gibson,[2] situated in the midst of Indian Territory (and incidentally the most remote fort in the United States), he did so for the sole purpose of reiterating the importance of the trip to the nation and to him, politically. Arbuckle received the courier cordially and remarked that he didn't need to be reminded of the magnitude of this unprecedented undertaking. Arbuckle was an old and trusted friend of the president, having served as his aide during the Battle of New Orleans,[3] but he was openly concerned that Jackson had succumbed to excitement surrounding the affair. General Arbuckle knew the inherent danger of the expedition, but he also wondered if Jackson had been away from the frontier so long that it dulled his senses relative to the imminent danger involved.

Obviously, President Jackson was affected by the great wave of publicity — some favorable, some not — that preceded the expedition, and he decided a disaster or failure would most certainly reflect on him and his administration. From the inception the conservative Arbuckle discouraged the idea, preferring to have Jesse bring the savage leaders into the fort for treaty talks.

Arbuckle was one of the bravest and most loyal commanders ever stationed in the Southwest.[4] Though totally lacking in the delicate art of politics and diplomacy, he felt the proposed trip into the home range of Indians was inviting disaster just to satisfy the yen for excitement of a few foolhardy adventurers.

Both Jesse and Arbuckle told Stokes, commissioner of Indian affairs, who conceived the idea and then convinced President Jackson that his brainstorm had merit, that his whole scheme was unwise and not destined to come to any good. However, Jackson was in command and was daring, even reckless, when he set on a course. His able post commander, Arbuckle, tried to follow orders while at the same time chart the course with the least likelihood of being dangerous to his command.

The romance of the expedition captured the imagination of blithe-spirited adventurers both in the young Republic and abroad.[5] Through diplomatic channels, requests for permission to accompany the troops had been pouring into the U.S. State Department. The national news media kept the populace at fever pitch, with daily coverage of the event. Congress, swept up by the reigning spirit, authorized the army to commission in March 1833 the first permanent cavalry regiment in American history, the "U.S. Dragoons."[6] Col. Henry Dodge was appointed as the first commanding officer, and his adjutant was Lt. Jefferson Davis.[7]

The new Dragoon uniform, whose designer was undoubtedly caught up in the excitement also, was certainly the most colorful and controversial garb ever worn by U.S. Army troops. The uniform was designed to "astonish the natives."[8] To put it mildly, these uniforms astonished the natives and more particularly old army regulars, not to mention unsuspecting frontier settlers. Years later, Jesse remembered the Dragoon uniform and the indelible mark it left on him. He said it attracted more attention than a freshet on the desert.

When Congress prescribed the dress, which included a dark blue, double-breasted wool coat, they certainly didn't reckon with the 100-degree-plus temperatures of the Southwest. The rest of the uniform consisted of blue-gray pants with yellow stripes, a deep orange sash, and black boots with yellow spurs. And if the natives weren't sufficiently astonished, they would be when they saw the Dragoons' caps. The simple motif of the cap included a high, black, stovepipe-like crown with yellow stripes, a shiny black brim, and the crown adorned with a gold eagle, a gilt star, and cord; it was topped with a drooping plume of white horse hair.[9] Here was the personification of bureaucratic bungling, framed for all to see.

Jesse looked upon the assembled entourage with incredulity. He had tried to refuse this assignment when he was first approached, and for a while he thought he would get out of the job. When the expedition took on an "international" flavor, the United States had to have the best scout-guide-interpreters available. This meant Jesse would be drafted to lead this most unexampled expedition.

The endeavor was first called the "Dodge Expedition" and later the "Leavenworth Expedition," and finally it was dubbed the "Leavenworth–Dodge Expedition." [10] Gen. Henry Leavenworth had been hand-picked to command this most sensitive journey and would replace Arbuckle as commanding officer at Fort Gibson. This military adjustment, as Leavenworth addressed the new assignment, in itself caused some problems. The Dragoons' organizer, Col. Henry Dodge, who was initially named to head the expedition, was dropped to second in command.

Lt. Col. Stephen Watts Kearney had been sent along as President Jackson's personal emissary,[11] and Montfort Stokes, former governor of North Carolina and presently commissioner of Indian affairs, now past seventy years, went along at Jackson's request to help ensure that adequate facilities and comforts were afforded those civilians in attendance.[12]

From the time General Leavenworth, with the rest of the advance party, stepped off the steamer at Fort Gibson, excitement mounted daily until the expedition departed. Hundreds of civilians flocked to the wilderness outpost hoping to gain passage on the expedition. Colonel Dodge had assembled his regiment at Jefferson Barracks, Missouri, and after all manner of confusion and chaos finally started on October 11, 1833, for Fort Gibson.[13] They arrived on December 18, their attire totally tattered and their bodies racked from hunger and exhaustion.[14]

The elite cavalry unit rode untrained horses through uncharted territory where there were no roads. In many instances the cavalrymen's mounts were more of a challenge than were inclement weather, diseases, or hostile Indians. To make matters worse, the men had no "issue" guns and their fancy uniforms were not ready when they left and had to be sent by boat to their rendezvous point. But the very fact that they survived this ordeal en route to Fort Gibson gave some encouragement for the coming test of nerves and sinew. Even after the Dragoons arrived in the territory in the dead of winter, they learned there was no room for them in the fort. Troops were rationed one blanket per man to repel the cold and were housed in tents pitched on the sandy Arkansas River bottom.[15] For man and beast this was truly a baptism of fire, enough to sober even the hardiest adventurer.

After numerous desertions, court-martials, and "punishment to suit the crime," the day of departure was at hand — June 24, 1834.[16]

Probably no expedition was ever assembled and outfitted under worse conditions. The wonder is that they ever got sufficient uniforms, food, medicine, mounts, and camping equipment to outfit the regiment as well as the excess passengers they were taking along.

The entire settlement was on hand to witness the departure. General Leavenworth, leading his command, saluted the assemblage and gave the command: "Forward march!" Rising above the rest of the column was Jesse Chisholm, riding his piebald mare at the head of the troops, flanked on either side by Leavenworth and Dodge. An ebullient artist, George Catlin, rode leisurely behind Dodge. At the last minute, the civilian "guest list" had been pared drastically due to inherent dangers posed by the trip. The fact that Catlin, the little Englishman, was allowed to go set off a wave of indignation by those scratched from the list.[17]

Catlin's work had already gained some prominence as the result of his earlier Indian paintings. He was invited on this momentous expedition in part for the acclaim his art had received and because of his friendship with Col. A. P. Chouteau. Catlin received an invitation from President Jackson to make the trip with the Dragoons at Chouteau's request.[18]

Actually, Catlin made his selection an easy decision to justify. His pleasant manner and optimistic outlook pervaded all who were in contact with him. He was a great promoter, too, fairly oozing with enthusiasm for whatever he happened to be promoting, in this case his paintings. Before the expedition was finished, though, he had many chances to get his damper dampened, including several brushes with death. But he never flinched in the face of adversity nor asked to be shielded from dangers they encountered.[19] Through Jesse's entrée with the Comanches and Kiowas in particular, Catlin was able to get closer to these Native Americans than he ever dreamed possible. Although he spent more than eight years visiting and painting Indians and their surroundings (more than 500 in his career, and twenty-seven scenes and individuals during this expedition),[20] Catlin remembered this trip as his most exciting and perilous, despite the calming influence the presence of Chisholm afforded.

Jesse had made his initial trip into this semidesert area in 1824, some ten years earlier.[21] Since then he had opened a trading post on wheels, which he regularly took to the Indians. When he loaded his two-wheeled wagon, a Mexican *caretta,* and headed south, he was like the "Good Humor man," traveling to trade with the denizens of the prairie. Screeching axles announced his arrival long before he came into view. In short, Jesse was as comfortable in these environs as a duck on water.

Under Leavenworth's command was the entire Dragoon Regiment, along with some detachments from the 3rd and 7th Regiments of the U.S. Infantry. The detachment from the 7th Infantry rendezvoused the main body when they approached Fort Towson,[22] bringing the traveling strength to more than 500. Catlin recorded the scene at the river crossing as follows: "We are at this place, on the banks of the Red River, having Texas under our eye on the opposite bank — The verdure is everywhere of the deepest green and the plains about us are literally speckled with buffalo."[23]

The season was unduly hot on that July 1, 1834, when the company crossed the Washita River. The heat extracted its toll and, coupled with a choleric or bilious fever,[24] men were falling out like flies. The main casualty was the commander, Gen. Henry Leavenworth.[25] With nearly half of the command struck down by illness, which proved fatal to some men in less than twenty-four hours,[26] a hospital camp was set up near the Washita. Colonel Dodge assumed command of the able-bodied force, and the expedition was continued. Lt. Col. Kearney commanded the sick forces and those men detained to nurse the sick.[27]

The whole purpose of the large and colorful military force was, by design, to impress Indians with a pompous show of strength.[28] Now, with about 250 able-bodied survivors, which certainly didn't indicate any particular strength, Colonel Dodge headed his forces for a rendezvous with unpredictable and dangerous Plains Indians. Jesse was greatly relieved that strength would be downplayed on this trip and, in its stead, peaceful diplomacy would be the method deployed by American treaty-seekers.

Dodge led his forces in a northwesterly direction for a point on the North Fork of Red River, now known as Devil's Canyon, site of the Toyash (Wichita) Indians' main camp. Raging bilious fever had so decimated the task force that they had to abandon the wagons, leaving them at the sick camp to be used as hospital wards.[29] A few pack animals carried all the food and livery necessary to sustain their operation.

For wary savages, this body of troops posed no more threat than a scouting party — a large one, certainly, but not a very dangerous force. The first weakness the Indians would note was their lack of water. In this heat, neither man nor animal would remain very mobile without water. Those two "regulars" of the frontier — searing heat and swarming insects — were so invisible but so formidable as to be the most equalizing force in any fight. Men and horses could survive days without food, but the lack of water claimed its toll as swiftly and surely as the rising of the sun.

Another telltale omen to scouting warriors was the way ranks were maintained, as well as the motion of the horses. Straggling or scattered ranks indicated illness within the body or laxness brought on by either overconfidence or novice behavior. In either case the sign showed the "hole in the armor." Also, foot-sore horses in large numbers revealed a spent force and indicated that they couldn't carry the rider far under the stress of battle.

Jesse and those other scouts on hand tried their best to keep the ranks in formidable array. The "other foe" was a seemingly ever present one: millions of swarming flies. These were of the vicious "horse fly" strain that could kill horses if they were tied or tethered and couldn't run away from their tormentors. One trooper wrote home telling of killing 500 flies with whom he shared his lunch, and at the dinner meal he found 5,000 relatives had come to the funeral. Death-dealing flies were ever present. At nightfall, smudge pots were put out to drive flies off while the horses and mules ate.[30]

So far, of the three big "I's" — Indians, insects, and illness — the latter two posed the biggest threat. In fact, troops needed relief soon or there wouldn't be anyone left for Indians to confront. The sheer anxiety brought on by tension gripped Dodge as he struggled with brilliant resolve in his effort to make ice cream out of sand dunes. All hope was not gone but neither was this surviving fragmented force, which had left "civilization" just over a week ago, bubbling with optimism.

When Jesse ran onto a small Comanche hunting party near present-day Hearldton, Oklahoma,[31] he brought them in for a confab. The tautness on both sides was tighter than a fiddler's bow strings. For Jesse, the meeting reminded him of the story of the dove appearing to Noah after forty days on the Ark.

The meeting would be peaceful because the Indians' very presence meant that Jesse had given them his word they would be safe with him. If he had not convinced these Comanches of the peaceful intent of 'this mission, arrows would already be flying.

After the first contact, not unlike two strange dogs "sniffing each other out," the troops and Comanches relaxed and began an unusually pleasant rapport. Several impromptu horse races between troopers and Indians helped entertain the crowd.

Colonel Dodge was ready to get down to business. While it was most encouraging to meet with these Indians, Jesse told Colonel Dodge that these young Comanches were not a part of the policy-making body of the tribe. At Jesse's bidding, Indians were fed and then Jesse suggested they lead his "friends" to their tribal campground. With nine Comanches leading the way, an apprehensive but happy entourage followed with an excitement which made them appear giddy to seasoned frontiersmen. It was necessary to break the trip with a night layover, then at dawn the caravan was back on the trail.

Just as dusk was closing, a large camp of Indians loomed in the valley, later designated Chandler Creek.[32] By a predetermined signal, unseen by any of the troops, a summon for common feasting and peaceful scrutiny was the order of the day.

So easy had been the transition from apprehension to joy, it was hard for either faction to believe the party was real. In spite of all the good feelings, Jesse was concerned that the Indians would learn of the troops' "fever." Some of the Dodge party was stricken since they left the sick behind at the Washita crossing. And while Comanches weren't necessarily unfeeling, they just didn't want their people exposed to the white man's illness.

Dodge decided it would be advisable to pursue their mission as soon as possible. The Comanches agreed to furnish an escort to the main camp of the Toyash (Wichita), located some seventy miles west of the Comanche camp.[33]

Jesse counseled Dodge to move out of the Comanche area and set up another "sick camp." Illness was raging in epidemic proportions again. Two soldiers had died during the night, and more than thirty were critically ill. About fifteen miles west of the Comanche camp, Dodge stopped to set up a relief station for his sick, leaving thirty-five able-bodied men and officers to nurse and/or bury the infirm should they die.[34] This event seemed to have a most depressing effect on the entire expedition.

As Dodge's remaining command, now numbered about 150, pulled out, it was really hard to determine what method was used to decide why one was staying and one was going. They all looked "pale around the gills."

Illness struck so swiftly and its effects were so lethal that the entire force became terrified. For the second time in two weeks, Dodge and his dwindling body of "fit to travel" left comrades and friends, not knowing if they would ever meet again.

Their concern was justified, for of the sick, more than 150 soldiers[35] and civilians died of the mysterious malady that maimed or mummified most members of the mission. The exact number of deaths was never certified, because many died after returning to Fort Gibson.

Dodge, Jesse, and other advisors to the commander reviewed progress thus far and tried to map strategy for future sessions. When the party arrived at the Comanche camp, it had been an awkward affair in which communications had been, on the surface at least, broken between Dodge and Chisholm.

The old Comanche chief, Taw-we-que-nah,[36] had isolated the two when he garrisoned troops in individual wickiups in a remote vicinity and had taken Jesse into his own quarters. The "peace party" headed by Dodge was obliged to prepare their "pitch" to Comanches without help from Jesse, who had been completely occupied in banter with the "enemy."

Looking back on the incident, Dodge was trying to get his signals memorized so he would be better able to cope with unforeseen developments like this one. What really threw Dodge out of tune with reality came when Chief Taw-we-que-nah announced, without notice, that the "pow-wow" would begin and lined treaty party spokesmen, including Dodge, in front of him, but with Jesse by his side. Dodge asked for a delay so he could talk to Jesse, but the chief said, "Let the talk begin, now!" Obviously embarrassed, Dodge groped for help interpreting the chief's words, since his standby, Jesse, was speaking the tongue of the Comanehe to convey Dodge's words.

As the meeting progressed, Dodge got slightly conflicting interpretations of the same sentence from several different interpreters. Colonel Dodge, not being very well versed in the delicate art of negotiating across language barriers, became confused. His problem stemmed from the inability of his interpreters to find alternate words for those for which there were no literal words to convey their exact meaning.[37] He had to rely on his interpreter to probe for a new word or words to isolate the speaker's intent and meaning.

Dodge ran into trouble immediately when he bluntly rejected the initial stand of the chief and then further complicated the matter when he allowed his impatience and anger to show. In an effort to save the mission, Jesse was trying to rephrase Dodge's angry words before they reached the chief's understanding.

The bird of peace seemed to be leaving the roost. Time and time again, Dodge put the success of their mission in dire jeopardy with his blunt, no-nonsense, military approach.[38] The court-martial atmosphere had no place in the Comanche camp, and Jesse scrambled around like a fly under a glass trying to turn Dodge's probing verbal barbs into balm before they reached the chief's ears. Dodge made certain demands that Jesse knew the Comanches could not accept. On these occasions he talked at length around the issue until he was able to present it in the light of his own personal conviction or proposal whereby he, and not Dodge, drew the chief's rejection. In this way he was able to get Dodge the answer to his demand — a resounding "no!" — without riling either party.

During this session, Jesse's presence was worth the whole cost of the trip. Without his uncanny wisdom and good humor, the entire mission probably would have gone up in smoke. His delicate play on words, in which truth and accuracy were paramount, was Jesse's forte. To both sides he was a tremendous asset, using his wit and good humor to divert ugly confrontations when language barriers set men further apart than they actually were.

Their main difference turned out to be minor in the light of understanding. Jesse's job was bringing understanding, and so far his work had been rated "well done" by both factions.

As jaded remnants of the once impressive Dragoon company started out to meet the mighty Toyash Indians, Dodge paused to thank Jesse. In the short space of two weeks, Dodge had developed a rapport and confidence with Jesse which could only come from being "battle tested." The mutual respect he and Jesse developed during this grueling experience would last throughout their lives.[39]

None of the treaty-seekers were ready for the revelation manifested by the contrast between Comanches they had just visited and the Toyash tribe which now greeted them. The nomadic Comanche had no tethers to either land or objects, while the Toyash (Wichita) Indians who welcomed Dodge's party on July 21 were the most docile and friendly-appearing "savages" one could find.

The Toyash camp consisted of more than 200 wood-framed, dome-shaped huts with grass-thatched roofs, which housed some 1,200 Indians. To add to the wonder of it all, a tour of the camp revealed well-cultivated fields of beans, corn, melons, squash, and pumpkins.[40] This cultural advancement of the Toyash reflected French influence in Texas dating back to LaSalle's expedition.[41] The French dubbed these Indians "Pani Pique," meaning tatooed Pawnee.[42] This name was in turn corrupted to Pawnee Pict, which was the name U.S. intelligence used at the time this expedition was charted.

Here again, Jesse proved indispensable when Colonel Dodge was asking the Comanche chief where he could find the Pawnee Pict tribe. The old chief was puzzled by Dodge's question.[43] He replied he didn't know them, much less where they could be located.

Jesse took it on himself to delve after the missing information Dodge and his advisors were seeking, hoping to glean some clue to guide the chief. Having no success, he turned to the Comanche chief and asked him the names of tribes who camped in the area. From the chief's answer, Jesse determined that "Toyash" was the tribe Dodge's information referred to as Pawnee Pict.

His handling of these semantics took on greater meaning when weighed against circumstances of Dodge's situation. This friendly tribe, by whatever name they were called, were healthy and the most relaxed body of Indians they would encounter. During the four days Dodge's peace party spent in the Toyash village, their tempo slowed measurably, and the overall mood was much more pleasant. The food served by the Wichitas was the most welcomed item on the agenda.[44]

When the peace council began, chiefs and other head men represented Toyash, Kiowa, and Comanche tribes, while Colonel Dodge represented the United States. The pacific mood was jarred when the powerful and treacherous Kiowas came in with their bows strung, ready for action. They had just learned their hated enemy, the Osages, were in the Dodge party.[45] This diplomatic blunder now threatened the peace efforts of all concerned. Kiowa were trying to get around Jesse, to get at the Osage scouts furnished by Chouteau.

While he was attempting to ward off the Kiowa attack, "Chouteau's Indians" were up on their feet, readying for battle. Jesse's stern rebuke settled the Osage back on the floor while he moved the Kiowa leaders out of earshot and counseled them to peace.

The two tribes were deadly and unreasoned enemies who should never have been assembled in this manner. Presence of both factions invited a fatal confrontation which could be dangerous for both participants and spectators alike.

Slightly behind his cue, Colonel Dodge produced his surprise or counter-irritant. He brought forth a little Kiowa girl, which Jesse at Stokes' direction had ransomed from the Osage for $200, to be used at some appropriate interval to further the efforts for peace.[46]

Return of the girl, free of charge, so thrilled the Kiowa delegation that they completely forgot their anger. This ploy was planned and executed by Stokes and Jesse, with Chouteau's cooperation, weeks before the expedition left Fort Gibson. Actually, they had the Kiowa girl's younger brother, too, but he was killed in an accident when butted by a ram, dying instantly, just as the troops were ready to leave on the trip. George Catlin described the sad event in his journal about the expedition.[47]

This seemingly insignificant episode proved to be a "stitch in time." Now, warlike Chief Dohasen would sit his Kiowa warriors down for a serious peace talk — even with Osage present.

A new start was begun to get the peace conference going again. First was the return of a Toyash girl to her parents.[48] Again bedlam broke out as joy and wild gestures of friendship engulfed the conclave. The scene brought unabashed tears of happiness from most unlikely sources — strong men, both red and white.

To keep the Indians on an even diplomatic stance, Jesse had paid the Comanches $400 for a white boy and a black they held captive, and on cue they brought the two boys forth and presented them to Colonel Dodge.[49] Chaos was the result, and after more tears and expressions of filial love the serious business which brought these men together could finally be addressed.

The white boy surrendered by the Comanches was Matthew Wright Martin, who was returned to his mother upon Dodge's return. Forty years later, the same M. W. Martin was living out his life in peace at Paul's Valley, Oklahoma.[50]

It was probably just as well that the United States had hostages and gifts to dispense, since that was about all they were empowered to do. But on the contrary, the head men of the Indians were ready, willing, and able to act.

All Dodge could offer was an invitation to come in to Fort Gibson[51] with him and sit down for a peace talk with American representatives, who were empowered to act in an official or authoritative capacity.

Indians didn't see any reason for not "biting the bullet" right then and there. Finally, Kiowas agreed to send fifteen chiefs, with Dohasen heading the group.[52] Comanches and Toyash were having no part of this proposal. After prodding from Jesse, Comanches agreed to send a chief with four warriors and the chief's woman to do the cooking and chores.[53] Then a Waco chief who was attached to the Toyash and two

Toyash warriors agreed to accompany Dodge home.[54]

Abruptly, Dodge shut the meeting down and said he must leave immediately for home base. He confided to his comrades that he, too, was ill and with as little more substantive accomplishment possible, he wanted to fold his tent and leave while he was still able to travel.

Dodge asked his advisors if there was a shorter, more direct route to Fort Gibson but learned there was none. At this point Jesse was asked if he had an alternate route. He replied that he did not but offered to lead them home by following his "homing instinct." The group unanimously decided to follow Chisholm, who by this time had established his credentials as a leader. His calm, self-confident mien exuded success.

As they were about to leave, a courier from Lt. Col. Stephen Watts Kearney at the sick camp on the Washita arrived with the news of General Leavenworth's death along with some ninety of his fellow officers and enlisted men.[55] The news, while not really too much of a shock, left rumpled survivors desolate, especially Dodge.

Just as they moved out, they came upon a "sea" of buffalo moving on a parallel line with their own movement. This rarely seen spectacle of an estimated 10,000 buffalo,[56] forming a moving river of animals which wafted across the prairie like a big ribbon ending at infinity, thrilled the troops watching.

It took all day for the buffalo to pass them. After this day-long diversion from their aches, pains and grief, the Leavenworth–Dodge expedition headed eastward and hopefully a quick journey to the relatively safe confines of Fort Gibson.

Dodge sent a messenger back to Kearney's camp, informing him of his orders to remove the sick and return to Fort Gibson. He then sent two scouts to get the other sick camp in Carter County to rendezvous them on their return trip.

Now Jesse was back at the helm, doing what he was famous for, as he set out for Fort Gibson. He was using dead reckoning to lead the tired and sick remnant of a once proud regiment on a straight path home.

Two days out, all the Comanches "bailed out" except one warrior who was designated to make the trip and represent Comanches at the conclave.[57] On August 16 the survivors stumbled into Fort Gibson,[58] just eight weeks since their noisy departure. The crest-fallen troops atop jaded ponies looked like anything but conquering heroes returning to claim the plaudits of the masses.

In the minds of those fortunate enough to return alive, their exploits weren't earth-shaking in impact. The trip had been both a mental and physical disaster from their viewpoint, that of participants. Possibly, objective views from unbiased judges gave the disease-racked survivors of this expedition high marks for devotion to duty and fellow countrymen.

The First Dragoons, on its maiden voyage, established a high precedent for future conduct. This mounted army quickly enhanced its image in the Seminole War in Florida and in 1845 during the Mexican War.[59] Probably the most famous Dragoon was Jefferson Davis. Ironically, it was Gen. Richard B. Mason, commander of the Dragoons, who court-martialed Davis for insubordination at a later date.[60]

The next appraisal was a resounding approval of the accomplishments: bringing two, heretofore unbridled and primitive tribes into Fort Gibson for peace treaty agreements and learning something of the terrain south and west of Fort Gibson. In terms of large and enduring feats, results were inconclusive, but the passing of time would give historians a chance to evaluate the net results.

In Jesse's case, his ability was clearly manifested. In isolated areas he was already in great demand for his unique services as a guide. Now, with international coverage of this spectacular excursion into the wilds, his performance should have earned him a lasting fame — but it did not.

For every man who made the round trip with the "Sage of the Prairie," Jesse was forever etched in his mind. Jesse had established a reputation as an Indian peacemaker and interpreter — a man clearly the possessor of a unique sense of direction, the likes of which few men would equal. His entrée into fame was noted in this way: "Jesse Chisholm, destined to be long known as a trader, guide, pathfinder and peace maker, made his first appearance as a factor in the public life of the Indian Territory when he played the part of an interpreter in the council at the Wichita Village." [61]

Catlin asked Jesse if he would be going to Washington to report to the president about the trip they had just completed. His negative response surprised the artist, who had been told by Dodge that Jesse had been extended an invitation.

Catlin reminded Jesse that he had reneged on his promise to sit for a painting. His response was, "I told you I would when I found the time." Then he concluded, "I haven't found the time." He never did. Jesse's main concern was getting back to his once lucrative trading business, which was now suffering from his neglect.

Those who had watched Jesse, hoping he would perform a miracle, but sure in their own reasoning he could not, now realized they had seen the impossible made to look so ridiculously easy that it confounded them. Already, Jesse was being called upon to grapple with seemingly insoluble situations. He did it by drawing on his innate senses for reasonable solutions. He never stoked ever-present and often flawed passions to carry out his theme. Jesse was now the personification of a peacemaker.

6.

Jesse Rescues Houston

ntimidating dark clouds tumbled over the churning angry waters of Trinity Bay. Great gusts of wind further agitated the foam-capped swells, as occasional thunderclaps added emphasis to nature's unrest. Colonel Houston paused momentarily from his deliberations to ascertain the proximity and course of the imminent summer squall.

After a few minutes of intense scrutiny, he opined, "I believe it's going to the south of us." Having disposed of the elements thusly, he continued his discourse on Jesse Chisholm.

"Jesse should have been a national hero as the result of his work during the Leavenworth–Dodge Expedition. When old Jesse told me about the role he played on this epic journey, he downplayed his contribution," Houston recalled. "Jesse reasoned that because he was paid for his services he wasn't due anything more."

Then Houston concluded, "He told me he was paid thirty dollars for his work on the Leavenworth–Dodge excursion. This must have represented one of the biggest bargains U.S. taxpayers ever obtained, for Jesse's services rendered."

At his home in the Creek Nation, Jesse reflected on his active participation in the negotiations of the United States and Indian tribes during the ill-fated Leavenworth–Dodge Expedition. His work carried

72

him to the southern part of Oklahoma and the northern portions of Texas.

What had he accomplished? His business was faring poorly in his absence, for one thing. If for no other reason, he resolved to tend to his trading business and leave treaty-making to those who had the patience and play-acting ability so essential to this pursuit.

He was busily sorting hides when he noticed his Uncle John Rogers, by then a Cherokee chief, riding into his quarters. He presumed Uncle John would be calling on his sister Martha Chisholm, Jesse's mother.[1] After a polite exchange, Rogers got right to the point; it was Jesse he had come to see.

Rogers had been sent by Colonel Dodge and Commissioner of Indian Affairs Stokes to engage Jesse's services as interpreter at the treaty council of Western Indians and the U.S. at Fort Gibson, September 2, 1834.[2] Rogers said, "Jesse, we need you." The way his strong-willed uncle phrased the invitation, Jesse was left little room to decline.

Jesse, even reluctantly, did attend and he did act as Chief John Rogers' interpreter. In fact, Jesse was assigned the task of locating, inviting, and then being responsible for getting Plains Indians to agree to attend. Assigning this task to anyone else but Jesse would have invited failure.

This council established Jesse Chisholm as "a must" when treating with wild native nomads of the Southwest. Col. Henry Dodge, Montfort Stokes (former governor of South Carolina), and S. C. Stambaugh were principal negotiators for the U.S.[3]

Chief Rogers and Jesse Chisholm represented Cherokees; Chief Clermont III, the Osage; Chiefs Roley McIntosh and Benjamin Perryman, the Creeks; Civil John and To-to-lis, the Seneca; Titche-tochecha, the Kiowa; We-ta-ra-yah, the Waco; We-ter-re-sharro, the Pawnee Picts; and Moosh-o-la-tu-bee for Choctaw and others, totaling about 150 delegates and guests.[4]

The group had scarcely assembled before the old Osage-Kiowa feud was touched off by Chief Clermont III, fiery young Osage leader. Jesse stepped between Clermont and his Kiowa foes and demanded Clermont be peaceful or face the wrath of the entire assembly. Some peace was restored after Jesse took his stand.

Lt. T. B. Wheelock recorded this unusual meeting in his *Journal of Lt. T. B. Wheelock.*[5] He devoted twenty-five pages to the "Proceedings of a Council held at Fort Gibson, Arkansas, in September 1834." In Wheelock's account he refers to Jesse's actions in a number of instances. At one point he reports Jesse asking Kiowa and Tawehas (Comanches) to be friends of Cherokees.[6] In another reference Jesse Chisholm, for the Cherokees, presents beads and tobacco to wild tribes and explains the friendly significance of his gift.[7] Later Jesse remembered to send the absent Comanche Chief Tabaquena a gift of beads and tobacco by his representative sitting in on the council.[8]

In all respects the peace try went smoothly. There were effusive shows of friendship, lots of speech-making, and general agreement that "we should do this more often."

Unfortunately, many of the Plains Indians came down with cholera on the way home and died.[9] Survivors blamed the deaths on food given them at Fort Gibson, while others blamed a poison dart coming from the eyes of Montfort Stokes, who wore glasses.[10] Whatever the cause of the deaths, these Indians wanted no more meetings at Fort Gibson. Largely through Jesse's influence, Plains Indians would agree to attend a peace meeting the following summer to be convened near Jesse's own trading post in the Creek Nation.[11]

Jesse was notified that he was already on the U.S. payroll. He responded that he hadn't been paid for his last job. Plans were already afoot for the new council to be held in August 1835 at Camp Holmes on Canadian River. Jesse was given the job of promoting the meeting to Plains Indians.

General Arbuckle was back as commandant at Fort Gibson[12] and along with Montfort Stokes represented the United States at this wilderness peace treaty council. Invitations to attend were accepted by the Wichita, Quepah, Seneca, Cherokee, Osage, Creek, and Choctaw. It was nearly a year later before Te-wak-on-i, Kiowa, and Kataka (Kiowa-Apache) were induced to come into Fort Gibson to sign peace pacts with the government on May 26, 1836.[13]

Living among Creeks for Jesse was not unlike a doctor trying to sleep at the hospital. He couldn't get any rest. Despite fresh treaties signed between Creeks and Osages, Chief McIntosh bitterly complained of serious breaches of peace by raiding Osage and Delaware Indians. Not without sufficient precedent or reason, Jesse was asked to intercede.

. His new role as arbiter had some bright sides but in the main tended to encircle him with problems of others. He solicited the aid of his friend Pierre Beatte,[14] who lived nearby at Cabin Creek, close to New Hopefield Settlement, and the two set about trying to restore order.

Beatte had a place in history already assured by Washington Irving's account of his deeds during Irving's 1832 visit to the prairie.[15] He and Jesse were regularly called upon when experienced interpreters were essential. Beatte, a close friend of the Chouteaus' and a longtime trader with the Osage, was a mighty man physically and in terms of influence.

He and Jesse were odd travel companions. Beatte was high-strung emotionally, quick-tempered, with catlike movements, while the massive Jesse Chisholm seemed to be just the opposite. Their common bond was respect and trust for each other. Along with their Delaware friend and guide, Black Beaver, they virtually stood alone as guides and interpreters on this frontier.

All three had their own families and businesses to care for, so these low-paying and, more often, no-pay jobs as interpreters were seldom sought after. Beatte traveled with P. L. Chouteau all the winter of 1835–36, gathering information for the United States,[16] and he was heartily "thanked" by Stokes when he returned. Jesse shared this experience too.

The source of most problems with the Indians, according to Jesse, was encroachment of "Texans" on Indian hunting grounds. The wholesale slaughter of buffalo had become epidemic, and Comanche and Kiowa were especially riled. The greatest single reason these two tribes turned on whites was due to whites' wanton killing of buffalo, then taking only the hide and occasionally a tongue.[17] Soon the base "sport" of killing only for the count of the dead had begun.

For people who relied solely on buffalo for the majority of their earthly needs, this carnage, done by whites, was unfathomable. For Jesse, who couldn't comprehend the slaughtering either, the job of squaring this behavior on the part of whites was nigh impossible. He also had a difficult season with white army officers and Indian agents who insisted on having things their way, leaving no room for discussion or clarification of their endless string of orders or mandates.

What should have been a relatively simple thing — setting dates for meetings — often proved to be a major consideration. A person could set his watch by the exodus of Plains Indians in early June each year as they began harvesting their winter store of buffalo. Jesse, who was primarily a trader dealing in hides, could certainly understand the reason these same tribes ignored treaty sessions arbitrarily set in June, July, or August. He skipped them himself or was just "out of pocket" when they sought his services during the buffalo harvest season. However, each newly appointed emissary to the Indian, flushed with inherent power accompanying his assignment, immediately called for runners to assemble Indians for treaty talks, often during their hunting season. After all, they probably came all the way from Washington and had a report due in the next sixty days. Tactfully, Jesse tried to explain to each succeeding apostle sent by the Great White Father that in dealing with these Indians, patience wasn't so much a virtue as it was a must. "After all, you are seeking an audience with them," Jesse reminded his host. "So you will have to do it at their convenience, not yours." [18]

Few army officers or civilians concerned with Indian policy-making ever understood this seeming indifference of these people. The chasm of misunderstanding had become so vast between Texans and Indians that Sam Houston had to take leave as commander-in-chief of the Texas army when problems with Mexico threatened war, to try to assuage the angry "pirates of the prairie." [19]

Houston had had enough experience with Indians to know that his mission was in serious trouble if they attacked his highly vulnerable flank. Fighting either Mexicans or Indians with his ragtag militia was a high-risk undertaking. Houston also knew his army was on a suicide course if he and his little band of volunteers had to man two battle fronts.

He summoned Jesse to help him treat with Comanches and Kiowas, but had to abandon his mission, leaving it entirely in Jesse's charge as he hastily returned to his flagging army. No doubt, Jesse used all his influence and flirted with the zenith of his ability when he steered hostile Indians off Houston's flanks.

By this time the Indians had become most hostile, numbering as high as 12,000. They far surpassed the army of Texas and occupying Mexicans in numerical strength and posed a serious threat to either faction they might set upon. Since both Mexicans and Texans were hated, Jesse's pitch was for neutrality. When he sold the Indians on a "Don't get involved in the white man's war" position, Jesse gave Houston the biggest prize of the war.

Significance of the Indians' inaction is still pondered when war buffs wrestle with Houston's miraculous upset of Santa Anna. History has accorded Houston some measure of credit, adding to his already long list of achievements, for his ability to keep Indians off his tail while he jostled a vastly superior Mexican army under General Santa Anna. Mexican officials had scoured the plains trying to enlist help from Indians. There were even rumblings among destitute Creeks, where Jesse lived, favoring military aid to Mexico.[20] Their own existing condition was so deplorable and apparently hopeless that Creeks were grasping at straws in an attempt to alleviate their suffering. But it was Jesse who successfully blunted the Mexicans' attempt to enlist Indian recruits to assault Houston's army.

Now grease from another skillet was burning Jesse. His task of selling the adage "Don't leap from the frying pan into the fire" was a difficult one. He reasoned that some haven, even a poor haven, was better than none. Selling this saw to hungry men was a challenge, one Jesse faced up to and won. He convinced the Creeks to stay home and plant crops, promising to buy their excesses.

Back at his trading post, he learned Chouteau was paying $48 for a bundle of twelve buffalo hides.[21] Jesse had bundled twenty packs when Colonel Dodge, leading a party of more than 100 Dragoons, rode up. Jesse was needed to lead them west to Bent's Fort.[22] Again he tried to pass the invitation, conjuring up every excuse he could find, but finally he agreed to go.

After two arduous weeks of rugged travel due to detours caused by high-water crossings, Jesse's party landed at Bent's place. This task behind him, Jesse headed home. Three weeks later he returned to his trading post, bone-weary and emotionally tired. He was nearing his thirtieth birthday and felt much older. He took the time to catch up on news in the area.

Maj. Richard B. Mason had filed charges on Lt. Jefferson Davis for insubordination, and his court-martial was in progress at Fort Gibson.[23] Davis was found not guilty, quit the army, and married Gen. Zachary Taylor's daughter Sara, who died three months after the wedding.[24]

Actually, another wedding in 1836 commanded more of Jesse's attention: his own to Eliza Edwards, daughter of the founder of Edwards Settlement, James Edwards.[25] He didn't get to bask in the tranquility of his own bed for long. Unrest in the territory was widespread. Creeks were divided among themselves, and the Cherokees were suffering internal political problems.

News from Texas bode more evil. Mexicans had overrun defenders at the Alamo.[26] A force of Texans surrendered to a Mexican force at Coleto (Goliad).[27] On Palm Sunday, March 27, those Texans taken prisoner were slaughtered and buried, some while still alive, according to rumors. Barely two months earlier, Jesse had visited with his old friend from Tennessee, fifty-year-old Davy Crockett.[28] Now Crockett was reported killed at the Alamo. He had jokingly told Jesse he felt safe because nobody bothered "old men."

Jesse knew many of the men who died at Coleto and at the Alamo, as well as the men under Houston's command. Their demise troubled his spirit. He recalled the many deaths from illness that struck the Leavenworth–Dodge Expedition. There was no way he could have fought illness, but the horrible man-inflicted killings he couldn't understand.

He didn't have long to ponder his options before he was paid $300 to guide a party of gold-seekers, led by John Wesley Durant, to Little Rock, of all places. This wild venture would be a source of friendly banter whenever Durant and Jesse's paths crossed.[29]

Houston's unforeseen victory over Mexican forces in Texas was the big news. Some reports told of Houston's death, while others had him wounded.[30] So chaotic and unreliable were news reports of the day that one had only to wait before conflicting reports came. One fact remained constant, however: As hard as it was to believe, Houston's force had conquered Santa Anna's army.[31]

There was also news from New Echota, Georgia — the kind that foretold deeds of infamy and disruption in men's lives. Just as 1835 was winding down, a group of dedicated but deranged Cherokees signed the final act of submission to the United States,[32] which wiped out the last Cherokee claims to their ancestral homes east of the Mississippi River. The Ridge-Watie-Boudinot alliance, in an act designed to negate power of Chief John Ross and two-thirds of the Cherokee Nation that elected him, proved to be a major force of division among the already split body. This was "Fort Sumter," the opening shot of the Cherokee Civil War, which drew active participants like President Jackson, Chief Justice John Marshall, President Martin Van Buren, President James K. Polk, and countless other fringe participants.

Arkansas had been accepted in 1836 as a state of the U.S. and immediately tried to cash in on Jackson's spoils system. Legislative action was quickly mounted to further alienate Indians and to simultaneously make a request for reactivation of Fort Smith to protect Arkansans.[33] Capt. John Rogers had sold the government half a section of his land on which to build.[34] News of the mass movement of Indians to the territory was the cause of alarm in Arkansas. More than 12,000 Creeks were being "herded in" by U.S. troops.

Jesse arrived at his trading site on the Brazos River near Waco,

Texas, in late September. During the course of business he inquired about Sam Houston. He learned Houston had convalesced at New Orleans, from battle wounds received at San Jacinto, and had returned to find that a grateful populace of the new Republic had nominated him to be their first president.[35] He was elected in due time. Jesse felt the prevailing spirit of happy anticipation that all Indians shared as Houston's star glowed on the horizon of the Southwest. They truly felt his victory was also their victory.

Jesse joined in the high expectation the Indians felt, but not for very long. He watched as Houston's enemies quickly closed ranks to begin decimating his gains. Houston's foes knew he defended the Indians from ruthless oppressors. Now Houston's enemies joined forces to try to destroy the Indians' strongest ally. Jesse hoped Houston's newfound fame would carry him, but he knew the combative nature of his friend and his ability to make enemies. He also sensed the fickle nature of those about Houston, waiting, like coyotes, for the kill. Jesse tried to caution his friends who dared store the "uncured" meat of Texas politics.

Back home in the Creek Nation, Jesse began putting his store together. Despite his absence from his home base, he found his crops doing well and his barn stacked high with buffalo robes. He was prospering greatly again. He planned a trip in the spring to St. Louis, and he was putting his barter goods in order.

In December he heard that the great Chief Opothleyohola and his mighty band of Creeks were nearing Fort Gibson.[36] A spontaneous movement of people went to welcome these Creeks. Stark terror numbed onlookers as wave after wave of emaciated, dirty, and sick humans staggered forth. Then there was a sea of soul-sick humans, numbering more than 10,000, pushed into a place they didn't want to be, dumped on a calloused cadre with scarcely enough livery for their own stables.

Jesse and many others quickly and readily depleted their own stores to alleviate suffering Creeks.[37] For many it was too little, too late. Hundreds of Creeks died that winter of 1836 due to exposure and starvation.[38] The rapacity of President Jackson and his ilk stunned Jesse. He just could not understand man's inhumanity to man, and his reaction to man's suffering was the same all his life.

To ease the Creeks' suffering, Jesse emptied not only his store but that of every other friend he had. He literally emptied his pockets of all his earthly possessions to help his less fortunate brother. This character trait would be the theme of his tombstone years later: "No one left his home cold or hungry."

Before the year was done, Jesse learned of the death of his friend, Stephen F. Austin, Texas' beloved leader and great benefactor.[39] Houston had just defeated Austin and Henry Smith in their bids to be elected the first president of Texas.[40] To assuage the sting of defeat, the magnanimous victor, Houston, had appointed both Austin and Smith to his cabinet of advisors. Austin became secretary of state. His sober, honest, and intelligent handling of his office gave Houston's tenure a positive start. Houston and the rest of the populace genuinely mourned the passing of this great leader.

Shortly before Austin's death, the vice-president under President Burnet's temporary rule, Lorenzo de Zavala,[41] died after a short illness. De Zavala had befriended Jesse in Mexico City on his first trip to Mexico. He had tutored Jesse, trying to give him some basic Spanish phrases, and told Jesse he picked up the language faster than anyone with whom he had worked. This Mexican intellectual, de Zavala, had cast his lot with Texans seeking independence from Mexico and had taken the wounded Houston into his home, across from the battlefield on Buffalo Bayou, to help save his life.

In 1837, Eliza Chisholm, Jesse's wife, bore him a son, William Edward.[42] After many "fits and false starts," Jesse now had his trading post at Camp Holmes, near the present site of Lexington, Oklahoma, running smoothly and very profitably.[43] Again he swore off "politics."

Col. A. P. Chouteau sent word to Jesse that he would be needed in early May of 1837 to act as host interpreter at a treaty council at Fort Gibson involving the Comanche, Kiowa, and Kiowa-Apache tribes and the United States.[44] A delegation of Kiowas and Comanches came by to ask Jesse to be in their corner at the May council. He would.

Montfort Stokes and Colonel Chouteau[45] represented the United States, with Colonel Dodge and Captain Bonneville,[46] the renowned French soldier of fortune, in uniform sitting as spectators. General Arbuckle was in Washington during this session.[47]

Jesse made a quick trip to Houston, the new capital of Texas, in answer to the summons of Texas' new president Sam Houston. While no written record is known to exist concerning the subject Houston and Jesse Chisholm discussed, family and friends of Jesse were told that President Houston entreated his friend to influence Creeks to resettle in Texas.[48] It was, if secret, the worst concealed idea Houston ever conceived. For what purpose Houston wanted the Creeks is moot now, but during this era Creeks as well as some Cherokees had been used as mercenaries: Creeks against Seminoles[49] and Cherokees against Creeks.[50]

Jesse returned to his home among Creeks, where he awaited the opportunity to discuss Houston's scheme with both Creek Chief Roley McIntosh and Opothleyohola. If he advised either chief on a course of action, it has never come to light. Probably the unfavorable atmosphere toward all Indians by Texans had a greater impact on the two chiefs' decisions than any other factor. Scarcely a year before, Creeks had seriously considered casting their lot with Mexicans against Texas. The issue didn't die at this point, but Jesse's role ended after one probe and his reply to Houston containing the chiefs' rejection of his removal plan.[51]

A new role involving Jesse was just beginning to take shape. His propensity for getting involved where human suffering abounded resulted in his trading house being used as a clearinghouse — for ransomed human beings. He salvaged many a human life by purchasing their freedom from their captors, Indian or white. His was a no punishment, no questions approach. "Bring in your captives and I will buy them," he said, "even Mexicans!" His idea spread, and as repulsive as the idea was to most whites, families of captives were elated with the hope of getting a loved one back.

The practice was virtually abandoned in most places due to duplicity on the part of some hostage agents. News spread quickly when agents returning hostages were killed after delivering the captive. This practice failed to get the real culprit in many cases, dried up hope for many captives, and in some instances riled the captor to kill his captives as retaliation for being double-crossed.

For more than thirty years, Jesse ransomed more souls than all other middlemen put together, primarily because he, and he alone, enjoyed the trust of all involved in this delicate business where human life hung precariously on whims of erratic and unreasoned men. So universal was his reputation as a ransomer of captives that Jesse regularly heard from persons in high stations of government acting for the United States, Mexico, Texas, Spain, France, and England.[52] Relatives of missing persons channeled most of their efforts through government agencies, who in turn contacted Jesse directly or through army personnel near him. At various times Jesse had letters from President Polk, President Harrison, President Tyler, Secretary of State Daniel Webster, Santa Anna, and Sam Houston[53] regarding persons believed to be held hostage by Indians or some other business relating to captives.

The volume of "business" became so great, he was obliged to accept help, financially, from those persons interested in saving human life. He never profited from this humane operation.[54] Rather, he would hock his home to effect the release of humans, especially children.

For this most unusual stand on moral and ethical behavior, Jesse drew heavy criticism in some areas. For this criticism he cared not a whet, and if he showed any reaction it was one of a man pushing with relentless zeal to erase human bondage where he could. He knew he was limited in what he could do, but he did what he could.

Jesse wasn't alone when it came to drawing criticism. He joined the world in wonderment at news of the latest blunder by Indian caretakers employed by the government. More than a million rations were dropped off at Fort Gibson in 1837, including corn, pork, flour, bacon, and salt (all perishable) and stored on the dock in 100-degree heat with no cover![55]

No problem. Washington bureaucrats had the solution handy: simply dispatch two officers over 2,000 miles into the wilderness by the slowest mode of travel, then build four warehouses 200 feet long to store the excess foods.[56]

Upon their arrival, two quartermaster trouble-shooters quickly realized they had a problem when they smelled pungent pork now seasoned by more than thirty days of baking. They moved with haste to build warehouses, but found that there was a shortage of building materials. Lumber was requisitioned, but months later the local trouble-shooters still didn't have any building materials. So they decided on their own volition to salvage what they could by shipping it to New Orleans for storage. What was deemed salvable was loaded on steamers for the trip to Louisiana.[57]

Unbelievably, the Arkansas River had dropped so low that all steamers were stranded. In desperation, U.S. agents began disbursing what was left to starving Indians in the area. In fact, Capt. James R. Stephenson,[58] one of the trouble-shooters, drew high commendation for the fair and efficient manner in which he handled food distribution!

Creeks came to Jesse, time after time of late, complaining about abuses from their agent, government officials, and contractors hired by the government.[59] Typical of the gripes were cows on the hoof selling for fifty percent more than they actually weighed; wagons capable of hauling twenty-five bushels reported selling for as much as a forty-bushel measure; a bushel of corn comprising three pecks; also, the oldest "skin game," where the uneducated were "short changed."

Jesse tried to help where he could, but offenses were so wide-spread and frequent that catching all the perpetrators of abuses was impossible. Even when caught "red handed," the word of an Indian just didn't count against that of a white man.[60] Jesse's joking advice to victims was simply "get smarter." With each new abuse came "Indian justice," or quick retaliation. Their code was quickly reformed to extract an "eye for an eye" type justice.

The entire territory was now convulsed with violence, most of which, while not unnoticed, went unpunished. The great economic upheaval in the United States brought on a wave of emigrants[61] through the Indians' homeland, some en route to Texas, some not sure where they were headed.

Drunken soldiers fighting, gambling, and carousing strained peace in the territory to the breaking point. Several violent free-for-alls had already erupted with a full-scale riot looming ahead.[62]

Chouteau's new and elegant trading post on Grand River in Cleveland County was drawing visitors and customers from every sector of the region.[63] His ample and wide variety of merchandise literally turned the wilderness into "little St. Louis." His shipbuilding ways were crowded with vessels in various stages of development.

The lordly splendor in this remote wilderness which was Chouteau's stood out like a corncob pipe at a champagne party. This was an empire rising out of the pyre, defying reason or description. Jesse often told his friends he couldn't be intimidated in any environment of society after surviving Chouteau's entertainment. He wasn't the only one awed by this colorful French tycoon.

News from Texas furnished some comic relief-sadistic humor at best. Houston had appointed Gen. Albert Sidney Johnston to be commander of the army of Texas.[64] The man he was to supplant, Gen. Felix Huston, felt he was best qualified to command and decided not to give up his post.[65] A lusty argument ensued to the amusement of bystanders, and in the heat of anger, Huston proposed a duel to determine who was ablest of the two. After Johnston accepted, he was seriously wounded and in a sense was embarrassed in front of men he was supposed to lead.

Now when Indian friends came to Jesse with complaints, he would chide them to cheer up by saying, "You could be in Texas." Despite the most primitive atmosphere surrounding residents of the territory, the scene portrayed of Texas seemed far worse than their own.

Most significant news emanating from Texas was the existence of separate nations within the state — red and white.

Chief John Bowles[66] of the East Texas Cherokees was on the State payroll as Houston's personal representative among wild tribes. This Houston appointment enflamed his enemies, who vowed to kill the old chief on sight.

Another unlikely employee of Texas during this period was Alexander LeGrand,[67] hired by Burnet, without Houston's knowledge or consent, to treat with northern Comanche tribes. Upon being hired, this will-o'-the-wisp struck out for the territory to find Jesse.

LeGrand had met Jesse years earlier when both were trading with Comanches. For a while the Frenchman was attached to these people. Always good for a laugh, the very mystique of this character of the plains monopolized Jesse's attention. Obviously, LeGrand had come to solicit his aid.

On one hand he boasted of his limitless influence and personal power, then alternately shifted his role to that of a soul abused, unappreciated, and neglected. Then he feigned surprise and hurt if his story didn't receive proper homage from his listener — for it was a safe bet that anyone around LeGrand would be listening for the most part. Jesse said to him, "My head rings for days after you are gone." [68]

Whatever he came seeking from Jesse remained a mystery. LeGrand didn't try to trade or borrow and did most of the "jawing," so Jesse didn't know what he contributed to justify this 500-mile trip by LeGrand. He learned LeGrand had met with Chief Traveling Wolf and tried to get Comanches to agree to peace terms. His efforts were fruitless since the bellicose leader of the plains tribe turned down the Texas agent's peace overture. Years later Jesse opined that book writers would have a field day writing about the cocky LeGrand and his endless claims to fame.[69]

A series of events culminating in a storm followed a relative lull in the Southwest. Lamar's ascendence to the presidency of Texas set off an economic prairie fire, but the new Republic wasn't the only one feeling the heat.

Events unfolding on the North American continent were causing a big stir: removal of some 15,000 Cherokees to the territory; abandonment of Fort Gibson; Col. A. P. Chouteau's death; a vicious drought in the Southwest; and arrival of Samuel Colt and his "Colt Revolver."[70] Each of these events had an impact on the tranquility of the area, and combined, the aggregate reached staggering dimensions and rocked foundations of these separate but closely correlated entities — territory and Texas.

No man ever cudgeled an adversary with more unwarranted and cruel treatment than did Mirabeau B. Lamar, second president of Texas. Lamar turned out to be as small in deed as he was in size and seemed to try to make up for his physical shortcomings with big acts of brazen barbarity. From the moment he had control of the reins of government, he declared war on all Indians.

The bitter irony here is the way Chief John Bowles and his Cherokees were treated, he who had been employed by Houston at Texas' expense to circulate among uncivilized tribes and exhort them to peace.[71] For his efforts and his tribes' longstanding friendship with whites, they were unceremoniously set upon. Bowles and most of his tribe were killed, leaving a few brutalized and terrified Indians, mostly women and children, homeless and destined to drift aimlessly.[72]

If this had been an isolated example of Lamar's behavior, it might have been glossed over. But his erratic bent became evident to all the world as he systematically destroyed every reasonable and logical precept by which sane men should be governed. His cruel nature surprised even his friends. His unreasoned acts nearly brought the struggling Republic to its knees before he resigned as president under an avalanche of criticism, leaving the helm of government to a less than erudite David G. Burnet.[73]

The end result of all this turmoil was a quickening pace of Indian leaders toward a meeting with Jesse. He was powerless to change the course of Texas leaders, but he did advise Indians to stay out of the new Republic.

The Comanches and Kiowas, being more wary of whites and Texans in particular, survived by staying away from Lamar's agents. For the most part southern Comanches were coexisting with Texans, and only northern tribes of Comanches and Kiowas were attacking travelers on the Santa Fe Trail.[74]

To Lamar and his ilk, all Indians were alike. Thus warfare against peace-seeking southern Comanches was the obvious intent.[75] This overt and unreasoned act endangered all settlers living beyond protected bounds of the Republic.

A large contingent of Penatekas,[76] as many as 300, rode to Jesse's home to tell him of their problems. He had already read Lamar's inauguration speech in which Lamar criticized Houston for his patience and mercy in dealing with Indians. Lamar promised an all-out war of extermination upon all Indians in Texas. True to his nature, Jesse stunned his friends with his snap response: "Get out of Texas or fight and die." [77] For the present they opted to make themselves scarce — and live.

A drought, which uniformly "blanketed the Southwest," practically eliminated all crops.[78] The corn crop was virtually nil. This "act of God," postmortem, had far-reaching effects on the peace of the area. Those who were hungry stole from those who had food, which caused unrest, not to mention the accompanying violence that these thefts provoked.

The great herd of buffalo was most unstable, wandering at random while looking for grazing[79] and "wet" water holes, since dry holes were now in abundance. As a result, they drifted far from their usual range. Indians who lived off these herds had to travel hundreds of miles in pursuit of food and hides, which they used and bartered. Trade activities of Jesse and others were drastically curtailed by the shortage of buffalo hides.

On the other side of the "big river," Gen. Winfield Scott was in the process of "packaging" Cherokees for shipment west.[80] Chief John Ridge,[81] who with Elias Boudinot "sold out" the last Cherokee claims, led 2,000 of his followers to the promised land in the territory. Getting there was quite an ordeal. Their privations were terrible, and many died on the way. This journey was a prelude to the mass pain and death experienced by Chief Ross' faction being moved under the benevolent guidelines laid down by General Scott. On May 17, 1838, General Scott issued a memorandum to his troops in which he said:

> The Cherokees, by the advances they have made in Christianity and civilization, are by far the most interesting tribe of Indians in the Territorial limits of the United States. Of the 15,000 of those people who are now to be removed — (and the time within which a voluntary emigration was stipulated, will expire on the 23rd instant) — it is understood that about four fifths are opposed, or have become averse to distant emigration; and . . . the troops will probably be obliged to cover the whole country they inhabit, in order to make prisoners and to march or to transport prisoners, by families, either to this place, to Ross's Landing or Gunter's Landing, where they are to be delivered over to the Superintendent of Cherokee Emigration.
>
> Considering the number and temper of the mass to be removed . . . It will readily occur, that simple indiscretions . . . acts of harshness and cruelty, on the part of our troops, may lead . . . in the end, to a general war and carnage . . . a result, in the case of those

particular Indians, utterly abhorrent to the generous sympathies of
the whole American people. Every possible kindness . . . must,
there-fore, be shown by the troops, and if in the ranks, a despicable
individual should be found, capable of inflicting a wanton injury or
insult on any Cherokee man, woman or child, it is hereby made the
special duty of the nearest good officer or man, instantly to inter-
pose, and to seize and consign the guilty wretch to the severest penalty of the laws.[82]

General Scott, while speaking only for himself, undoubtedly was
expressing sentiments of a great number of American citizens. Some
case could conceivably be made to justify abuses heaped upon Chief
Opothleyohola and his Creek followers. These Indians fought when
they were pushed — by U.S. courts — to defend their honor and their
legal right to stay on their land.

It was by President Jackson's order and by his ruthless hand that
these tyrannical acts were used against Creeks, wiping out constitu-
tional guarantees by executive order.[83] Jackson's flagrant abuse of executive power moved the country as close to a dictatorship as had ever
been seen. For a man who hated the British for the tyranny they heaped
upon him,[84] it seems ironic that Jackson would become even more des-
potic and tyrannical when he assumed power.

The mass movement of people, who were carrying all their
earthly possessions into the territory, coupled with the removal of Fort
Gibson's troops,[85] the only semblance of authority then existing, made
for a desperate environment, lawless for all intents. That Fort Gibson
now decommissioned had attracted an unruly mob of camp followers
was undeniable, but timing of the move couldn't have been worse for
highly civilized and orderly Cherokee Indians.

Colonel Arbuckle sent his swashbuckling sidekick, Captain
Bonneville, and a company of infantry to reactivate Fort Smith.[86] Cherokee Agent Stokes was evicted from the fort and relocated eight miles
east on Bernard Bayou.[87] Stokes vigorously protested abandonment of
Fort Gibson, primarily because it would remove protection afforded
Cherokees, Creeks, Delawares, and other friendly and cooperative Indians. He also reminded his superiors that the Indians used the fort as
their market and also received allotments there.

All to no avail was his advice. The fort was abandoned and chaos
supplanted the delicate calm which had existed. Vultures circled the
doomed fort. For his part, Jesse stayed clear of Fort Gibson.

Upon learning that Cherokees were being treated with some semblance of dignity and humanity, the vindictive, old former president Andrew Jackson wrote:

> The contract with [Chief John] Ross must be arrested, or you may rely upon it, the expense and other evils will shake the popularity of the Administration to its center. What madness and folly to have anything to do with Ross where the agent was proceeding well with the removal on the principles of economy that would have saved at least 100 percent from what the contract with Ross will cost . . .
>
> I have only time to add as the mail waits that the contract with Ross [must be arrested], and General Smith left to superintend the removal. The time and circumstances under which Gen'l Scott made this contract shows that he was no economist, or is sub rosa, in league with Clay and co. to bring disgrace on the administration . . .
>
> P.S. I am so feeble I can scarcely wield my pen, but friendship dictates it and the subject excites me. Why is it that the scamp Ross is not banished from the notice of the administration?[88]

In early summer of 1838, Jesse, still grieving for his Cherokee friends, in company with his friend J. W. Durant, went to Texas to talk business with Houston.[89] They also talked with Gen. Thomas Rusk. The three friends spent most of the morning discussing business opportunities. During the course of this visit, Rusk informed them he was leaving for Velasco on business. He had a horse running at the new track at Velasco, so he needed to check out his investment. Rusk's invitation to accompany him was readily accepted by Jesse and Durant.

If Jesse had a serious vice, the love of horse racing, with friendly wagering, was his greatest sin. From his youth he loved to race horses or just to watch them run. As he moved among Indians to trade, he soon learned that fast horses were a commodity he could always sell — after he made a few "bucks" backing his "sleeper." As a judge of horse flesh he had few peers, and during his lifetime trading horses accounted for about eighty percent of his gains. Jesse said he could see further into the future and get there more quickly astride a great horse.

While at the track, Rusk introduced Jesse to William H. Wharton,[90] who was proudly showing off his repeating pistol. He had one of Sam Colt's revolving pistols, which were just being introduced in that area. This gun, or one of its type, would drastically alter the power structure relating to Indian warfare and hand-to-hand combat. Jesse wasn't too impressed with Colt's gun, firearms not being his long suit. On the other hand, his lawyer friend, Durant, probed Wharton eagerly to find how he could order the unusual gun. Rusk obtained one and gave it to Durant about a year later.

As the party was leaving the track, they discussed Rusk's entry, which finished far behind the leaders. Jesse chided Rusk with the observation that he owned plow animals that could beat his horse.[91] He recognized Rusk's horse at once, as one he had sold Bill Cannon some six months earlier. Jesse's evaluation of the horse was the same as it had been six months before: "No stamina." Durant thought all the horses should have run faster to escape the avalanche of vicious mosquitoes. In fact, he built a fire to drive mosquitoes away from his viewing area.

News from home rocked Jesse's composure. Col. Auguste Pierre Chouteau had died on Christmas Day, 1838.[92] The control he exercised with Osage Indians, coupled with his patriarchal posture with other Indians in the region, had exalted him beyond reach of any other aspirant to his lofty realm. His personality was molded into a dominant pose that commanded respect of all who associated with him — even fiery Andrew Jackson, his longtime friend and political ally. Chouteau's strong hand and lavish parties would be sorely missed in the territory.

Chouteau was scarcely cool in his grave before his empire was plundered,[93] leaving little to remind future generations of his great opulence and magnetic power. Jesse had depended on Chouteau for financial backing and business counsel for most of his life. He would come to know how much the loss of his friend Chouteau meant, particularly when his own path became cluttered with thorny problems, where wisdom and experience were needed.

7

Cherokee Civil War

He sat back in his old rocker and gazed intently at his audience to gain undivided attention. Now satisfied, the old colonel leaned forward to share his confidential tidbit of information. "You know, Jesse Chisholm was making regular trade trips to California for years before Kit Carson and Captain John Fremont gained fame opening a trail to California." He added, "Jesse probably traveled more extensively in the southern region of the North American continent than any person living during his lifetime and was blazing new trails most of the time."

There was an aura of urgency surrounding Andrew Jackson Houston as he tried to convey the proper place Jesse Chisholm must occupy. "Jesse never got the 'due' he had coming because nobody told his story," he said.

The Cherokee civil war shocked Indians and whites alike. War between Indians on an intra-tribal basis was old hat, but conflict within the Cherokee Nation was most unexpected and difficult to understand.[1] "The Cherokees," as had been described by Gen. Winfield Scott to his command on May 17, 1838, "by the advances they have made in Christianity and civilization, are by far the most interesting tribe of Indians in the territorial limits of the United States."[2]

Jesse was caught up in the strife between blood kin and friends within the Cherokee Nation. The strife was brought on by duplicity on the part of certain Cherokee individuals acting in behalf of and solely for the United States government and Andrew Jackson in particular.

For a period of thirty years, up to the time when U.S. troops forcibly ejected and transplanted some 100,000 Indians to the newly designated territory, a series of "treaty" agreements had systematically stripped Indians of all their property while pounding their pride. People all over the country realized it was happening, but the reason for this upheaval escaped the general public.

Some idea of the Indians' real plight can be gleaned from Pierce M. Butler, agent for Cherokees, who reported a conversation between Governor James Merriwether of Georgia and President Jackson.[3] Governor Merriwether said, "We want Cherokee lands in Georgia, but the Cherokees will not consent to cede them." Jackson replied, "You must get clear of them [the Cherokees] by legislation. Take judicial jurisdiction over their country; build fires around them, and do indirectly what you cannot effect directly."

When Jesse heard Butler's charge against President Jackson, he sought him out to learn if he had gotten Butler's story right. Butler's verification did nothing to ease Jesse's shock and hurt.

As far back as 1789, the secretary of war, Gen. Henry Knox, wrote this to President Washington: "The disgraceful violation of the 'Treaty of Hopewell' with Cherokees requires the serious consideration of Congress. If so direct and manifest contempt of the authority of the United States be suffered with impunity, it will be in vain to attempt to extend the arm of government to the frontiers. The Indian tribes can have no faith in such imbecile promises, and the lawless whites will ridicule a government which shall, on paper only, make Indian treaties or regulate Indian boundaries." [4]

On December 28, 1791, John Chisholm, grandfather of Jesse, had led a delegation of Indians to Philadelphia to call on President Washington and protest treaty violations.[5] Now, forty-five years later, the Treaty of New Echota (Georgia), proclaimed on May 23, 1836, in fact divested Cherokee people of their last vestige of birthrights, taking all of their land east of the Mississippi River.[6]

Jesse and his family had already migrated to Indian Territory with a group of Cherokees some twenty years earlier. Ignatius Chisholm, his father, recognized the inevitable fate of the entire population of Indians on the eastern seacoast and moved his family ahead of the panic.

After unauthorized cessions of land by Chief Doublehead and a group of his chiefs, Doublehead was executed by the edict of his Cherokee followers.[7] The traditional or verbal law of the Cherokee was implemented: death for traitors. In a legal manner, Doublehead was found guilty and killed after he participated in cessions of land to the United States in 1805. Ironically, just thirty years later, Major Ridge, one of the latest to sign away Cherokee land, and John Rogers, a supporter of Ridge, were two of the men who carried out Doublehead's execution.[8]

Jesse had already effected his withdrawal from his birthright with the Cherokees when civil war erupted in the Indian Nation. With the inevitable chaos accompanying the arrival of some 15,000 Cherokees, as well as Creeks, Delawares, and other groups, Jesse sensed the coming storm and chose to vacate the congested area of Tahlequah, the capital, and relocate his family in the remote area then occupied by Creeks.

His competition as a trader was virtually nonexistent among Creeks. On the other hand, all manner of whites, Indians, and half-breeds flocked to the relatively safe confines of the friendly, educated, and affluent Cherokees in and around Fort Gibson,[9] to establish barter with these Indians and at the same time enjoy security afforded by the U.S. army fort.

The tranquility of Cherokees who lived around Fort Gibson was appreciated and nurtured by General Arbuckle. Therefore, when peace was interrupted, with the arrival of Eastern Cherokees headed by Chief John Ross, the old post commander predictably and naturally sided with "old settlers." [10] These old settlers had served as Arbuckle's allies on Indian matters for years. The highly intelligent and prosperous Cherokees, like their white brothers, were completely compatible with democratic rule.

When the influx of the remaining two-thirds of the Cherokee Nation joined the one-third who preceeded them by ten years, local balance of authority was upset. Ordinarily, the overwhelming majority which came with head chief Ross would have assured him control of the Cherokee Nation.[11] But the splinter group that negotiated the New Echota Treaty with the United States joined forces with old settlers, or Western Cherokees, to form a powerful minority, which drew support from the U.S. government in the form of General Arbuckle.[12]

As war raged out of control and seemed destined to grow in dimensions, the only man possessing the conciliatory temperament to deal with enraged factions was Jesse Chisholm. He was summoned by Arbuckle at the behest of Stokes, and was so stunned by this summons that he could scarcely communicate. "What can I do?" he wondered. Neither knew the answer, but they wished him luck in his efforts and promised him the support of the United States Army. No man more resembled David taking on Goliath than did the meek and humble Jesse as he set out to still the turbulent Cherokee War.

He refused assistance from the army. His lot was similar to the man who had to eat an elephant: He didn't know how to do it, but he would start by taking a bite. First Jesse looked up his oldest and closest friend, Sequoyah, to talk the problem over with him. He believed his old mentor should have been acting in the role he once occupied. But because Sequoyah had already taken a stand, his was no longer an unbiased attitude. Because of reverential awe with which all Indians, particularly Cherokees, held Sequoyah, he still had the respect of all three factions involved. However, those who opposed his views no longer sought his advice or consent for their course of action.

One thing Jesse received of a substantive nature from Sequoyah was the old sage's observation that outside interference, particularly on the part of the American military, made shambles of peace efforts.[13] This coming from Sequoyah, who already had backing of the military, seemed ludicrous — but it was the truth.

Next Jesse talked with old Chief George Lowery, considered by Cherokees in the same way that Americans saw George Washington — like a father. His was a rational and logical analysis, probably prejudiced in favor of Eastern Cherokees or "newcomers," but nevertheless reasonable and flexible. He, too, observed that outside influences, more especially the unsound and erratic ravings of General Arbuckle, while predictable, would do little toward bringing about a peaceful solution.[14]

His Uncle John Rogers was Jesse's next source as he sought a peaceful solution to Cherokee problems. As head chief of the old settlers he had cast his lot with "treaty signers," or the "Ridge-Watie-Boudinot" faction. Talking to Uncle John was tough for Jesse, not because of his stand or anything he said, but rather from John's habit of "talking down" to his young nephew. While visiting his cantankerous uncle, Jesse got a spate of opinions out of which he learned the real motive for the stand assumed by John Rogers: power and money.[15]

General Arbuckle confided to Rogers, Brown, and other leaders of the old settlers that the government was putting out vast sums of money for removal of Eastern Cherokees. He said further that Ross wanted to grab the money and go "south," to Mexico or some other lo-

cale. Arbuckle added, "This money rightfully belongs to all Cherokees, not just the Ross group." [16] Predicated on his own lust for power
(he didn't need money), Rogers had been conned into doing Jackson's
dirty work. The former president was rallying all his friends, picking
up most of his "marks" while using his lackey, President Van Buren,
to front for him in an all-out assault on Chief Ross.

For General Arbuckle, gullible to the point of being dangerous, [17]
this Cherokee "uprising" was nothing he couldn't handle. His duties
were never clearly defined or confined by rules or laws, so Arbuckle
challenged each new situation with the experience he had at his disposal.

Jackson used Arbuckle, his former aide, shamelessly in his efforts
to bilk Cherokees of everything they owned. He had become fanatical
in his zeal to destroy John Ross, along with some 13,000 of his followers.

The more Uncle John Rogers talked, the more clearly Jesse saw
the reason his uncle heaped abuses on Ross and party — anticipated
"spoils" for the victor. After taking leave of Uncle John, he wondered
how to tell him he was the unwitting "tool" of Jackson, a man John
Rogers hated above all men. Jesse knew he wasn't the man to tell
Uncle John he had been used, at least not while he was in such a volatile mood. For his own part, Jesse had heard enough to form his own
conclusion.

On a long shot, certainly an unsure gamble, he opted to give his
story to Indian Commissioner Stokes privately, then bow out. His
meeting with this highly sensitive, alert, and intelligent patriot
proved easier than he had imagined. After he recounted his findings
and conclusions to Stokes, fully expecting some argument, he saw the
old man smile knowingly, nod his head and say, "Just as I had it figured." Jesse's tension evaporated as he listened to his wily host give
point after point, which secured his earlier deductions. While he
didn't feel like he had really accomplished anything, Jesse left believ-
ing the "cause of right" had a mighty ally in this incredible man.

In truth, Stokes set out to strip the facade employed by Jacksonian forces. [18] For his efforts he was fired. However, by his selfless act he
opened enough eyes to vicious acts being perpetrated on all factions in
the Cherokee dispute to get reform measures under way.

Jackson forces hoped these intelligent Indians would "self-de-
struct," proving to the world that one couldn't trust an Indian. They
almost succeeded.

A few years later a shaky truce was completed, though spurned by some like Rogers and Stand Watie. Fifteen years after the truce, deeply embedded hatred again cropped to the surface. While the United States was gripped in Civil War that divided the nation, so Cherokees split along old lines.[19]

Looking back on the Cherokee split and the diverse course it ran, one can see that Stokes and Arbuckle were both winners and losers. After Stokes was fired, it became Arbuckle's turn to be let out.

In defense of Arbuckle, then past the twilight of an illustrious career, his stand was both predictable and justifiable to many. He lived with the old settlers more than fifteen years, during which period he came to rely on these intelligent and peace-loving Indians to serve as an ally in handling his less civilized charges. No doubt about it, Cherokees made General Arbuckle look good to his bosses and civilian observers in the territory.[20]

Arbuckle was not a mean person, but rather a good man in the military sense — loyal, capable of following orders, brave. At times he acted the buffoon, particularly when he was used to spread false rumors of a Cherokee takeover of Arkansas and surrounding country.

Now they were both gone, fired after years of effective, constructive, and useful service to their country. Stokes and Arbuckle can be remembered predominantly for good deeds they performed rather than the nit which cropped up at the end of their careers.

No sooner had Jesse returned home from the Cherokee ruckus than he was called on by Col. James Logan, agent for Creeks, to enlist his aid in getting Upper and Lower Creeks to talk peace.[21] Split along the same lines as their Cherokee neighbors, some 10,000 of Opothleyohola's new arrivals were trying to share land with about the same number of Lower Creeks under Chief Roley McIntosh. In short, McIntosh didn't want the newcomers,[22] and the newcomers weren't happy to be there. Neither group was in control of its destiny. President Jackson had already taken care of that.

The local dispute threatened peace of the entire territory. Seminole Indians under Chief Wildcat were siding with Opothleyohola, and so were Clermont's Osages, making for a dangerous confrontation. All Logan needed Jesse to do was prevail upon the two warring chiefs, McIntosh and Opothleyohola, to come together and talk out their problems.

By some miracle the two met with Logan and agreed, if reluctantly, to peace. The American War Between the States in 1861 gave opportunity for old Creek hate to resurface,[23] they too splitting their alliance to the United States and Confederacy. Lower Creeks served under CSA Cherokee General Stand Watie, while Upper Creeks opted for neutrality.

Pressures caused by Creek and Cherokee disputes mounted to a point that Jesse could no longer tolerate the stress. His friend J. W. Durant was visiting with him while en route to Texas. The two agreed to an alternate proposition after talking with Josiah and John Gregg, who were also calling at Chisholm's post. [24]

Durant had attached himself to Josiah Gregg's caravan near Fort Gibson. [25] Gregg had asked General Arbuckle for a military escort to get him to the Mexican border, and this request was being considered when Gregg's party left the area in late April 1839. Durant went along as far as Jesse's trading post at Camp Holmes. For several days Gregg tried mightily to induce Jesse to go along with them. [26] During his stay, Jesse introduced Gregg to Comanche Chief Tabaquenah and some of his followers, [27] who had come to trade at Chisholm's trading post.

The most memorable incident occurring during this period was Jesse's fervent try to buy hostages from this party of Comanches. [28] When Jesse refused to give the Indians guns in trade for the hostages, trade relations collapsed, for the time being at least.

Gregg and Durant watched in awe as Jesse badgered and berated the Comanches for their inflexible stand and finally in desperation ordered them to leave his post. The Comanches meekly and with no apparent rancor mounted their ponies and rode off.

After Gregg departed with his escort, headed by Capt. Jim Bowman and forty troopers, [29] Durant asked Jesse why he had spurned Gregg's request for a guide, since the money seemed generous. Jesse's answer was formed slowly: "He's too smart, he isn't looking for help, he's looking for an ear." Jesse alluded to Gregg's habit of asking a question and then answering it himself before the answer could be given by the person to whom it was directed.

Jesse reminded Durant that when Comanche Chief Tabaquenah was visiting his trading post, Gregg tried to converse with him in French, Spanish, and with his limited knowledge of sign language. Durant remembered with amusement how Jesse watched with glee as Gregg groped to communicate with the Comanche chief, but Jesse never offered him any help. The stocky little Comanche chief, understanding more than he let on, enjoyed Gregg's untrained efforts to "make talk." [30] Gregg didn't learn much from Chief Tabaquenah that day. If Gregg had sought assistance, several onlookers could have helped him, but he chose to go it alone.

Soon after Gregg departed, Jesse and Durant decided to "break new ground." Having agreed upon a course, they returned to Fort Gibson, where they applied to General Arbuckle for a passport to California.[31] The passport was issued in Jesse's name.

Just before leaving for Texas, they heard that Capt. George McCall had been dispatched by General Arbuckle to put down a Cherokee "uprising" which simply didn't happen. Ever the gull, Arbuckle was still chasing rumors.[32]

Cool days made travel a pleasure as Jesse and Durant, along with several friends, moved briskly toward Texas, arriving at San Antonio on May 26, 1839. After a brief layover where they viewed ruins of the Alamo, they hit the trail for Mazatlan, Mexico, by way of Laredo, Monterrey, and Durango. They arrived June 20, and the following day the party took a schooner for San Diego on the California coast, arriving there June 27.

After satisfying the purpose which brought them this far, they prepared to return to Texas. Jesse was anxious to explore more coastal land owned by Mexico, but his party was anxious to get back to Texas.

The real reason Jesse hurried to California by boat was to explore the feasibility of opening up a trading center, and at the same time give him an opportunity to "home in" a trade route to his trading post. He found the Mexican province offered him a great trade mecca for his hides, salt, and horses. Chisholm's party of six men and pack animals left California and began to lay out the route to his home.

They left San Diego June 29 and were at Albuquerque on August 17. Some forty-one days were spent traveling an estimated 900 miles across the torrid desert wasteland.[33] The route basically crossed the Colorado River above Yuma and trailed south of Phoenix, then took a winding route through mountains to Socorro, New Mexico, and finally to Albuquerque. Jesse planned to rest his men at Santa Fe.

Whatever their aches, they didn't nurse them long before they were on the well-beaten path to Texas. They had already reached San Antonio when Jesse decided to head back to Laredo to look for some horses he had seen in that vicinity. Durant left his party at San Antonio en route to Austin, where he hoped to find Sam Houston.

At Arturo Robles' "Rancho Escondida," Jesse traded for sixteen beautiful, "half wild and crazy" mustangs, then started for home.[34] The day started off easy enough, men and beast moving cautiously over hot, sandy plains with nothing to interrupt the view. Then, for no apparent reason, several of the new mustangs bolted and ran in a westerly direction. Others instinctively followed suit, and the race was on.[35]

At no time were Jesse or his companions able to close the gap on the flying mustangs. Chasing the horses in the arid heat and scorching sands caused his own mount to give out. He waved a halt to his men, and they reasoned together that their mounts had no chance to overtake the unburdened mustangs. They would leisurely trail the horses and, if able to overtake them, try to get them into corrals.

Some two hours later, the group was about forty miles northwest of Laredo when they noticed a cloud of dust rising to the north of their own position. In another half hour they could see horses. Suddenly, Jesse lurched forward after recognizing the horses as his own strays.

Jesse's men fanned out in time to turn the near-jaded animals. Three riders got ropes on the lead horses and began to circle them to a halt. Surprisingly, the mustangs quit the pace, almost too quickly. Jesse figured they were looking for a chance to bolt and he began tethering the animals. He didn't need to bother: They were through running for the day.

No sooner had they hobbled his horses when a small band of Indians burst onto the scene. Jesse called Little Bear by his Indian name and the entire party, numbering about thirty, infiltrated their ranks. He learned from the Comanches how they happened on his camp. Just out of Eagle Pass (more than 100 miles from Laredo) the Indians had spotted this herd of "wild" horses and set out after them. The best they could figure, these horses had run nearly eighty miles! Small wonder they gave up so easily. They had been pushed for nearly five hours in the 100-degree heat with no rest stops.

Jesse's party made camp with the Comanches. The next morning all parties moved northward to where the Comanche main body was located near Carrizo Springs. The following is an account of his activities:

> Two Negro boys were taken by the Comanche in February, 1839 after a battle at the home of Dr. Joseph W. Robertson, who lived on the Colorado River. Their captors, traveling in a body of about six hundred, afterwards met James Vann, a mulatto, James Tiblow, mixed blood Shawnee and Delaware Indian, and George Brinton, a Creek, who were hunting on Colorado River. These Hunters bought Abraham, one of the boys about fifteen years of age, for $150 and brought him to Edwards' trading post and sold him to Edwards for the purported consideration of $500 on March 10, 1840, though the bill of sale was made to Edwards' daughter Lucinda. The other boy,

Sambo, about ten years old, had been purchased in 1839 from the Comanche by Jesse Chisholm when he encountered them on the prairies of Texas. Chisholm was obliged to borrow some guns from his companions with which he effected a trade with the Indians for the boy at a valuation of $150. The band from whom he purchased the boy were called the "Hoo-seesh tribe, or Comanches of the Woods" numbering about fifteen hundred men, women and children. They had in their possession also several white children, whom Chisholm endeavored to buy, but these the Indians would not sell. He took the Negro boy with him to Mexico, and afterwards brought him to Fort Holmes and sold him to Lucinda Edwards, his sister-in-law, January 24, 1841 for $400.

This man Chisholm is very intelligent, and is as I believe, a man of sterling integrity. At the time he visited the Comanches, when the boy was purchased, he was on his way to Mexico under a passport from Gen'l Arbuckle, dated at this Post 23 of September 1839. He was accompanied by individuals, all named in this Passport, who will testify to the correctness of his statement. The People of Texas, it seems have been in the habit of contracting with Indians belonging to the Delaware, Shawnee, Chactaw and Chickasaw tribes to procure from the Comanches their friends & slaves and to pay ransom.

In 1845, while the title to the Negroes was still being agitated, Chisholm made an affidavit that it was while he was on his way from California in 1839 that he met the Comanche Indians on a "branch of the St. Salva," and bought Sambo. At Edwards' trading house witnesses to the bill of sale of the Negro to Lucinda Edwards were Robert Buckham, Peter May, Danny Richardson, Nicholas Miller, John Brown and Elijah Davis.

The other men named in the passport were Robert Beckham, living at the mouth of Little River, Nicholas Miller living in the Cherokee Nation, John Caunot of Missouri, Peter May of the Cherokee Nation, George Bullet and George Connor, Delaware Indians.

> Lieutenant Carleton to Colonel Mason,
> report of investigation of prisoners at
> Edwards' trading house.[36]

Already Jesse had turned a profit from his horses. He raced a paint mare against Comanche Chief Ten Bears' best. He had no way of really knowing what his big paint could do, especially after her "workout" four days earlier. Little Bear was most eager to buy her, so Jesse reasoned she must have showed some promise.

Already well used, the track was around a clump of trees, about one-quarter mile distant, then back to the finish near the chief's tent.

The track was a total distance of nearly three-quarters of a mile, with a stretch 300 yards long where the horses were obscured from viewers by trees.

Bets were placed, with Ten Bears' nag enjoying the bettors favor about ten to one. Jesse called as many bets as his means of exchange would permit. The greatest problem Jesse had betting with his friends was agreeing on what was comparable exchange. When all bets were down, the race was finally begun.

It was a good start. Both horses moved out in fluid grace, pushed on by the powerful movement of their legs. As the horses reached the tree line, the two steeds were moving as one. The track called for a left-hand turn around the trees, and as they executed the turn, Jesse's mare appeared to be on the outside. Now there was daylight between the horses, with the chief's pony ahead.

The race ran out of public view for thirty seconds. Then one horse came out of the woods, fairly flying. The natural question was, "Where was Chisholm's horse?" Now fully ten lengths behind came the other horse, still looking strong. On they ran until the lead horse won by nearly twenty lengths.

On close scrutiny the viewers found that it was Jesse's horse which had run away with the race. Everyone was puzzled as to what had happened. Had the chief's mount been fouled or had it possibly stumbled? She obviously wasn't hurt or lame.

Even Jesse wondered how his horse had pulled away so easily to win. Bets were held while Ten Bears polled his rider and the judges. "The other horse just ran ours in the ground," was the answer. There would be no protest. Jesse's mare had won. In specie, he won more than $600. He knew the horse was worth more, but he made the chief so happy by letting him purchase the speedy mare for $500 that it was worth the sacrifice. Also, he had paid only $480 for the sixteen horses he bought earlier from Robles![37]

The trip home promised to be somewhat easier. "Sambo" seemed to sense the safety his new master represented. He never failed to give "Mr. Chisholm" credit for rescuing him from the Comanches.

Before Jesse reached home he stopped at Robert Jones' place on Red River and caught up on local news. This Choctaw Indian had a growing spread, which made him one of the wealthiest men in the territory.

Chisholm learned that Chief Bowles was dead, killed in July by Col. Edward Burleson in Texas.[38] His followers were ruthlessly killed or scattered. At home on Cherokee lands, Elias Boudinot, John Ridge, and Major Ridge were all killed by assassins[39] in late June. General Arbuckle was now acting as Cherokee agent since Stokes' removal.[40]

Then Jones gave Chisholm the worst news: President Lamar had issued a mandate evicting all Indians in the Republic of Texas.[41] An order, Jesse opined, was easier to give than to effect. He knew that Comanches were already skirmishing with Texas Ranger posses.

At home, Jesse tried to lay low and recoup his trade routine. He didn't get to rest long. The dire circumstances of some of Bowles' tribe, who stumbled into the territory destitute, raised his sense of pity. He housed the ones he could and set out to find friends to help the other poor wretches. As the new year dawned, he fervently hoped it would be more tranquil than 1839.

In quick succession, Texans slaughtered some sixty Comanches in an ambush set up in San Antonio.[42] The Comanches and Kiowas raided Indianola and Victoria, Texas, killing and plundering at will.[43] As these Indians left Texas, they headed for Chisholm's trading post. He learned of their foul deeds and remonstrated them to stop this practice.

Dohasen, the Kiowa war chief, asked him to accompany them to a peace try with Cheyenne and Arapaho near Bent's Fort. If peace was the intent, he would go. While there he would visit Bill Bent.[44]

Just as Jesse was leaving for Bent's home, Satanta asked permission to accompany him. When he agreed, he was not aware of bad blood between Bent and Satanta. When the two antagonists met, a near free-for-all ensued before Jesse physically restrained both men at the same time. Bent's family and friends rushed to his aid, but he called them off. Still fuming, Bent ordered Satanta out. Jesse started to leave with him and Bent quickly asked him to stay. Jesse would stay only if his friends could stay. Bent assured him his guest could stay as long as Jesse would assume responsibility for the Indians' behavior. Then Bent proceeded to give the burly Kiowa chief a cursing in every tongue and sign language he knew. After a prolonged verbal tirade by Bent, his cases fully stated, he lapsed into silence. Jesse laughed aloud when Bent's "lesson of the day" ended. A shaky peace prevailed for the remainder of Jesse's visit.

Back among the large contingent of Indians, Jesse told Comanches and Kiowas they were welcome to trade at Bent's trading house if they behaved. At the same meeting, the Indians agreed to peace terms with each other.

This singular event bode trouble for Texans, since the coalition of

Indians could now devote all resources and energy to their war with the white settlers.

The only good sign Jesse noted was the deplorable condition of the majority of Kiowas. The past winter, a smallpox epidemic had drastically reduced their fighting strength.[45] Still recuperating, many of the braves were in no condition to fight off mosquitoes.

At his trading post Jesse found a New York newspaper, *Journal of Commerce,* in which writer John H. Payne accused the secretary of war of abusing Chief Ross and Cherokees in general.[46] The account also cited Arbuckle's tyranny as U.S. agent-in-charge, pertaining to his behavior in dealing with Ross. Jesse had met Payne when he was a guest of Chief Ross, but he was hardly prepared for Payne's angry charges.

Now on the heels of national attention, new president John Tyler appointed Pierce M. Butler to replace Stokes[47] and relieved Arbuckle of his duties, transferring him to Louisiana. The year 1841 already seemed like a good one.

Probably the biggest news was the scandal that Col. Ethan Allen Hitchcock uncovered during his investigation of affairs in the territory.[48] Gen. Zachary Taylor had just assumed command,[49] making his headquarters at Fort Smith. Their respective orders were to "clean house."

General Taylor first met with various leaders in Arkansas and the territory. Taylor and Jesse had been acquainted some seven years, since Taylor had assumed command there, and he invited Jesse to visit with the new commandant at his convenience. In late July 1841, Jesse dined with Taylor in the general's tent. They sat on bare ground — wet ground, Jesse remembered. No man to put on airs was Taylor.[50]

Among questions the general posed was the advisability of "beefing up" the defense at Fort Smith. Jesse had to laugh. He asked Taylor if he was expecting Mexico to attack him. For whatever reason, Taylor ordered building stopped at Fort Smith, saving taxpayers much money.[51]

In short order the crusty little general was making a survey of his own command, and on his own knowledge he ordered construction of a new garrison to be located not at Fort Smith but instead near the Texas border, about 100 miles west of Fort Towson. The fort would be called Fort Washita.[52]

In quick succession, Colonel Hitchcock began his personal investigation into charges of bungling, malpractice, and fraud by government agents and civilian contractors. His report was fully documented and well prepared, but evidence was so shocking and so far-reaching — even into the oval office — that President Tyler suppressed the report, even though neither he nor his administration was involved.[53]

Tyler had no grounds for refuting any of the charges, but he could not believe the situation could be as bad as Hitchcock's report indicated. Congressional pressure upon Tyler to release the report to the public was intense. Its contents were already circulated, but Tyler would not make it official by releasing the damning report.

To add to woes in the territory, more than a thousand Seminoles from Florida had been dumped at Fort Gibson in a destitute condition.[54] Troops using bloodhounds rounded up these Indians out of their haunts in the Florida Everglades and shipped them like cattle to the territory.

Once there, Chief Alligator and his depleted tribe begged and stole from Cherokees and Creeks on either side of them to survive. Many didn't survive. Men with compassion, like Jesse and his friends, openly wondered how long the ordeal must continue before the inhumanity and cruelty to Indians would cease.

The widely publicized Santa Fe Expedition, sponsored by Texas' President M. B. Lamar and his entourage of bellicose mercenaries, had suffered a violent catastrophe at the hands of Mexico.[55] The entire complement of troops was captured by Mexicans before they reached Santa Fe and were then brutally force-marched to Mexico City. Many died on the way, and none were left unscathed.

Texas was broke, its credit destroyed, thanks in the main to Lamar's failure as an administrator. The Republic couldn't even mount a force to go rescue those poor souls Lamar had sent to destruction.

Settlers in Texas felt the aftershock of Lamar's foolishness. When wild tribes learned what Texas troops had done to Penateka Comanches, they reacted with savage fury. Settlers who found themselves isolated from large communities now had to worry about aroused Indians, bent on revenge.

On his trading rounds, Jesse frankly advised settlers that he met to move to higher ground before the flood of angry savages flowed over them. In too many cases, new Texans bought guns from Jesse and decided to defend their homes. This tragic mistake was the last many ever made.

Jesse tried to divert head men of both Kiowa and Comanche tribes but learned that bad blood had already washed over banks of the prairie. A real blood bath was in progress. Angry Texans now clamored for Lamar's blood. The settlers had enough problems from Mexico without adding Indians to their list.

In desperation, Jesse went looking for Sam Houston, hoping his wise counsel might help. He couldn't find Houston. Even if he had, the blood bath on the prairie probably would have to run its course. The only hope he held was to be on hand to help survivors.

Media sources were sparse in Texas, but reports of Lamar's insane actions were getting wide coverage. The public outcry was so great that Lamar resigned, leaving his tough but dense vice-president, David G. Burnet, to face the wolves.[56] The election was necessary, but only as a formality.

Houston was overwhelmingly swept back into service as president of the Texas Republic. He took office in December and began his biggest challenge ever — keeping Texas afloat. The flood of public debts, rampaging savages, revenge-seeking Mexicans, and unsavory settlers had all but washed the little Republic of Texas out of existence. Many doubted that even Houston could turn the tide of bankruptcy away from the Republic.

Houston's election did signal a change immediately for affairs of Indians in Texas. Jesse met with Houston at Nacogdoches shortly after his election.[57] For once he could not agree to help his friend, Houston, though he truly wished he could. He explained to Houston that Indians had been so badly wronged by Texans, they weren't likely to listen to any man. Houston, in the grandiose posture that few could assume with a more colorful stance, now chided Jesse to "try, before you give up." Houston told Chisholm why he must not "quit" and railed on about how he couldn't "let them down."

Finally, to shut Houston up or to take his leave, Jesse agreed to talk to his Indian friends. He promised nothing but an attempt. Houston relaxed. If Jesse said he would try, one could "hook the rooster up on it."

8

Sam Houston's Trouble-shooter

We walked into LaPorte one hot and sunny morning, a trip covering more than two miles. Several people stopped their cars on the dusty shell road to offer the colonel and me a ride. He politely refused each offer. Years earlier, I had learned that Colonel Houston did not like to be interrupted when he had a trend of thought engaged. To him, well-intentioned people who stopped to offer him a ride constituted an interruption.

At Isensee's Grocery he bought an apple for me and a sack of groceries for himself. We then began the hot, dusty, and arduous trip back to Houston's bay-side home.

On this day, Colonel Houston was trying to deal with the reality and legend of Zachary Taylor that he had learned from his father, Sam Houston.

"Popa respected him as a man and military figure, but thought he was too rigid to successfully manage the nation as president," he said. Then, after a reflective pause, he blurted, "Jesse was very fond of General Taylor and believed he was capable, fair and honest." In summation he added, "You will have to study more than I can give you to make a fair judgment of Zachary Taylor."

True to his word, General Taylor was moving and shaking the "business as usual" syndrome of the territory. Jesse found Taylor's house-cleaning most invigorating, and watched him act with positive

105

measures to correct old evils only recently uncovered by Col. Ethan Allen Hitchcock's investigation a few months earlier.

So far, neither Taylor nor anyone else had been able to ease the plight of nearly 3,000 starving Seminoles who now plagued peaceful territory Indians. The civil unrest the Cherokees were experiencing was not visibly improved, but Taylor was content to let them work out their own solution.

On the Creek side of the territory, Agent Logan reported good progress restoring peace among these people. He delivered an invitation to General Taylor to attend a treaty session that the Creeks were hosting in May. To the surprise of many, Taylor attended along with representatives from more than eighteen tribes, by far the most representative council held to date in the territory.[1]

For the first time in a long time, Jesse spent most of his effort observing, only helping Agent Logan with sticky language interpretation. By now Jesse admitted speaking at least a dozen different languages, which he utilized in his work. With his mastery of sign language, Spanish, and some French, he was a most valuable asset at a council like the one in progress.

At Jesse's suggestion, Creek Agent Logan wrote President Sam Houston to relay the desire expressed by several chiefs for peace with Texans.[2] Tawakoni, Wichita, and other Indians living in Texas stated this desire during their meeting at the Creek Nation. Houston, too, sought peace.

By the time Houston got Agent Logan's letter, he was up to his ears in "snakes," both from within and without his Republic. The horrible mess he inherited from former president Lamar was now fully manifested for the world to see.

The ill-advised and equally ill-fated Santa Fe Expedition was causing more problems. In retaliation for the Texans' botched attack on Santa Fe, General Santa Anna sent Gen. Rafael Vasquez with 1,500 troops into Texas. On March 5, 1842, the Mexican army overpowered the citizenry at San Antonio, taking 100 hostages with them, and then retreated into Mexico with no hindrance from Texas.[3]

Now Houston had the war he had feared was inevitable — but no army, no guns, no provisions or means of obtaining these vital necessities for fighting the war. And he reasoned, with some logic, that the much abused Indians would also "strike while the iron was hot." They, too, had a few scores to even with Texans.

More or less anticipating the little Mexican dictator's moves,

Houston by executive decree called the Republic's legislature into emergency session at Houston.[4] With good reason, he suspected that the new capital located at Austin would be no bigger a challenge to Mexican forces than had been San Antonio.

When he moved the capital to Houston, a new village rising out of the swamps on Buffalo Bayou, some fifty miles north from the coast at Galveston, Houston envisioned it as a permanent move. Lamar adherents were wary of this move, fearing Houston would be unbeatable if he successfully transferred the seat of government to his personal base of power. The move sufficiently aroused Lamar's fire-eating followers to cause them to unload all their wrath on the president. For the time being, Houston prevailed and established the new capital at the corner of Main and Texas in the heart of the town bearing his name.

Now the snakes from within were threatening. As a youth, Jesse was busily clubbing a pile brush when Houston asked him what was going on. He told Houston he was breaking snake eggs. "It's easier to break eggs than it is to kill snakes," Jesse had said. Now the president used this analogy to describe his dilemma with his volunteer army, which threatened the very future of Texas.

Mindful of the charge he had given Chisholm earlier, to help him convince Indians that Texas wanted peace, along with the added inducement of Creek Agent Jim Logan's letter denoting the Indians' desire for peace, Houston wrote:

> City of Houston,
> July 1, 1842

> TO THE CHIEFS OF THE BORDER TRIBES:
> My Friends:
>   The path between us has been red, and the blood of our people remains on the ground. Trouble has been upon us. Our people have sorrowed for their kindred who have been slain. The red men have come upon us, and have slain and taken some of our people. We found them and slew them, and have their women and children. They are with us and are kindly treated. Our people held by you have been sold; and those with you are held in suffering. This is all bad, and trouble must be while we are at war.
>   I learn that the red friends want peace and our hand is now white, and shall not be stained with blood. Let our red brothers say this, and we will smoke the pipe of peace. Chiefs should make peace. I send counselors to give my talk. Listen to them. They will tell you the truth. Wise chiefs will open their ears and hear you shall have peace; and your people who are prisoners shall be given up to you on

the Brazos, when the council shall meet there. You must bring all the prisoners which you have of ours.

You shall trade with our people at new trading houses, and no harm shall be done to you or your people. If you are friendly and keep peace with us, your women and children shall not be harmed. You shall come to our council-house, and no one shall raise a hand against you. Let the tomahawk be buried, and let the pipe of peace be handed round council of friends. I will not forget this talk — nor my people.

Your brother,
Sam Houston.[5]

Jesse proudly carried this letter on his junkets and shared its contents every chance afforded him. If the Texans really wanted peace, he would try to help them in their search.

Neither Houston nor Jesse found reason to rejoice with events taking place south of the Rio Grande. Mexican forces numbering 1,400 under Col. Adrian Woll took San Antonio again on September 11, 1842, in broad daylight with ridiculous ease. Woll's troops took forty-five prisoners this time, then leisurely retreated back into Mexico.[6] Now the Texas Congress had to be convened, but where?

A compromise was worked out between Houston and his opposition to meet on neutral ground. Washington-on-the-Brazos, safe enough from surprise attack, yet out of the Houston stronghold that was the city named for him, was agreed upon by both factions.

With all his heart, Houston hoped Jesse could help him keep the Indians off of his exposed flanks. Even the arrival of the first run of Colt's Walker Model revolver didn't guarantee to alter odds for Texas' survival of simultaneous attacks from Mexicans and hostile Indians.[7]

Houston and Jesse's efforts seemed ready to reach full fruition. On March 28, 1843, the treaty council on Tehuacana Creek was convened.[8]

With some needed support and cooperation from the United States, Texans now probed for the peace they needed so badly. Governor P. M. Butler, agent for the Cherokees, along with Capt. G. A.H. Blake, his military escort, arrived at Warren's Trading House on March 15 and met with Houston's host representative, George W. Terrell. Indian tribes represented were Keitsash, Waco, and Wichita. Chisholm, along with John Connor, Jim Secondeyon, Jim Shaw, Luis Sanchez, and Red Horse were interpreters. Comanches demanded the presence of Houston before they would attend.

In a rare document housed in the Texas State Archives is the following voucher:

Asa Brigham . . . . Treasure
April 12, 1843
REPUBLIC OF TEXAS   To Jesse Chism [Chisholm] Dr.
    To money expended in service of the Republic in visiting and
bringing in Frontier Indians to council, in 1842. $150.
    Approved . . . . Sam Houston
Executive Department, Washington, April 14, 1843

To Maj. H. Brigham, Treasurer & c.
    Pay the above amount of one hundred and fifty dollors to Jesse
Chism [Chisholm] out of the funds in your hands to my credit for
protection of the frontier, & hold this as a voucher.
                                     Sam Houston[9]

Since there were no scheduled Indian councils for Texas during 1842, the money paid Chisholm represented pay for confidential and personal services rendered to Houston and the Republic. The fact is Jesse was paid out of Houston's private discretionary fund, one in which delicate matters, not deemed appropriate for public airing, could be used by the chief executive without specific accounting.

"For keeping Indians off our tail," Jesse's pay wasn't impressive, but that Houston had his services available and the wisdom to call on them is readily apparent. In selecting Jesse for the seemingly insurmountable task, he chose an ally to have in a "bear fight." Houston never went bear-hunting with a switch!

As the result of Jesse's "ground breaking," Texas anticipated major Indian treaty sessions in 1843. Already Houston's appointee, Col. Joseph C. Eldredge, a comparatively young, twenty-five-year-old soldier of fortune, was setting up the processes for treaty meetings.[10] Houston's selection of Eldredge demonstrates again his ability to pick winners. Eldredge left Texas for good after four years to seek new adventures. Among his other adventures, Eldredge played an active part in the laying of the Atlantic cable and was with Commodore Oliver Perry when he opened Japan to world trade.[11]

Another of Houston's appointees to work with Eldredge was twenty-one-year-old Hamilton P. Bee from Charleston, South Carolina. Bee's father, Barnard Bee, had gone to Texas with J. W. Durant in 1837.[12] At age seventeen he had demonstrated enough ability to be appointed secretary of the commission which established the boundary between Texas and the United States. Bee, too, enhanced Houston's record for picking winners, going from this assignment to an illustrious career.

Houston's third appointment for this delicate and most urgent Indian treaty work was Thomas S. Torrey, a twenty-four-year-old adventurer from Connecticut.[13] Torrey was still showing the ravaging effects of his "death march" with survivors of the Santa Fe Expedition and his subsequent confinement in Perote Prison in Mexico City.

Torrey and his brothers, John and David, were operating a series of trading houses in Texas. Records reveal that Houston was a stockholder in two of these businesses. Young Thomas Torrey would be dead six months later from ill effects of his earlier abuses at the hands of his Mexican captors.

All three appointees were directed by Houston to coordinate their efforts with Jesse Chisholm. Now Houston's peace-seekers set out to entreat with the Indians, with Jesse guiding the organizational process — when his young associates would allow him the opportunity. Without consulting Jesse, Eldredge and a small party set out to chase down the eminent Comanche chief of the Penateka, Pahayoko. Three months and over 1,000 miles of fruitless travel later, they were still chasing this old nomad when Houston learned of their folly. He stormed at his aide to tell Eldredge to get Chisholm to bring the chief to them. Jesse was located at Fort Washita, where he was visiting his friend Col. Wm. S. Harney, newly arrived at that post.[14]

In short order Chisholm arranged a meeting on neutral ground in the territory in what is now Comanche County, Oklahoma. Houston's treaty party assembled at the Comanche camp designated by Jesse on August 3, 1843. On August 7 Jesse escorted Chief Pahayoko to meet Colonel Eldredge, Bee, and Torrey with their entire traveling party.

The only positive note recorded here was an agreement to meet with Texas treaty-seekers the next year — if Houston also would attend. With these guidelines, Eldredge reported his progress to Houston.[15]

John W. Durant was dispatched by Houston to locate Jesse and learn his thoughts about how and where the treaty meeting with Pahayoko should take place. Durant returned with Jesse's opinions, which stressed the urgency for Houston to attend in person. The Comanche chief had demanded Houston's presence as a basis for his participation.

The Texas treaty commission met again in September 1843, this time at Bird's Fort, located about twenty miles west of Dallas on the

Trinity River. The following tribes were represented: Caddo, Anadarko, Cherokee, Ironeyes, Waco, Tawakoni, Biloxi, Keitsash, Delaware, and Chickasaw. Still the Comanches stayed away because Houston wasn't able to attend, so this meeting proved to have little meaning.

By far the most significant and heart-rending sight was that of a group of survivors of Chief Bowles' Cherokees from East Texas who had befriended and helped Houston. For their crime they had been annihilated by Lamar and his aide, Col. Edward Burleson, commandant of the raiding Texas army. Now these Cherokees showed up naked, starving, desolate, and begging. This proud clan for nearly a century had been most civilized, mastering agriculture and ranching for a profitable livelihood. They were also well educated, which made their desperate plight the more distasteful.

A meeting including all Indians in the vicinity of Texas was rescheduled. A grand council was to meet at Tehuacana Creek, located in what now is McClennan County, Texas. The event was held in April 1844, but little was accomplished because Comanches again did not attend. The council was reset for May.

This time Buffalo Hump and Old Owl were induced by Jesse to come in, but neither was in a peaceful mood.[16] A disappointed Houston pondered his remaining options. Discussing the problem with Jesse, he heard him reiterate the Comanches' demand that Houston appear in person. Houston agreed, and a new treaty attempt was scheduled for October 1844.[17]

To add to general confusion already rampant along the border between Texas and the United States, some white men wantonly killed three Delaware Indians in the summer of 1844. Known widely for their peaceful and cooperative attitude toward whites, these Indians were hunting south of Red River on the Texas side near the mouth of Blue River when killed for no apparent reason.

The U.S. government, on behalf of families of the slain Delaware Indians, complained to Texas authorities for relief. In turn Houston engaged Jesse to give him a report as quickly as possible of facts surrounding the incident. Jesse and his helpers, Daniel G. Watson and L. S. Williams, submitted a report to Houston on October 9, 1844.[18] The white offenders had been caught and hanged, but there was still a minor problem. Since friends of the dead Indians were unconvinced that justice had been done, they demanded permission to tomahawk three Texans. Request denied.

Houston finally spoke with Comanches and agreed upon a treaty with them in October 1844. Of interest was the report giving details of the meeting. After the treaty, verbally agreed upon by Houston and the Comanches, was committed to writing and presented to the participants to be signed, some three days after the agreement, Chief Buffalo Hump refused to sign. The chief's main objection was the boundary line named in the written document. Houston tried to assure Buffalo Hump that the document was a true account of what they had agreed upon. Whether by accident or intent, boundaries set forth were not what the Comanche chief agreed to and he engaged in a heated exchange with Houston. He even accused Houston of lying and proceeded to prove his contentions relative to the disputed boundaries. The bellicose Buffalo Hump knew every landmark, not to mention the distance between them, and had a most complete knowledge of what he was discussing.[19]

After consulting with Jesse, Houston was obliged to back down from his lofty position and agree with the posture contended by the unlettered Indian. Few men, save Houston, could have had the good grace and good sense to listen and then act as he did, thereby salvaging this peace effort.

The close relationship between Houston and his friend Chisholm is reflected in this document:

In Agreement with Jesse Chisholm
Washington
May 25, 1844

I agree to give Jesse Chisholm two hundred and fifty dollors in specie, for four months service with L. H. William, out of appropriations for Indian purposes.

Sam Houston[20]

An article that appeared in the *Telegraph and Texas Register*, February 22, 1845, reported that a treaty council was held November 9, 1844, on Tahwakkarro (Tehuacana) Creek near Torrey's trading post. Texas Indian commissioners in attendance were Thomas I. Smith, J. C. Neill, and E. Morehouse. Interpreters were Daniel G. Watson, L. S. Williams, Jesse Chisholm, Luis Sanchez, Vincent (Chisholm's adopted son), and John Conner.[21] This treaty was heavily laden with the usual rhetoric peculiar to the events, but one strong clause that authorized guns and ammunition to Indians for hunting purposes was included. Anson Jones, president, and Ashbel Smith, his secretary of state, signed the treaty into law on February 5, 1845. Even though Houston had engineered this treaty, Jones allowed it to be ratified by Congress, with his stamp of approval.[22]

During his three-year tenure as president, Sam Houston was instrumental in reestablishing peaceful relations with wild Indian tribes inhabiting his Republic. Unfortunately, when Anson Jones succeeded Houston as president, the peace link was broken again.

Jones had more of a business approach, rather than the humane instinct so vital in dealing with Indians. He tried to use the same personnel and methods employed by Houston when dealing with Indians, but he chose to remain at arm's length — which resulted in like treatment of him by them. The most serious problem Jones developed came when he ignored advice he had asked from Jesse. Whatever Jones did seemed to be wrong. Indians raided and killed on a renewed scale, while at the same time agreeing to peace — when it suited their purposes.

Jesse gave up his efforts to advise President Jones and returned to his trading post. He found affairs in the Cherokee Nation so violent as to make him wish he hadn't come home. Jesse found it difficult to find enjoyment, even when visiting his family and close friends. On a recent visit with Sequoyah and Uncle John Rogers, he learned of their desire and intent to forever remove themselves from this place.

Now old, and badly crippled to boot, Sequoyah should have been enjoying some peace. Instead he had induced his son, Tessy, and some friends to go with him to Mexico to call on Santa Anna, the Mexican ruler, with the purpose of buying land on which they might migrate and settle. His plan was so grandiose that few of his friends believed he would really try to implement his scheme.

In as gentle a fashion as he could act out, Jesse had told his old mentor that he would not be able to accompany them because of prior commitments he had with Houston. Sequoyah accepted this but did ask Jesse to make him a map showing the best route to Mexico City. He also asked Jesse to recommend an area of Mexico where he should try to buy land.

When he did as he was asked by Sequoyah, Jesse honestly felt he was merely catering to his passing whims, never imagining the old man would try to carry out his brainstorm. Jesse left his old friend, one he would never see again, and took his leave to pursue his own business.

To the astonishment of his family and friends, Sequoyah was indeed going to Mexico. After twenty years in the territory, he could abide it no further. Now the little giant who had contributed as much as, or possibly more than, any man toward the advancement of Cherokees was going to leave. Sequoyah, who in his nation's great hour of need had served as president of the convention which ultimately effected the reestablishment of union between warring clan members, was hell-bent on going to Mexico.

Some authors recounting Sequoyah's deeds stated that he went to Mexico looking for lost members of his tribe, hoping to talk them into returning to the territory. It makes for a more tender tale, but it does not square with facts. There is general agreement that Sequoyah, now past eighty years, left the territory late in 1842 and was never seen again by his friends and family, save his son, Tessy, who went with him. [23]

In December 1844, Chief Ross summoned Jesse to Tahlequah, the Cherokee capital. All Chief Ross wanted Jesse to do was go to Mexico and find Sequoyah. After two years' absence, his friends and family had become concerned for his well-being. So wild and unreasonable was Ross' proposal that Jesse could only shake his head in disbelief. Ross told Jesse to take as many men as he wanted to assist him, and the Cherokee Nation would outfit his party and pay them for their services. The remote chance that Sequoyah might be found alive was all that prompted Jesse to accept the chief's offer ($200 to defray expenses).

Sequoyah became too infirm to continue his trip at San Fernando, Mexico, after their horses were stolen. All but one of his party continued on the mission to Mexico City. Standing Rock remained with Sequoyah. A few days after his troop took their leave of Sequoyah, he died.

Here is Jesse Chisholm's report to Chief Ross:

SEQUOYAH'S LAST DAYS
(Copy)

Warren's Trading House
Red River, April 12, 1845

We the undersigned Cherokees, direct from the Spanish dominions, do hereby certify that (Sequoyah) George Guess, of the Cherokee Nation, Arkansas, Departed this life in the town of San Fernando in the month of August 1843, and his son (Chusaleta) is at this time on the Brasos River, Texas, about 30 miles above the falls, and intends returning home this fall.

Given under our hands day and date above writen.

(Signed)	Standing Rock,	his
		x mark
	Standing Bowles,	his
		x mark
	Watch Justice,	his
		x mark

Witness:
    Daniel G. Watson,
Jesse Chisholm.[24]

While Jesse was scouring Mexico looking for Sequoyah, Chief Ross was badgering Cherokee Agent P. M. Butler to utilize U.S. diplomatic channels to prod Mexican officials to help them search for Sequoyah. From Washington, President Polk urged Butler to give every assistance his office could to help the Cherokees find their lost leader.

At the behest of these parties in their endeavor, Butler sent his own search party looking for Jesse. He received this report from his search party:

(Translation)   P. M. Butler, Cherokee Agent
Sir:
    Having reached the Red River on my way, I met with the following Cherokees from Mexico: Jesse, the leader of the party, The Worm, Gah-na-nes-kee, the Standing Man, and the Standing Rock. The last named, the Standing Rock, attended Sequoyah during his last sickness and also witnessed his death and burial. Tsee-sa-le-tah, the son of Sequoyah, remains on Red River. He is very sorry that the remains of his Father are buried so far from his own country and remains where he is on this account. As Sequoyah was the object for which I had started in search and having learned the fact of his death, which I communicated to those who sent me, it will be useless for me to proceed any further. I will return toward home. He is dead without a doubt. His remaining family, widow, two daughters and a young man live some where in Skin Bayou District.
                            Oo-no-leh
                            15th May, 1845[25]

News of the death of the venerable old soldier and politician, Andrew Jackson, was received with mixed emotions. For those who loved him with boundless enthusiasm, there were an equal number who detested him. One thing was agreed upon by all: With the passing of Jackson also went the Jacksonian power and influence that dominated the United States for thirty years.

Lest the residents in the territory got too carried away with the idea of being out from under Jackson's influence, they needed only to look and see Col. Matthew Arbuckle, Jackson's old comrade in arms, back in command at Fort Smith, replacing Gen. Zachary Taylor. The latter was placed in charge of U.S. armed forces now massing in Texas, which had become the newest state. Texas had accepted U.S. terms for being annexed on July 4, 1845. In a matter of days after Texas joined the Union, General Taylor was massing his forces on the Nueces River near Corpus Christi in order to "protect" Texans from Mexicans.

News that affected few but was a devastating loss to Jesse Chisholm followed: word of the death of his beautiful and gracious young wife, Eliza.[26] She died suddenly after contracting smallpox, leaving a son and daughter as well as thirteen adopted children motherless. For an appropriate period Jesse was confined to his home, caring for his family in the disconcerting way one will when faced with such tragedy.

It was during this period of grief he found himself alone yet surrounded by people. He was the indispensable man to both white and red, yet a part of neither. He was regularly called upon to solve problems of others but could not be accredited by any race. He was regularly called to lead the way, but the fruits of his success seemed to fall to those he led.

As Jesse fretted about trying to care for his children, he realized he didn't know them nor they him. His life had been too enmeshed with those outside for him to have had time to develop strong ties with his own. For these reasons he was a lonely and disconsolate actor in search of the stage.

For all his depression and doubts, the periphery in which he ensconced himself was no barrier for those demanding his services. It was Mrs. Shelton, his longtime friend, who would live at his home and care for his children.

George, his oldest, would accompany him. The smiling lad, smaller than most boys his age, had already seen a life of many varied experiences. George had scrambled through life's brambles until he was ransomed by "Papa Jesse" from Comanches a few years earlier. The happy and trouble-free George caused his father to lose his own grief in the joy his son exhibited. They were going to Texas!

Jesse felt the excitement he had experienced the first time he attended a treaty council. His son's wide-eyed mirth permeated his own spirits. But this treaty try gave no more hope of bringing about lasting peace than the first he witnessed. He even wondered why he was involved again. Long ago his mind augured the hopelessness of his dream, only his heart failed to concede.

He was calmly reading a past issue of the *Telegraph and Texas Register,* dated October 15, 1845, when this report caught his eye: "The military power of this tribe [Comanche] has long since been broken, and it is a matter of but little consequence whether they remain at peace or at war with our government." With this newly proclaimed truth, Chisholm wondered why his services were needed. If the Comanches were no longer a threat, who was killing Texas settlers?

The council at Comanche Peak, where Hood County now is, drew many spectators to witness the taming of the wild or harnessing of hellish Comanches. The most capable and productive Indian official available, P. M. Butler, was chosen to head the commission representing the United States. He would be assisted by Col. M. G. Lewis. By the time this treaty party composed of "domestic Indians," U.S. cavalry escort, white traders, newsmen, and spectators reached the assigned rendezvous, more than eighty people were in the caravan.

Not everyone wanted peace with these Indians. A group of scurrilous men engaged in clandestine trade with Indians saw their bootlegging and gun-running profits about to go up in smoke if Indians succumbed to an orderly existence.[27] To prevent this interference with their illicit business practices, these men lied to the Indians. At one place they warned the Indians that they would be poisoned if they attended treaty sessions. At another site they were warned whites had smallpox. Other Indians were told by those cruel vendors that their throats would be slit while they slept. When the Comanches heard these stories, they reacted in a predictable manner. They stayed away in droves.

For the time being there would be no new peace treaty. It was better than a long-shot bet that Jesse would be called on to supply his own private balm to get the wary Indians to come in for talks. On cue, Jesse and other scouts were sent out to round up the missing Comanches.

The search began in February, but before the three commissioners had time to locate a new treaty site, Jesse arrived with Indians in April.[28] For a change, when the treaty session was begun on schedule, both factions took the peace council seriously.

Elijah Hicks, editor of the *Cherokee Advocate,* was on hand and assisted Plains Indians present: Caddo, Waco, Wichita, and the late arriving Comanche. Jim Shaw, Luis Sanches, and Chisholm were interpreters. John H. Rollins, Indian agent, and Robert S. Neighbors, Comanche Indian agent, who was making his first conclave, were all participants. The Penateka strain of Comanche came out en masse.

Never before had so much "brass" of the Comanche been represented. Here at last was Pah-hah-yo-ko, Buffalo Hump, Old Owl, Santa Anna, and Yellow Wolf, all agreeing to "love, honor and obey" — almost. They did agree to follow the path of peace.

While this solemn event was unfolding, one of Buffalo Hump's four wives took on the other three, and the shaky peace was in great jeopardy.[29] In a most chauvinistic manner, the old chief told his harem to "shut up." Jesse recalled this incident as the only real action that occurred during the two-week session.

Jesse had serious doubts whether the restraint of trade written into the treaty would stand up in the Supreme Court. But since no one abided by these treaties much anyway, he decided it was useless to make an issue of its legality. Besides, there were four more very active strains of Comanches still out there — not agreeing even among themselves, much less with whites.

To cap off the conclave, Santa Anna, Comanche chief, and six other chiefs accompanied Butler and Lewis to Washington so they might be impressed with the power of the United States. Sam Houston, already a U.S. senator from Texas, welcomed his red brothers when they got to the "big teepee."[30]

Jesse returned home to look for some lost pieces of his life. There he learned that his Uncle John Rogers died in June, while on a visit in Washington. Rogers' former brother-in-law, Sam Houston, assisted with his funeral arrangements.

General Taylor's war was gathering some momentum. Congress declared war on Mexico on May 13, 1846, only after Taylor baited Mexican General Mariano Arista to step over taw. For a while it looked as if Taylor was going to have to start the hostilities himself.

Those fire eaters from Texas, more than 8,000 enlistees, joined ranks with Taylor. Out of the woodwork came Lamar, Ed Burleson, A. S. Johnston, Ben McCulloch, and a host of the old Lamar warmakers. Texas' new governor, J. P. Henderson, got carried away with the spirit of the moment and gave up his office to fight Mexico.

Jesse neither offered his services nor were they sought by anyone in Taylor's ranks. Perhaps he was too valuable in his capacity of peacemaker, particularly if Indians used the whites' diversion with a war to go on a rampage to try to settle old scores. He would be the essential link from then on to communicate with the wild tribes.

Politics, the roughest foe Jesse knew, now claimed the career of P. M. Butler, he of the disciplined school but with a heart as kind as his ability was outstanding. He was fired from his post as Indian agent. With his dismissal Butler rejoined the army from whence he had come to help Taylor's war. Butler was killed fighting in Mexico on August 20, 1847.

A new life loomed for Jesse. He married a neighbor whom he had known from her childhood, Sahkahkee "Sari" McQueen, a Creek.[31] To some this union appeared one of convenience. If it was, more than thirty years of marital bliss spoke well for the arrangement.

The new Cherokee Indian agent, James McKissick, was on hand inquiring for Jesse. With a new wife and a new agent, whom he must come to know, Jesse had his work cut out for him in adjusting to new people in his life.

Another new agent, Robert S. Neighbors, would have charge of Comanches. Jesse had met Neighbors only the past year, but formed a liking for him immediately. When Old Owl, Penateka chief of the Comanches, came to Jesse complaining that Capt. Ben McCulloch wouldn't let his people hunt buffalo (a treaty violation), he referred him to Neighbors, primarily to see what the new agent would do. Neighbors' honest and dedicated effort in the old chief's behalf was a welcome sign for Jesse. It was most significant that he acted as he did, because Jesse learned from Comanche chief Old Owl that Mexican soldiers were offering to pay them to fight whites.

By this time battlewise troops under the iron-fisted rule of General Taylor threatened to drive Santa Anna's Mexican force into the sea. With each new conquest, hero-worshiping Americans cheered Taylor's every move. Obviously, his was an instant love affair for those minions of war.

In an attempt to blunt the little general's wave of popularity, Gen. Winfield Scott, ranking officer in the armed forces, was dispatched by President Polk to Mexico to lead 19,000 seasoned U.S. troops.[32] They would land at Vera Cruz and hopefully beat Taylor to Mexico City. Scott was eminently successful, but two years of good "press" was too much for anyone to supplant.

Taylor's star was too bright to be covered, even by the 300-pound commanding general. His was a future now assured of top billing, justifiably or not.

Old-timers in the territory, like Harney and Hancock, remembered Taylor and Jesse as mutually respectful and considerate. Jesse liked Taylor, but was one of a handful not intimidated by this man who was destined to be the next president of the United States.[33] Jesse only hoped that Taylor would lead the country in the same effective way that he had guided troops in the territory.

9

Gold Rush
Mania

We had barely gotten into the story on this morning when a flash rain squall drove us to cover inside Houston's home. He asked his daughter, Margaret, to hand him several books, along with a box of old newspaper clippings.

When she took too long finding the books requested, he asked another daughter, Ari, to join the search operation. When no better results came from two searchers, he joined them. All three of the Houston family rummaged for more than an hour, looking through boxes of books, papers, and letters before he either found what he sought or gave up his search.

From time to time, Colonel Houston would cease looking to peruse some document and would hand it to me for my inspection. In this manner, I was able to see much of the Houston memorabilia, particularly those items that pertained to Jesse Chisholm.

As he tendered each book or clipping for my perusal, he would say, "Remind me to tell you about this . . ."

When the search was completed, Ari brought us two homemade wafers and a cup of broth. The old man continued: "This article in the Clarksville {Texas} paper in 1849 tells about Jesse taking a group of sixty people to the goldfields in California." And so began the story of how Chisholm guided this party through hostile Indian Territory as far as Santa Fe.

From an unexpected source, Jesse was being openly challenged. For the first time in his storied career, he found his word being questioned by an Indian, Seminole Chief Wildcat.[1] He had watched with some concern not for his own well-being but for the possible danger to those who fell under Wildcat's influence.

Wildcat was an articulate, educated, and personable giant who was in the right place at the right time. Countless broken treaties, lies, and bilking of Indians by whites had at last brought out an Indian with enough guts and brains to implement some serious opposition. His reputation spread like a prairie fire, and his aim was just as perilous.

Chief Wildcat, as fearless as he was intelligent, faced down Roley McIntosh, head chief of the Lower Creeks, while at the same time daring the United States or other Indians to help the beleaguered Creek leader. Earlier, McIntosh had issued a warrant for Wildcat's arrest, charging him with insurrection, among other things. Wildcat rode to McIntosh and dared him to try to carry out his arrest orders.

For several years, Chief Wildcat had been advising, protecting, participating with, and in general making himself known to all Indians in the territory, leaving his "marks" as he made his rounds — including regular trips to Mexico. If the established pattern of whites ran true to form, Wildcat would soon claim his "marks."

The "system" which dealt so harshly and unfairly with all Indians was creating the perfect atmosphere for an amalgamation of offended peoples or malcontents united, in which a dominant leader could transform them into a mighty army. Jesse watched this deadly game being played out, which could ignite the entire Southwest in warfare.

Wildcat wasn't the only spur to Indian emotions. The entire world knew by then that gold had been found in California in sufficient quantities to "excite a dead horse."[2] Col. R. B. Mason was acting as military governor of California when gold changed this quiet extension of the great American desert into a hotbed of lust, death, and unbridled growth.

Based on his past record for ineptness while commanding at Fort Gibson, Mason was a poor candidate to successfully maintain peace in the goldfields. The U.S. Army had sent Mason to California to allow him to finish his career in peace, but fate put him back on the firing line. Mason's job in California became a nightmare as men went wild in their lust for gold.

St. Louis, Fort Smith, and Memphis, all suitable ports of embarkation for California, soon became flooded with gold-seekers. The subsequent avalanche of humans that headed across the territory en route to "sure riches" became both a financial boon for some and an endless source of death and destruction for many.

Wave after wave of "men gone crazy" charged across uncharted wilds heading west — right across the hunting grounds and home of the most untamed and unfriendly Indians left on the North American continent. Comanches, Kiowas, and Cheyennes were the biggest menace to the uncontrolled trespassers. Foolish and unguarded men furnished too easy a prey for these denizens of destruction and death. The mortality rate of those on prairie schooners was nearly as great as that of ticks at a dipping vat.

Like news of the gold find, reports that Indians were on a rampage spread rapidly. It was not reported that the Indians were protecting their homes — on land they had claimed for centuries.

Such was the situation on the plains in early 1849, when some intellectual giant suggested that the United States bribe these savages to leave gold-seekers alone.[3] The U.S. would begin promising them complete immunity from punishment for past depredations. The incredible aspect of this poser was that Indians — not whites — "looked for the loophole."

A large group of these Comanche raiders found their friend Jesse near Graham, Texas, at his trading camp on the Brazos River. They told him about the offer of amnesty delivered by some territory Indians. He was so thunderstruck by the unreality of the idea, he could not believe it was a valid proposal. Indians, to a man, were also full of doubts and joined Jesse trying to find logic where there was no logic. The Comanches wondered what the white men were up to. Was this an ambush ploy like they had experienced in San Antonio a few years before?

Jesse was so intrigued by the whole matter he curtailed his trading trip to accompany Comanches back to the Indians who first delivered the whites' offer.[4] En route back to the territory with Comanches, he was intercepted by a messenger. The message for Jesse sent him scurrying to his home. Once there, he saw his new daughter, Jenny, for the first time. She was born during his absence of three months. The new father enjoyed a brief interlude with his family while his Indian friends camped in the front yard. After a week, Jesse headed for the Creek Agency.

Philip H. Raiford, newly appointed Creek agent, had not arrived at his new post when Jesse and his large band of Comanches arrived at agency headquarters in the Creek Nation. It was just as well. The docile, friendly, English-speaking Creeks were one thing, but the rude, brash, and surly Comanches were something else — a challenge that Raiford wasn't ready for.

A courier from General Arbuckle had enlisted the Creeks' aid in contacting Comanches with the offer of a peace treaty. This was the peace offer referred to earlier in which the U.S. guaranteed complete amnesty for Comanche raiders in exchange for peace. When Creek Chief McIntosh verified the offer, Jesse and the Comanches were shocked all the more, if possible, than when it was first tendered. Jesse refused to advise them what to do.

Comanches decided to ask Chief Roley McIntosh for his advice. From this session they were advised to make peace with whites — and the sooner the better.

Comanches then wanted to talk to Seminole Chief Wildcat. This was a move Jesse hadn't anticipated. With all his being, Jesse dreaded this confrontation. He had nothing against Wildcat, but on an earlier occasion the chief had told others that Chisholm was weak and curried favor of the whites. In the council circle of Indians, there is no room for "the weak." Jesse knew he would be forced to challenge the veracity of Wildcat's charge or lose face with Indians.

When Jesse and his guests arrived at Wildcat's place, he greeted them all cordially but paid special attention to Chisholm. When he learned the reason for the visit from Comanches, Wildcat made a long speech giving many reasons these Comanches should sue for peace.

As Wildcat talked on, Jesse waited for the other side of his counsel, for the other shoe to fall. It never came. Neither did Wildcat veer from his positive stand for peace. And he had nothing but the highest praise for the Comanches' host, Chisholm. Never one to buy trouble, Jesse left Wildcat as he found him — friendly.

This amnesty offer by General Arbuckle and the military, while legitimate, was too preposterous to be believed. Jesse opted to return to his home and avoid getting any further involved.

Even with the sage advice the territory Indians gave Comanches, they still could not bring themselves to believe their enemies could forgive their many transgressions. Like children, they knew and frankly expected they would be chastened. For three days they continued to agonize over their dilemma before they agreed to sue for peace — and take their chances.

Where the seasoned or experienced agents in the Southwest had recognized and immediately began steps to correct ills, a new set of agents was now in charge, content to leave decisions for a later date. Death removed Cherokee agent James McKissick in January 1848, before his "seat was warm." After three months with no military agent for Cherokees, a new agent, Richard C. S. Brown, took office in April 1848, a new broom ready to sweep. Brown found many crevices that needed the attention of his new broom. Comanches lost the services of Robert S. Neighbors to politics. This dedicated public servant sought solutions, being ever among his charges. His replacement, honorable and highly esteemed Judge John H. Rollins, through no fault of his, had become old, chronically ill, and usually unable to travel.[5]

The first problem Rollins faced was the oversight or outright refusal of Congress to allocate funds for Indian annuities voted by the same Congress. Instead of trying to allay Comanches' justifiable indignation, Judge Rollins hid from his charges.

These two incidents were not isolated cases. The agency system was as mixed up as those bureaucrats who managed the system. Chaos had been created out of a reasonable working order. As this deplorable situation grew in intensity with every agency upheaval, so did the Indians' need for sound counsel and guidance. Many turned to Jesse, but he couldn't be spread far enough to help all those needing help. Another source of help were the headmen of the civilized tribes, especially those heading the "five civilized tribes." But not all of the leaders of the civilized tribes could be considered strong advocates for peace. One of the tribes, the Seminole, was headed by Chief Wildcat — an Indian certainly not renowned as a peace advocate.

News from another front indicated that Jesse was attracting more national attention. The following announcement appeared in the *Northern Standard,* February 10, 1849:

> The organization of an expedition to California leaving Preston (Grayson County) Texas on April 1, 1849. It is anticipated that the services of Jesse Chism [Chisholm] as a pilot will be procured, who is perfectly conversant with the whole route to be traversed, as well as the languages of the different tribes of Indians through which the expedition will pass.
>
> James G. Thompson
> S. Kinzey
> James H. Mars

As this article illustrates, the name Jesse Chisholm had become synonymous with "safe passage." It was now being employed by speculators hoping to draw a crowd just by using his name, more often than not without his consent.

Once again Jesse's name cropped up in official documents among Indian agents. In a communiqué between Seminole Agent Marcellus Duval and the War Department, he explained his "inability to communicate with the Keechies because his interpreter, Jesse Chisholm, was away in Missouri." [6]

Also looking for Jesse's services was Lt. James H. Simpson, in charge of the Corps of Topographic Engineers' work crew, doing a survey from Fort Smith to the Rio Grande. [7] Jesse couldn't go but put them in touch with his friend Black Beaver, Delaware guide, who was available. This was the same survey party that utilized Capt. Randolph B. Marcy as escort on his first trip conducting some 400 gold-seekers to California, over a route Jesse had been using for years.

Demands had become so great for Jesse's services that he was unable to tend to his own business and simply could not be all the places he was wanted and needed. He had become deeply involved with the rescue of Indian-held hostages. His top priority, hostage rescue, was expensive, time-consuming and burdensome, particularly after he was able to ransom captives. He would and often did stop his work when a human life hung in the balance. When there was no claimant for his hostages, Jesse clothed, fed, and housed them himself.

Jesse had hoped his friend President Taylor would begin righting some of the wrongs both knew existed in the Indian Territory, but so far the path seemed to be leading to oblivion. The president seemed to be preoccupied with other pressing business.

Jesse followed with interest some legislation pending in the U.S. Congress. One congressman, Senator Thomas Hart Benton of Missouri, was one who couldn't be accused of lacking vision. Senator Benton in quick succession introduced two Senate bills espousing astronomical feats. [8] Bill number one proposed building a railroad from the Mississippi River (starting, naturally, at his home town St. Louis) to the Pacific Ocean. His second bill called for building a highway from St. Louis (quite naturally) to San Francisco along the 35th parallel or new "Marcy Road." Passage of either of these two bills would have been a license for speculators to steamroll Indians in their path. Jesse knew that by the time Indians got the news, the die would be irrevocably cast.

News from Texas was not good for Indians either. P. H. Bell, a

Houston-hating fire-eater, was elected governor. His first official duty was to recommend the enlargement of Capt. Jack Hays' Ranger force, and with the new Colt revolver he planned to rid Texas of "Houston's Indians."

To help facilitate this endeavor, the U.S. was setting up a series of nine new military posts in Texas during the next ten years. Texas was going after Indians like Georgia had done twenty years earlier.

One constant remained: Texas' inconsistent posture in treating with Indians. On one hand, the United States was making grand gestures for peace; on the other hand, they were implementing means for the total destruction of Indians through their newest state, Texas.

In ten years more than twenty percent of all U.S. military personnel would be stationed in Texas.[9] This massing of troops had nothing to do with Mexican threats, either real or imagined. Mexico no longer posed any threat to American citizens. Mass build-up of troops in Texas was for the purpose of fighting Indians. According to the Treaty of Guadalupe-Hidalgo, made with Mexico after the war of 1845, the United States agreed to protect Mexico from attack by Indians of this nation. Some wag called the military "hired guns" to protect Mexico.

United States policy toward Indians, never clearly defined, became more diverse than ever. (The riddle of Indian policy is still confusing today, after more than 150 years in the making.) In light of this, Jesse chose not to jeopardize his friendship with Comanches by recommending they enter into any peace agreement based on U.S. promises. He could see there was no real intent on the part of either faction to deal honorably at this juncture of their ever-widening war. He reasoned there was no more he could contribute in behalf of peace, so he returned to his family and business, where he knew he was needed.

Jesse had neglected his business so badly that he found his trading post almost bare of supplies when he arrived there. He was forced to leave the friendly environment of home for a much needed buying trip.

During his trip to St. Louis, he traded with various tribes along the route. On one of these encounters with Kiowas, he learned of the great epidemic of cholera which left nearly half of their number dead and many still suffering debilitating after-effects. So touched was Jesse by the suffering he found among Kiowas that he stayed among them nearly two weeks, helping to nurse the sick. He gave freely, never counting cost. His simple philosophy was: "They were hungry so I fed them."

In St. Louis, Jesse arranged for supplies he had bought to be sent by boat to his new trading post at Camp Holmes. He hurried back to his store to help stock his shelves with the goods from his trip.

His trading post was on the well-beaten path to California, where hordes of people scurried by nearly every day. His business boomed faster than he could supply demands for food, clothing, cooking utensils, and horses — or for that matter anything else needed for the junket.

Time and time again he tried to dissuade ill-prepared prospectors from making the effort. In most cases, his free advice was freely rejected. There was simply no "turning" this stampede of gold prospectors, so Jesse actively plied his trade to help travelers along the road to riches — or ruin.

In spite of frequent stabs at maintaining his trading post business, he found his time being used more for trading for human beings. His reputation as a man concerned for humans in bondage was reported by Santa Fe Indian Agent James S. Calhoun in a report to his superiors on March 31, 1850: "Chisholm, Wm. Donaho and Josiah Gregg ransomed Comanche prisoners out of the goodness of their hearts at $200.00 each." [10]

Looking backward in time, one ponders why Jesse's spectacular behavior, that of ransoming lives, not unlike an eclipse in rarity, was not more newsworthy. Killings, raids, retaliations, and death were endlessly covered like weather reports.

Enjoying a brief respite, Jesse worked at his own business awhile, buying more than 3,500 hides, most number of kind being 3,000 buffalo robes. [11] The harvest of buffalo was at an all-time peak. In St. Louis alone, one company reported buying 100,000 hides. The American Fur Company was the biggest but certainly was only one of many in the largest trading center on the Mississippi River.

Despite his neglect, Jesse's business was now prospering more than ever. He even found time to build a large and attractive two-story frame house for his family.

At the request of Comanche Chief Buffalo Hump, he went to San Antonio to try to learn from Agent Rollins why their annuities were being withheld. Rollins said money had been made available to him and that he planned to disburse the money in early December. He told Jesse he planned to use the occasion for signing a new treaty agreement with the Indians, and asked Jesse to assist him. Jesse reluctantly agreed.

The meeting began December 10, 1850. Out of this meeting

came the ribald joke of an ethnic nature pertaining to Mexicans.

The meeting, conducted by Rollins, who was representing the United States, was well under way when the agent confronted Comanche Buffalo Hump about his promise to return all white captives. The old chief assured Rollins he had complied with the promise. At that point Jesse asked him about four Mexicans he knew were being held in the Comanches' camp. Rollins interrupted to remind Jesse, "Mexicans don't count."

Years later, "badmen" boasted so many notches on their gun "not counting Mexicans." [12] In different areas, "exempt" lists included blacks and Indians interchangeably with Mexicans. It was in a mutual feeling of loathing for Mexicans where Texans and Indians found common understanding. There is no evidence that Mexicans held Texans or Indians any dearer than loathing.

The irony of this naiveté shown by Indians on one side, compared with that expressed by eminent Judge Rollins, is a paradox of the times. Social advancement of Rollins appears to be equal to that of his savage charges.

It was at this meeting, in the wilds of Texas, that Jesse had learned of the death of President Taylor, nearly five months earlier. At the same time, the passing of John Calhoun, South Carolina politician, was reported by Judge Rollins. Jesse was saddened by Taylor's death, while Rollins mourned the passing of Calhoun.

Shortly before President Taylor died, he publicly ridiculed Texas fighting men under his command in the Mexican War of 1845–48. [13] Taylor's criticism included Houston's enemies Lamar, Burleson, McCulloch, and many others, men with whom Houston had experienced similar problems as those mentioned by Taylor. However, when Taylor dragged Texas' name into his diatribe on fighting men, he found the fighting side of "old Sam." Houston got the Senate floor on a point of personal privilege to answer President Taylor's charges against the fighting Texans. [14]

On July 8, 1850, Houston leveled a vicious attack on Taylor. Much to his sorrow, Houston learned the next day of Taylor's death. Nevertheless, he found no reason to recant his defense of Texans in general.

The next few months were relatively calm for Jesse, as he patched wagons and fences and made other minor repairs to his home. He was called upon at his trading post by some Penateka Comanches complaining of harassment from other Comanches — Yamparika in particular. Jesse was once again busy trying to "mend the fences" of someone else.

After Agent Rollins learned that Mexican prisoners were supposed to be released by Comanches, he led an army detachment into their camp to effect the prisoners' release. The Comanches gave up the captives without a struggle, and Rollins left without paying any ransom. For this fact, other Comanches were furious at Penatekas. In every case where Indians gave concessions to whites, they hammered out links in the chain that would eventually bind them. Any concession of one tribe caused internal cleavage which weakened the protective wall their unity afforded.

The internal cleavage of Indians' solidarity was getting more serious with each new onslaught. On a front nearby, another Indian was doing such an outstanding job of uniting Indians in Mexico that he was looked upon with ever increasing alarm.

Seminole Chief Wildcat was now reaching the apex of his career. [15] More than 500 Kickapoo joined his band of outcast Indians and more than a hundred blacks, giving him an army of more than 1,000 warriors. [16] Other Indians were being urged to join him.

Based on reports of these activities, the United States sent Col. Samuel Cooper and a company of troops to try to contact Wildcat and learn what they could of his intentions. Jesse went along as guide and interpreter. In March 1851 they found Wildcat near Eagle Pass on the Mexican border. For his own reasons, Wildcat put on a show of goodwill and was outwardly accommodating toward Cooper.

The report this party made concerning their meeting with Wildcat was most unusual. The intelligent and personable chief completely won over his adversary. The military reported he was polite, friendly, and most concerned for welfare of his followers. Wildcat told Colonel Cooper the only reason he left the territory was to avoid war with "McIntosh Creeks." Jesse listened with interest as Wildcat captivated his army interrogator, feigning shock that his peaceful and innocent stance was being questioned.

José Maria Jesus Carbajal was in the welcoming party at Piedras Negras when Colonel Cooper encountered Chief Wildcat. Carbajal, longtime friend of Chisholm, had fought with Sam Houston at San Jacinto. He is also recorded as one of Santa Anna's officers in the war of 1845 and was a Mason. This unusual individual, like Jesse, defied categorization. Born in San Antonio and reared in Texas, he was allied with Houston's cause. Yet he was too "Mexican" to be trusted and by then was an outcast in his native Mexico. Nevertheless, Carbajal moved back and forth between Mexico and Texas all his life with little resistance from either faction. He befriended and was accepted by wild Indian tribes. Carbajal's private report about Chief Wildcat's pending pact with Mexico had spurred Jesse's personal doubts about Wildcat's real motives.

It was what Wildcat didn't tell Cooper that worried Jesse. Reports reaching him from some Creek chiefs related Wildcat's pending deal with Mexico, whereby he would protect their borders from Indian attack in exchange for land on which to settle his followers. This was the news Carbajal corroborated during his session with Jesse. U.S. army officers could detect no visible danger from Wildcat's behavior. But Jesse saw graphically the groundwork begun to cause further rifts among Indians.

Now the internal rupture caused by Chief Wildcat would further divide Indians. Various Indians assembled by Wildcat would be paid to protect their hated enemy, the Mexicans, from attack by other Indians including Comanche, Kiowa, Osage, and Apache.

Politics of war and art of survival uncovered some strange fellows occupying the same bed — at the same time.

When Jesse related his meeting with Wildcat to Comanche Chief Bull Hump and his followers, they all pulled their lower eyelids with forefingers, a gesture appropriated from some white man. The old chief grinned widely as Jesse looked puzzled by their act. Bull Hump explained that the movement was one that suggested a story or transaction needed to be looked at more closely. It was Jesse's turn to grin and nod agreement. The eye-opening gesture became widely used to express doubt, surprise, or incredulity.

As Jesse wearily worked his way home, he was resigned to spend much more time at home. At his home and trading post, which formerly housed Col. A. P. Chouteau's business enterprises,[17] Jesse was prospering in a magnitude he never imagined possible.

Traffic to the California goldfields had abated some, but the stream of humans moving west was more than sufficient to keep his business booming. He had made $3,000 on two occasions guiding large caravans as far as Santa Fe, and could have taken at least four more groups if he had chosen to do so.[18]

At home he learned that Gen. Matthew Arbuckle had died at Fort Smith.[19] News of the old man's death didn't come as too much of a shock, but it did sadden Jesse greatly. He loved and respected Arbuckle. While not always agreeing, the two had been like father and son since Jesse was nineteen years old. Arbuckle was seventy-five years old when he died, with more than forty years spent on the frontier, longer than any other regular army officer. His judgment was occasionally suspect, but never his honor or loyalty.

The year 1852 was one in which Jesse spent on personal business. His family now numbered nineteen, including wife, mother, and children. There were many mouths needing food. He did find time to visit with Senator Houston at Washington-on-the-Brazos in October, when both men were guests in the home of J. W. Durant.[20]

While on the way home from this meeting, Jesse met E. H. Altgelt at Waco and negotiated the purchase of four wagons. Altgelt had the wagons, a large Pittsburgh variety, in storage at New Braunfels. He hired two teamsters at Waco, young Peter Smith and Charles Goodnight, to help him transport the wagons home.[21] Smith continued to work for Chisholm the rest of his career. This was probably the first meeting of the cocky but highly capable Goodnight with Chisholm, but their paths crossed many times in the next fifteen years.

Jesse was working his way home when he met up with his friend Col. R. B. Marcy, while crossing Red River at Ryan. During this reunion, Marcy introduced Jesse to his new son-in-law, Capt. George B. McClellan. His career was just beginning, but in ten years he would be a general, commanding Union forces during the Civil War.

During 1853, Lt. A. W. Whipple and Lt. J. C. Ives were surveying a road bed for the railroad from Mississippi River to the Pacific Ocean. The following are excerpts from Whipple's report concerning Jesse.[22]

"Jesse Chisholm, half breed Cherokee trader and frontiersman occupied the site of Chouteau's after the discovery of gold in California, and when the overland travel became considerable, etc." He went on to say, "Because of his profound knowledge of the Indians and the country and his extraordinary sagacity, Chisholm either was a part or had been avidly sought for every Western exploring expedition."

Whipple was also impressed in other ways. "He is a man of considerable wealth, and extensively engaged in trade. In the prosecution of his regular business, he could realize twice the amount the Government would be willing to pay for his services. His determination (not to accompany the expedition) is to be regretted the more, from the influence he possesses with wild tribes westward.

"He is a man of excellent judgement, and has traveled much

among the western savages. At the great Indian council, held about six weeks since, he was selected as the general interpreter for all: Comanches, Kioways, Kichais, Creeks, Delawares, Shawnees, Chickasaws and Choctaws. He has traded with, and been much among the Comanches, and understands not only their language, but their manners, customs and ceremonies, probably better than any one not belonging to their tribe."

In Whipple's journal he reported he had tried to enlist the services of the great little Delaware scout, guide-interpreter Black Beaver, with no better luck than he had trying to enlist Jesse's services. Now Whipple decided to try for Jesse again (August 12, 1853): "Since then, we have sought for Jesse Chisholm, celebrated as a guide and good Indian interpreter. His services we hope to secure, by waiting a day or two, in order to communicate with him. He has gone to hunt for lost horses and is expected back tomorrow."

Finally, on August 19, Jesse declined to go but gave Whipple a crash course in key Comanche words and their correct pronunciation. Apparently, he didn't feel his lesson had been too well mastered because he offered to send his teenaged son George, the Mexican boy he ransomed some four years earlier.[23]

Both father and son beamed happily as George rode away with Whipple's party. For all practical purposes, Whipple was running the same line Lieutenant Simpson surveyed five years earlier. They even had the same Jesse in mind to guide their way.

The business in which Jesse was involved that had prevented him from helping Whipple was a commitment he made to Chief Ten Bears of the Yamparika Comanches to attend a treaty council at Fort Atkinson, Kansas,[24] in July 1853. Creeks had extended Chisholm an invitation to act as their interpreter, and sent him to invite some 200 lodges of Comanche camped in the Wichita Mountains.

Maj. Thomas Fitzpatrick and John W. Whitfield, both Indian agents, represented the United States at this parley, with Jesse acting as interpreter for all eight tribes represented at the council. More than 1,500 Creeks came to the spectacular conclave at Salt Flats. In all, there were more than 3,000 Indians to be fed and entertained.

It was at this meeting Agent Whitfield told Kiowa head chief Little Mountain that the Great White Father (the president) was going to teach his tribe to farm. Whitfield was left speechless by Little Mountain's reply. The old chief said "he was glad to hear it and while the Great Father was so generous he hoped he would send the Indians some land that would grow corn, since they had none, suited for that purpose." [25]

Even while their troubles mounted, Indians could laugh and joke. Their rapier-like wit often stunned unsuspecting agents charged with teaching them the ways of the white man.

Upon returning home, Jesse learned of the death of a member of a Creek chief's family. He stopped by to pay his respects. The service was a Christian one, "a practice in vogue among advanced Indians of the Five Civilized Tribes." [26] To satisfy spiritual needs of the chief, the young preacher spent several full days "preaching the eulogy" for the departed. The grateful old chief set up tables to feed mourners, some 1,000 who stayed to the end, including Jesse.

It is recorded in several places that Jesse never embraced the Christian faith. Whether this funeral or some other incident turned him away is uncertain, but as busy as he was he didn't have time to attend too many funerals.

10

Texas Trails and Trials

The old storyteller had rambled around half the morning, seemingly unable to get into his story. He had several interruptions. There was a news reporter from the Houston Chronicle *who wanted to schedule an interview with him. He upset Colonel Houston when he tried to conduct the interview that day and was sent away.*

It was obvious that Colonel Houston had some important message he wanted to relate. Before he could get into his story, he had to stop again and render first aid to one of his daughters, Ari. She moaned loudly after she burned her arm when it brushed against the iron pot in which she was boiling clothes.

Almost timidly, the old gentleman glanced slowly from side to side. He seemed to be wondering what would interrupt him next, as he began telling about the acts of his father, Sam Houston, whom he admired most.

As the new year moved around, Sam Houston was telling the U.S. Senate and the world about Indians — for two days straight.[1] Speaking before the Senate on March 3, 1854, Senator Houston said, "Cherokees have never been idolators, neither have the Creeks, nor the Choctaws, nor the Chickashaws. They believe in one Great Spirit — in God — the white man's God. They believe in His son Jesus Christ and His atonement and propitiations for the sins of men. They believe in the sanctifying efficacy of the Holy Ghost. They bow at the Christian altar, and they believe in the Sacred Volume."

He continued, "But even if they were wild Indians, untutored, when you deprive them of what would give them knowledge, and discourage them from making an effort to become civilized and social beings, how can you expect them to be otherwise than savage?"

The booming voice of Houston roared, "When you undertake to tame horses, do you turn them from you and drive them into the desert," he continued, "or do you take care of them and treat them with humanity?"

Next, Houston lowered his voice to a raspy whisper and became very specific in making his next point. "These Indians are not inferior in point of genius to John Randolph. His father, in point of native intellect, was not inferior to any man!"

Texas legislators were having none of Houston's expertise concerning the Plains Indians. Instead this august body of heavy thinkers drafted legislation which awarded a total of sixteen leagues of land for Indian reservations, four for Comanche use exclusively, and the other twelve for use by all other Texas Indians.[2]

Land awarded Comanches was barely suitable for grazing but nothing else. This move hardly fazed the Kiowas and Comanches because they cared not a bit what Texas solons did since they had no intention of complying with the edict.

Once again, Jesse was drawn into the fray when his red brothers came to him for help. He was roused from his peaceful pursuits at home for a pow-wow with a party of Comanches headed for San Antonio, where they would meet Chief Wildcat and his Seminole followers.

At the meeting Wildcat told Shaved Head and Ten Bears of the fine home his tribe was making at Piedras Negras, just across the Rio Grande River from Eagle Pass. There was no mention of past differences he had encountered with Comanches, but Jesse sensed a veiled threat if they didn't accept his offer.

Pressure of his own business dictated Jesse's departure before the meeting adjourned because his services were required no longer. Ten Bears had already expressed his opposition to joining forces with Wildcat, so no major agreement was likely to gel.[3]

Jesse visited friends in San Antonio. Among those he visited was Francois X. Aubrey, an old guide he had met first at Bent's Fort years earlier.[4] Aubrey turned the tables on Jesse and tried to induce him to go to California with him. Jesse turned him down, because he had more urgent business in Texas.

He traveled to Huntsville to visit Houston and accompanied him to Brenham, where Houston was to speak on April 15. Jesse had planned to stay with his friend Durant at Washington-on-the-Brazos but learned he had moved to Centerville in Leon County. "Old Sam" chided Jesse when he saw his embarrassment from learning of Durant's move. Houston laughed and said he could have told him two years ago that Durant had moved. As they rode back to Huntsville, Houston suggested they ride to visit Durant at his home in Centerville. They stopped overnight at Houston's home before continuing their trip.

Houston showed Jesse an ad in the *Leon Pioneer* newspaper announcing the services of John W. Durant, Law Firm. He was now a partner with lawyer William D. Wood, who doubled as editor of the Leon County newspaper.[5]

When Houston and Jesse spent the night at Durant's home, the old cronies recalled events which still inspired and invigorated them, even though their paths had branched in diverse directions. The three men's friendship had begun in Tennessee more than thirty years earlier.

During this visit, Jesse remembered Mrs. Houston was with child, due in late June or early July. Senator Houston had to leave before his newest arrival came. He had just returned to Washington when he received news that his son, Andrew Jackson Houston, was born June 21, 1854 (the same person narrating this story).

Following this happy interlude with old friends, Jesse rode toward his home. He took painful notice of scorched earth from Dallas all the way to Red River. It was late in May and no rain had fallen for months, but worse things would follow. Drought proved to be very severe and destroyed the majority of Indian crops in 1854.[6]

The arid condition was apparent right up to his own home, only more so it seemed. The warm greeting he received from his family temporarily dulled his thoughts about the parched earth around his spread.

He heard his son George tell of his journey with Lieutenant Whipple. The newest Chisholm scout and interpreter had grown homesick after three weeks of camp meals and had secured his leave to return home. He told his papa that that was the last trip he was going to embark upon. Papa could only smile; he knew the feeling. Father and son both agreed to stay home, for a while anyway.

Agent Robert Neighbors had done an excellent job entreating

Comanches to stay on the reservation near Fort Chadbourne (by San Angelo). A shaky peace prevailed. But now Buffalo Hump and Sanaco, with up to 900 followers, were in Jesse's front yard telling him their problems. They had been run out of Texas by the army. This seemed too incredible even in Texas. Jesse advised them to camp near his place and he would try to find out what was happening.

Here the old saw "a little knowledge in the hands of a fool is a dangerous thing" proved so true. The renewed outbreak of hostilities came about when a trader at Fort Chadbourne overheard Agent Neighbors talking with army officials about punishing some north-based Comanches for depredations on settlers in North Texas. With this as information, the trader told Indians trading at Fort Chadbourne that the military was going to kill them and they had better run for their lives.[7] These were friendly Penatekas who were trying to abide reservation life.

This one misguided act set off another wave of frenzied fighting, which made the entire frontier resemble a shooting gallery. It would get much worse before it got any better.

By the time Jesse had unraveled this tragic turn of events, Buffalo Hump and his Comanche followers had grown impatient and headed for Bent's Trading Post to rendezvous with their northern cousins.

For the first time in his life, Jesse became fighting mad. The only thing that helped restrain him was the question of who to be mad with. Through Jesse and other sources, Senator Sam Houston learned of the military blunder that set Comanches on the war path and took his anger to the floor of the U.S. Senate. Now Jesse wasn't the only one mad.

Houston vented his feeling for the military when he probed: "Do you think a man is fit for such service who has been educated at West Point Academy, furnished with rich stores of learning; more educated in the science of war . . . ? Are you going to take such gentlemen, and suppose that by intrusion they will understand the Indian character? Or do you suppose . . . they could track an Indian, or would they know whether they were tracking a wagon or a carriage?"[8]

The Senate gallery rocked with laughter as Houston jibed the military, but this day he sought to win his colleagues' support for Indians, not to amuse Senate gallery crowds. A few days later, Houston was back on the stump again.

On December 31, 1854, he told his fellow senators, "I have stood alone in this body against a powerful array of talent and influence, contending for what I conceived to be a great principle, and which must obtain, or the Indian race be exterminated." [9]

News out of Fort Gibson told of the arrival of Col. Albert Sidney Johnston heading the Second Cavalry Division en route to Texas to fight Indians. [10] Also in this command, besides Johnston, were many future heroes of the U.S. military, including Maj. George H. Thomas and Capt. E. Kirby Smith.

This new contingent of troops bode ill tidings for Indians. There would be no let-up now until the Indians were totally subdued.

Lt. Col. Robert E. Lee joined the division at San Antonio in March 1856. He distinguished himself even more during his tenure in Texas.

Jesse was asked to lead Col. Pitcairn Morrison with more than 200 officers and men in search of Indians that were preying on Santa Fe Trail users. [11] He declined because he didn't believe there was even a remote chance of settling this dispute peacefully. Colonel Morrison carried out his mission and in fact confronted two different bands: the Kiowa under Satanta and later the Comanche under Shaved Head. These Indians were told to behave themselves and to proceed to their destination. Both of the wild rebels would and should be prime suspects where Indian trouble cropped up, but in this instance there were either too many for Morrison to fight or they convinced him they were innocent of any bad deeds. Either way, both tribes were left free to continue their depredations.

For a change, news coming out of Texas did not dwell on Indian uprisings. Years after Robert E. Lee left Texas for "a nobler and grander cause," he reminisced that he came to Texas with the camels in 1856. These same camels were the prime topic of discussion all over the nation.

When Jefferson Davis, now secretary of war, came up with the brainstorm of importing camels for use in Texas, [12] he succeeded in stopping the war, at least for a spell, while amazed citizens gazed at the newest visitors to the frontier. These desert creatures were supposed to be the answer to conquering the great Texas desert. The docile and at times ornery beasts both amused and puzzled every person who saw them. The two most startling events on the frontier in the mid-1800s were the first Dragoon uniforms in 1834 and camels in 1856. Jeff Davis wore one of the uniforms *and* was responsible for sending camels. That this could draw a crowd was not a subject for much debate.

Unfortunately, the camels offered but a brief respite from bigger problems plaguing the Southwest. At Bent's Fort, Jesse learned from

Bill Bent he was feuding with Kiowas again. Seems old Ben Hatcher, Bent's clerk, had allowed Kiowas to store their tepees and spare gear at Bent's trading post. Bent tripped over the Kiowa gear for a week and then asked some Cheyennes to haul it off.

When Lone Wolf, Big Bow, and Stumbling Bear returned and found their gear gone, these Kiowas declared war on Bent and his Cheyenne neighbors.[13] Bent was sorry for his error, but not sorry enough to replace the Kiowas' lost gear. He made no attempt to make amends with Kiowas. If they never came back he would be happier. But they did come back, with a vengeance, looking for Bent's scalp.

Jesse reminded Bent that Indians had enough troubles without adding his to their list. Bent finally confided to Jesse that the buildup of Comanches, Kiowas, and Apaches in his already troubled region was causing him great concern.[14] He was extremely vulnerable if these wild ones turned on him. Jesse told his friend Bill that was all the more reason not to rile Indians without cause, as he had done by giving the Kiowas' gear to their enemies, the Cheyenne.

Before 1857 was well under way, a second shipment of camels landed at Indianola, Texas. Now there would be seventy-five of the unpredictable beasts in Texas.[15]

Those close to the situation had grave reservations about the ability of Americans to adjust to camels. The camels were doing fine. To be more accurate, camels were doing about as they pleased. One of the herdsmen told his commanding officer that they were going to have to import the men who trained the camels, because the animals did not understand English. The experiment was hardly begun, and most handlers were ready to ship them back from whence they came.

Any diversionary effect these camels furnished the nation was gone, but they continued to perplex and rile their handlers for years after the experiment was dubbed a monumental bust. There were bigger busts to be dealt with now, particularly the one relating to the nation's economy.

In addition to expanding Indian problems, financial panic hit U.S. industrialists, and the ever widening gap between abolitionist and ultra-secessionist made natives restive. The climate was generally unfriendly and unfeeling for problems of others.

Jesse found the role of peacemaker was needed now more than ever, but had never been less popular. People in general were massed in rigid lines looking for an opportunity to vent their spleens. They wouldn't have to wait much longer.

As an example of the rationale and unreasoned thinking of a few, Jesse Chisholm was adjudged the culprit responsible for inciting Indians.[16] He had sold seventy-odd guns to various tribes over the period of a year. His sin, compared with that of Indian agents who dispensed more than a thousand guns during the same period, is hard to justify.

Rapidly vanishing buffalo made Indian survival more difficult. Bow and arrows simply could not sustain their needs. A few people closely associated with the tribes knew their problems and recognized they needed guns to hunt game if they were to retain any reasonable degree of self-sufficiency.

The distemper which gripped white society spread to savages. Kiowas and Nokoni Comanches erupted into open warfare initially. In fast order, Kickapoo, Apache, Cheyenne, and Yamparika Comanches joined them. The frontier was ablaze again.

Jesse stayed as far from the fire as he could, but the very nature of his business required some contact. He would ship more than 6,000 buffalo and other hides in 1857.[17] His business was booming, and he was becoming very wealthy in his own right.

During the following year he moved his trading post even farther away from congested areas. He set up business at a new and very remote post on Chouteau Creek, near the Canadian River at Council Grove, Oklahoma.[18] On this historic site, Jesse was at the crossroads of east-west and north-south traffic. Discovery of gold in Colorado in 1858 set off another frenzied wave of people on the move — right by his trading post. In less than ten years, this location would be just off the north-south trail to Abilene, Kansas, the "Chisholm Trail" that would bear his name.

Late in October 1858, a new wagon road survey was being conducted from Fort Smith to the Colorado River by United States surveyors.[19] Lt. Edward F. Beale was in charge of this survey and reported as follows in a journal kept by his assistant, F. E. Engle:

> · [October 28] about ten day ago I dispatched Mr. George Beale to Fort Arbuckle to obtain the services of a guide or three, if possible. He returned day before yesterday, bringing the disagreeable intelligence that neither of the men for whom I had sent would consent to start out this season on account of the hostilities existing between our people and the Comanches: Black Beaver and Jesse Chisholm both agreeing that the Comanches would burn off every blade of grass as we advanced, so that we would soon not have an animal left.

After Beale had begun his journey, he made the following entry in his journal (November 12, 1858): "This day the expedition passed within a mile of Jesse Chisholm's home south of the route." He went on to record his location in the southern part of Potawatomie County and noted it was the last settlement they would pass.

Here Beale's luck changed for the better. Jesse, though somewhat reluctantly, agreed to accompany Beale as far as Albuquerque. The next day, Beale made this notation: "[November 13, 1858] . . . we encamped in good grass near a small stream . . . near our camp, I found R. Frank Green, esq. with his mail stages awaiting my arrival and intending to take advantage of my escort to pursue their way to New Mexico. Mr. Green had been waiting nearly a month, the late fight of Major Van Dorn (U.S. Army) and the hostilities consequent thereon making it impossible for him to pass the Comanche Nation unprotected."

The fight Beale refers to was the slaughter of sixty Comanches and four Wichita assembled for a peace council on Rush Creek at Rush Springs, Oklahoma. On September 29, 1858, Maj. Earl Van Dorn attacked the sleeping Indians, wantonly killing men and women.[20] Comanches lashed out in unbridled fury, particularly at Wichita Indians, whom they felt had set up this ambush-like attack.

Retaliation against whites was top priority, but imagined treachery by Wichitas could not be overlooked. Both Black Beaver and Jesse knew the warlike mood of Comanches and didn't want responsibility for lives of any whites in this area.[21]

Finally, Jesse relented and accompanied Beale, but only after failing to dissuade his going. He knew his presence gave Beale's party a reasonable safety — if he could be identified before they were attacked.

Jesse was successful in getting Beale's group through safely, but it was the only group so lucky for the next two years. Other expeditions ended abruptly when the lives of travelers were wasted by warring savages.

By the time Jesse got back home in June 1859, his adopted family of Creeks were holding their first democratic election to select a new head chief.[22] Motey Canard won, ousting longtime headman, Roley McIntosh.

Jesse scarcely reached his home before he received an invitation to accompany Elias Rector and Robert S. Neighbors in their search for a new reservation site for Comanches and Wichitas in the territory.[23] He met with Rector, Neighbors, and Maj. W. H. Emory, commander at

Fort Washita, to discuss several sites under scrutiny.

Jesse contributed his ideas and then abruptly asked to be excused due to pressing problems arising from his expanding business and the needs of his family. He was tired of looking after other people's problems while having to shelve his own.

Back home he found a visitor waiting for him. Bill Bent, accompanied by his "bodyguards," some twelve Cheyenne, wanted to talk business with him. The two men planned a trip to Denver to survey the possibility of a joint venture in that area, where they would supply prospectors near Pikes Peak.[24]

Another prominent reason for Bent's visit was revealed when he asked Jesse to use his influence to calm raging Comanche and Kiowa over whom Bent had no influence. Bent became alarmed when he found some 4,000 very hostile Indians settling in the vicinity of his trading fort and feared trouble was imminent. Jesse agreed to do what he could — from his front porch.

He did not want to move any more than was absolutely necessary. Now fifty-four years old, he felt compelled to slow down. His family had grown up and he scarcely knew them. He dared hope this deplorable situation would change.

News was rushed to Jesse relating to the murder of R. S. Neighbors, Texas Indian agent.[25] This man, more than any other, with the exception of Jesse, was effective in dealing with Comanches. He tried to get a peaceful and workable contract between the United States and these Indians and in many instances was marginally successful. There were those who hated Neighbors or anyone else, for that matter, who proposed fair treatment of Indians.

It was one such man who ambushed and killed Neighbors at Fort Belknap in 1859. Neighbors had just returned from escorting some 1,300 Indians, including more than 200 Comanches, to their new reservation south of Washita River in the territory. Maj. George H. Thomas had furnished the military escort to evict peace-seeking Indians from Texas. A group of white ruffians insisted these Indians be killed instead of being removed. Of such was the temperament of the area and times in Texas. The man who killed Neighbors expressed prevailing sentiment of some when he sneered that any man who took up for Indians was no better than the Indian and should be killed too.

On a larger scale, citizens of the United States, North and South, were forming irrevocable stances not unlike the ones in which Indians and whites had found themselves involved. Abraham Lincoln, committed to abolition of slavery, was pitted against President James Buchanan and Whigs' candidate John Bell of Tennessee. The outcome of this election gave promise that it would reshape moral content of the nation — whatever the outcome.

In Texas, the off-again, on-again politics which alternately swept Sam Houston into or out of public office was again "on" for Houston. He was elected governor in August 1859 and was "enthroned," as one detractor noted, in December.[26]

For those who revered the Union, for Indians, for his friends, and for Jesse, the election of "Old Sam" was most welcome news. Now one could see light at the end of the tunnel, especially if that person resided in Texas. Sam Houston's presence and strong leadership bode good times ahead.

11

Jesse Chisholm: Bigger Than War

*L*ike a child cringing before a dose of castor oil, the old man seemed unable to come to grips with the emotions engulfing his mind. Recalling the War Between the States and the role his father acted out seared his soul.

The taunts, privation, and anguish he felt as a child rushed back to flood Colonel Houston's conscious being. He unashamedly recoiled, trying to fight back tears that streaked his weather-beaten, time-rutted cheeks, as he recalled how his family suffered after his father was impeached for refusing to swear allegiance to the Confederacy.

Only a child could feel the full measure of pain as he watched the father he adored be vilified as a traitor and spat upon by a fickle populace. Only a short time before, those same voters had swept him into the office of governor of Texas, by an overwhelming majority.

Every place the beleaguered Houston family turned, they faced new threats and abuses. Two years into the fated war, Texas' great patriot, Sam Houston, died in 1863. His son always believed that his father died of a broken heart.

Andrew Jackson Houston's scarred memory recalled the Houston family's darkest hour. He was now trying to tell about Jesse Chisholm's heroic efforts to aid those suffering Indian refugees from the nation's Civil War.

The culmination of secessionist hopes, a civil war, triggered drastic changes in the South. Some lives were wrecked in the inception;

others took a little longer. Backers of Governor Houston's bid for the U.S. presidency learned he had support in all three conventions. Houston chose to ignore the convention process, preferring to gain election as "the people's" choice. But by so doing, he eliminated any chance of being elected on a national scale.[1] Lincoln was elected.

The Southern hierarchy immediately began dismantling the Union, as state after state seceded. In Texas, the same legislature that had voted to secede also impeached Houston and selected a governor who agreed with the action they had taken.[2] Houston agreed with neither the decision to secede nor the action taken to remove him from office.

Predictably, Jesse Chisholm chose to remain neutral, and for once his services would not be needed by either faction — or so it seemed. Just as predictable was the fact that both warring factions tried to enlist Jesse's help.

Suddenly, the nation found itself locked in a most unusual struggle in which both sides allowed each other time to rally their forces and arm their warriors. Many military men who were on duty in the South and had been for years were now forced to take a side. In the case of Robert E. Lee, on duty in Texas, both sides made bids for his services.[3] He would get top billing either way he went. Other officers had the same option, if not as big an offer.

After sides were manned with the personnel to fight a war, strategy was planned. From the beginning, Indians, both civilized and wild, were top priority of both sides, particularly the South. After years of abuse, harassment, and brutal treatment, the various tribes found themselves being courted by both sides.

With a potential Trojan Horse, in which up to 80,000 warriors were living in their midst, leaders of the South moved swiftly to garner support from leaders in the territory. President Jefferson Davis, newly elected head of the Confederate States, appointed "Old Arkansaw Traveler" Albert Pike to deal with "Indians west of Arkansas."[4] With the rank of general, he set out for the territory.

Parties sympathetic to the South were already occupying army posts evacuated recently by Federal forces. One of these was Fort Cobb, where the Wichita agency was housed. It was at Fort Cobb that Pike made his first presentation to try to strike a deal with both Wichitas and Comanches, who had been invited to listen to his proposal.

Pike had asked President Davis for unlimited power to make treaties, and Davis gave him such power. Now Pike had the wherewithal to get various tribes to sign on with the Confederate States of America.

Beginning in March 1861, when he got his commission and authority from CSA's President Davis, General Pike set up a concentrated program of enlisting all Indians under the Confederate banner. Immediately, Pike acquired the services of old Texas Ranger friend Ben McCulloch, newly commissioned general in CSA, and the two set out to meet with Chief John Ross, head man of Cherokees.[5]

When Pike first announced his intentions of talking to various tribes, he gleaned information from men who knew the best way to approach each one. President Davis personally knew Chisholm, Ross, and Stand Watie of the Cherokees, as well as Roley McIntosh and Opothleyohola of the Creeks and several other lesser chiefs. Without exception, Pike was reminded of the internal disputes between Ross and Watie and that of McIntosh and Opothleyohola. He was told by CSA officers that Chisholm was his best bet to interpret for him with wild tribes.[6]

Pike learned that Cherokees had not been paid their annuities. And, having recently represented the Choctaws in dealing with the United States, he knew their tribal leaders first-hand. With all the knowledge and power to which Pike came into possession, he also got permission to offer Cherokees $500,000 plus interest for the past twenty-five years for "neutral land" in their nation.[7] This was a ploy designed to negate Ross' position of neutrality with his executive council, who knew the tribe was in dire financial straits. He also had a similar bribe to undermine the neutral stance of Opothleyohola and further widen the dispute between him and the McIntosh half of Creeks.

When Pike and McCulloch first contacted Jesse, he refused to help them. The loquacious and overbearing Pike so annoyed Chisholm that he couldn't take leave fast enough. Even McCulloch tried to tone down Pike's abrasive "pitch" which annoyed Jesse so much. After visiting with Stand Watie, Ross, Robert McIntosh and his neighbor Chief Opothleyohola, he was convinced Indians had a better chance of remaining neutral if he was present to screen offers. So, tentatively, Jesse agreed to accompany Pike when he met with the wild tribes.

Finally, Pike got Comanche and Wichita tribes together at Fort Cobb in August 1861. For two days Jesse listened to lies, half-truths, and promises of Pike as he tried to sign Indians to peace agreements. When the treaty sessions ended, chiefs representing Nokoni, Kotsoteka, Tenewa, Penateka, and Yamparika Comanches signed pacts, as did the Wichita representatives.[8] The only concession Indians made was to stay on their assigned reservations.

A month later, Pike had arranged for a treaty signing with Kiowas and a few Comanches at Fort Wise, Kansas. No sooner had Jesse finished this odious task when a messenger from Col. W. H. Emory asked him to introduce several agents representing the Federal cause to Plains Indians. In order to maintain his independent stance, he agreed to introduce the North's representative. Lies and half-truths promised by these men were equal to any he had translated for Pike and were even more bazaar at times. Chisholm finally quit, being thoroughly disgusted with both factions.[9]

In talking to Buffalo Hump after these meetings, he learned Comanches thought Chisholm had changed his mind when he brought agents from the North in for treaty talks. Therefore, they signed an agreement with them too. Buffalo Hump told Jesse not to worry about agreements he had signed with both North and South, because his Comanches weren't going to stay on the reservation anyway.

At this point it was apparent to Chisholm that these agents had used his entrée to give their mission the "cloak of respectability" with various wild tribes. True to form, both sides — in this case three sides — were still dealing dishonestly with the other.

Recruitment of Indians for the North was handled primarily by Col. W. H. Emory, Gen. James G. Blunt, and Col. William Weir, who for the most part were honorable and sensible men. However, some of the men they assigned to enlist Indians were governed by neither honorable nor sensible rules of conduct. In their zeal to win converts from ranks of Indians, these foolish men resorted to any ruse to complete their mission. The old saying of "all is fair in love and war" was readily applied by agents of both North and South during their efforts to enlist Indian support.

Serving as interpreter while these various agents were making their pitches, Jesse heard one North agent tell Comanches they could use guns given them against not only Texans but other Indians. He added that they could keep the spoils, including any prisoners they took.[10] This last statement gave Jesse some doubt about what the abolitionist movement really meant. On the one hand, "the cause," in words at least, was freeing of slaves held in bondage by the South; but here one of their agents was authorizing enslavement of red, white, and black peoples.

By no means was this hypocrisy confined to agents for the North. Prevailing attitude of the South followed closely that of the North.

Indians were told by Southern agents that their total extinction was in store if the North prevailed. The North had pushed them out of their former homes and now intended to push them completely out of this country, after taking all their slaves and other possessions, they said.

Propaganda was vicious, designed more to incite than to inform. Which side told the biggest and best lie? Chisholm declared the ugly contest a standoff — too close to call. In his mind it was sheer insanity to incite and arm Comanches and Kiowas to make war. Like giving a child a loaded gun to play with, someone was likely to get hurt. These wild Indians were not used to any restrictions, even among their own camps, much less to guidelines imposed by white "dreamers."

Despite all efforts to bribe him to join their side, Jesse maintained his own neutrality, and for a time both sides tried to intimidate him to sign with them. In Chisholm's case his neutrality could be tolerated, but the neutrality of Chief Ross of the Cherokees and Opothleyohola's Creeks could not be accepted.

Both sides believed it was most important to them to have Indians allied with their cause. Long before war commenced, Jesse routinely advised his Indian friends to stay clear of the white man's argument and steadfastly maintained his own neutrality. With some justification he likened the North-South war to a domestic quarrel between a husband and wife, where intrusion of a third party usually ends up with the couple turning on the intruder.

The Five Civilized Tribes, made up of Creeks, Choctaws, Cherokees, Chickasaws, and Seminoles, had many customs and habits similar to those of their white Southern neighbors. For one thing, Indians were large slaveholders, too, using slaves to work their crops.[11] But there was an important difference in respect to social and political status of Indians and whites. The Indian was, like the Negro, part of a social experiment the United States was testing, in which the Indian was placed in protective custody and maintained by force.

Centuries before, Dante had warned that "in time of great moral crisis" neutrality is difficult if not impossible to maintain. Jesse and his friends, both white and Indian, scrambled for middle ground but found their position was in the middle of the "hurricane's eye," where they were battered from all sides. Once battle lines were drawn, no position of neutrality was tenable.

As wards of the federal government, Indians should have been excluded from participation in the war by North and South, especially by the North. Residents of the South should have known better than to rekindle savage instincts of "Redskins on the warpath." They, better than anyone else, knew first-hand the latent fury now resting with relative peace in the territory.

Taxpayers in the North should have recalled vast sums of money it cost to put down Indian uprisings in the past, to say nothing of the frightful cost in human lives spent keeping peace on the Southwest frontier. Instead of the caution and restraint recommended by Chisholm, both sides rushed hell-bent into Indian Territory, intent on enlisting and rearming Indians.

The awesome pressure Pike and his Southern confederates applied to Chief Ross and Chief Opothleyohola ran the gamut, from gentle persuasion to hard and threatening rhetoric. These two old chiefs told Jesse they would maintain a neutral stand, but cleavage of the Stand Watie faction threatened to again pit Cherokee against Cherokee, this time with no real motive. For this reason Chief Ross gave in and joined Watie's group as allies of the South. [12]

Chisholm had tried to reason with the fiery Watie long before he opted to join forces with the South. He warned Watie he would be offered huge bribes to bolt the unified Cherokee ranks. Always combative by nature, Watie didn't need to be bribed. The chance to cut Ross deep was all the incentive he needed.

Watie got nothing from the Confederate States except the rank of general and the command of mustered Indians. He fought with daring and reckless abandon, inspiring his men to feats beyond bounds most could have been led. But even if the South had prevailed, Watie would have been by-passed when the spoils were divided, if the way he and his troops were treated during the war was any indication of influence he wielded. His troops had to live by their own means, looting and plundering. [13] The lot of his Indian brothers who joined ranks with the North was worse, if possible. They got no significant rank or leadership roles.

With the split in Cherokee ranks, Pike was able to divide and conquer. Next was the powerful Creek Nation. The same wedge was driven into this peaceful clan. Pike used Daniel McIntosh and Chilly McIntosh as his means to split Creek solidarity. The old hatred festering along lines between Upper Creeks of Opothleyohola and Lower Creeks was the pressure point.

After Ross folded from unrelenting pressure, Pike figured old Chief Opothleyohola would give in with a gentle nudge. To the surprise of all, he did not give in — then or ever, for that matter. This man of honor and principle refused to yield to any force, pressure, or other coercion and determinedly maintained a neutral pose.

The South could not accept this stance by Opothleyohola and followers, numbering 4,000 or more, in their midst.[14] These Creeks could offer aid and succor to the North, or worse, they could influence other Indians to remain neutral. It was decided to give Opothleyohola one last chance to change his mind. If he didn't join ranks with the CSA, he would be provoked to fight and then be destroyed. This was the option Opothleyohola faced when he called Jesse to seek his help and advice.

Upper Creeks voted to give up their homes, tilled fields, and other earthly possessions and move into the wilderness. This is where Jesse was needed. He was asked to lead them to a remote area, away from war. Word spread rapidly with news of the Creeks' intentions of leaving.

When news of the departure of Creeks reached the Southern military command post, the consensus of opinion was, "Good, good riddance!" Opinions changed quickly when they learned that a large number of Indians were clamoring to follow Chisholm and Creeks to a haven in the wilderness. The Confederates suspected that some dire intrigue on the part of Chisholm to deliver these Indians to the Northern army was in the making. CSA leaders issued the order to take the Indians into "protective" custody and kill them, if necessary, to effect this order.[15]

Creeks and a large body of Seminoles under their chief, Halek Tustenuggee, were in the process of departing the territory. As they assembled on Deep Fork of Canadian River, they learned of the order to stop their departure. They were forced to flee across Cherokee land to avert the war they dreaded.

Gen. Ben McCulloch, Southern commandant of troops in Indian Territory, gave Col. Douglas H. Cooper the duty of stopping Opothleyohola's exodus. Cooper was formerly agent for Choctaws and was a close friend of President Davis. The two had served together in the war with Mexico in 1845.[16] Like Davis, Cooper was a man of very positive disposition and was not in the least bit timid about expressing his opinions.

From his headquarters at Fort Gibson, Colonel Cooper amassed some 1,400 troops to go after Opothleyohola and his followers. He led his forces out on November 15, 1861, including six companies of his own regiment made up from Chickasaw and Choctaw enlistees along with the Creek regiment under Col. Daniel McIntosh. Col. William Quayle led a detachment of the Ninth Texas Cavalry, Lt. Col. Chilly McIntosh led a Creek battalion, and a Seminole battalion was guided by Maj. John Jumper.[17]

When Colonel Cooper and his men reached the Upper Creeks' point of embarkation, they learned the Indians had already left. Four days later, November 19, Cooper's troops caught up with Opothleyohola's runaway, rag-tag collection of men, women, children, cows, horses, chickens, and slaves. At Round Mountain, near the mouth of the Cimarron, Colonel Cooper issued orders to attack. Attack they did, and the issue was never in doubt. Some men tried to protect women and children against Cooper's horde of untutored, undisciplined, blood-lusting troops. Quickly, the troops reverted to baser instincts normally associated with Indians, and the new CSA charges claimed more than a hundred scalps. Then looting and pillaging occupied Cooper's troops. They abandoned the fight to chase after horses, cows, and even some loose chickens.

While Colonel Cooper's noble army was thus occupied, some of the "dangerous" fugitives fled in panic with only the clothes on their backs. It could have been worse, but a large number of Cooper's army gagged at the sight of their kin being slaughtered. This proved to be just a preview of coming events.

The pause in Cooper's slaughter was caused by a message received from General McCulloch, ordering him to stand by for possible service in Arkansas.[18] On November 25, McCulloch lifted his standby order so that Cooper could finish his monumental slaughter.

So dirty was this business that Cooper left some of the Seminole troops with delicate stomachs behind to guard Fort Gibson. He added some 500 fresh troops from Col. John Drew's Cherokee regiment to his 1,000 mounted soldiers to go after Opothleyohola. They caught the cold and hungry remnants of Creek defectors near Tulsa and got on with their business of slaughtering. On this occasion, Creeks clung to life as a drowning man would. Men, women, and even children resisted death with a fury that startled Cooper's forces. He opted to rest his weary command overnight and finish the mop-up operation on the next day.

Overnight Colonel Drew's command, nearly 500 men, disappeared.[19] Many had crossed over to help the desperate forces of Opothleyohola. The rest of Cooper's command looked pale around the gills, so he decided to return to his base and get more ammunition and supplies and then come back to finish his annihilation of the Creek refugees still on their feet, if indeed there be any.

This pause on Cooper's part led to further defections within his own ranks, and he was compelled to appeal to the South's command post at Fort Smith for reinforcements. Col. James McIntosh, with some 2,000 troops, came to Cooper's aid,[20] in pursuit of about 700 wounded, sick, hungry, and hopeless humans. When Cooper and McIntosh met after the first wave of troops ran the women and children into the ground, Colonel McIntosh said he had seen enough and rallied his command to return to Arkansas.

Not the sadistic Cooper, who came for blood. He would pursue any women and children who might endanger his army. Until Colonel Chivington's ignoble attack on Cheyennes three years later, this inhumane orgy by Colonel Cooper stood unparalleled in modern warfare.[21]

When Chisholm met with Opothleyohola before he left the territory, he had planned to lead these Indians to a site on Arkansas River near Wichita, Kansas. Jesse learned of the plight of Opothleyohola and took his family and a small band of followers on a trail west of the one over which Creeks were chased. He experienced no incidents moving to the site he had chosen in Kansas.

Creek refugees landed far to the north and east of the site where they were planning to settle with him. Now news of the carnage inflicted on Creeks reached Jesse. He was not prepared for the tragic scene he found in Chief Opothleyohola's camp. Death seemed sweet in comparison to the utter despair he witnessed.

The faint hope for life spurred these few surviving Indians to greater dimensions than human endurance could normally be expected to carry them. They had made it — alive — but they were cold, freezing cold, with no shelter and no food.

After a super human effort to cling to life, hundreds more now died, including Chief Opothleyohola.[22] It was Chisholm's turn to display some magnificent efforts to assuage hunger and suffering which abounded. He dogged George Cutler, Indian agent in Kansas, to help him care for the Indians.

So horribly was the camp bespoiled by death that the sick had to be removed to a new location. There was no one to bury the many dead so the corpses were dragged aside and left. When winter passed, the stench was discernible for half a mile.

With complete disregard for his own welfare, Jesse drove himself night and day for weeks foraging food, clothes, and medicine for the poor, sick mortals called survivors. Time after time he collapsed from exhaustion, but after nature's enforced rest he rallied his aching body to help his less fortunate brothers. Largely through efforts Jesse made, some 400 Creeks survived a "winter of death."

Scars inflicted by man showed up on their minds more than their bodies. Memories of this devastating experience would haunt not only those who lived it, but also those who watched Creeks fight to survive.

The real test of Jesse Chisholm's amazing charisma was forthcoming. In order to help surviving Creeks, he had to go back into the South's stronghold to his own bailiwick to get food and clothing to provide for needy now camped in North territory. His ability to move back and forth at his will permitted him to feed many starving Indians.

The same magic spell he had over all Indians now extended to warring whites. He moved across their firing lines with reckless disregard for his own well-being. Along both lines, sentries came to recognize him. When the challenge of "Who's there?" was hurled, the calm reply of "Chisholm" said it all. "It's just old Prairie Jesse, let him pass," would be the response, and pass he did.

Both sides questioned him concerning conditions where he had just been. His reply of "about the same" was all either side learned. Some writers and historians have erringly claimed he was pro-North, while others said he was pro-South. In truth he loved them both, but hated their conflict.

He had spent most of his life living between conflict in the Cherokee Nation as well as that within the Creek Nation. He also traveled the lonely road between Indian versus Indian, at war, and then he witnessed the internal blood-letting between red and white men.

As if by chance, Jesse was seemingly shielded from all harm as he moved freely among fighting friends, while also commanding the highest respect and regard from all factions.

Despite his herculean effort to help Indians remain neutral, they became involved. When they were hurt for being victims of involvement, he fed them and nursed their wounds. Soon he returned to his original plan to seclude himself with his family in the wilds of Kansas.

The sylvan retreat he selected just off Arkansas River, where it passed through Wichita, Kansas, would become a heavily traveled cattle road between this point and the territory, then on through to Red River and Texas. For years Jesse had used this trail on his way to trade excursions among Kiowas near Medicine Lodge. When Colonel Emory asked Chisholm to lead his fleeing Union loyalist troops out of the

South's territory, he declined but recommended his friend Black Beaver for the task.[23] The fleeing Union army, led by Beaver, probably followed Chisholm's well-marked trade route to Kansas and safety.

In March 1863, Jesse developed pneumonia from overwork and exposure.[24] The illness carried him close to the consuming jaws of death, before leaving him spent and troubled. For six months he watched helplessly as his personal wealth and health were totally ravaged. It was a gaunt and trembling, bare facsimile of the former Chisholm who set out to redeem his fortunes with only his indomitable will to sustain his resolve.

Upon reaching the territory, he learned there was big money available from supplying food to forts in the South, particularly cattle. With two friends, he drove sixty of his cows and twenty old horses to Shreveport. He met his friend J. W. Durant, who was a procurement agent for the South.[25] This chance meeting with Durant proved very beneficial for both.

Chisholm's illness had taken him out of the market so long that he lost contact with changes brought on by war. Inflation was rampant. For cattle he brought to sell, he expected to get six to eight dollars each, and for old horses forty to fifty dollars. Durant could have bought them from him for these prices, but instead paid him prevailing prices — eighty dollars per head for cattle and four hundred for each horse, in CSA specie.

Fortunately for Jesse, he spent his CSA currency on any tangible items he could find, including used tools, guns, food, clothes, horse shoes, cloth, and gunpowder. With this haul of goods he headed back to get more livestock. He made one more trip to Shreveport with cattle and horses. This time he couldn't find any place to spend his CSA scrip, nor could he discount it and get gold. So he left with the few goods he bought and, as he later stated, "a trunk full of Confederate paper."

Now sufficiently recovered from financial distress, he resumed his peaceful life in Kansas. As the tide of battle began to sway in favor of the North, all interior troops in the South were pressed into service to try to stop the onslaught. This meant frontier garrisons were abandoned. Also abandoned was any semblance of law and order.

Indians left on reservations with no food or clothing now drifted aimlessly in search of sustenance. Finding none, they reverted to old practices of taking what they wanted where they were stronger than the victim. The scene in the territory became one where survival went to the fittest, with self-preservation being the main concern.

In every recorded account where great disasters have occurred there are stories of vile vultures preying on dead or dying victims. Here the situation was no different. Unsavory men who never affiliated with any decent cause or element flocked to the territory, where they found many Indians with little or nothing on which to live, then proceeded to take that little from them. In some respects this scene was re-enacted in most cities of the South at the end of the war, but occurred at least two years earlier in the territory.

Indians of the prairie, those wild tribes who knew no shackles, genuinely missed the opportunity to barter for their needs. They had accumulated great piles of hides but found no one to buy or trade for them. Before the war ended, Comanches and Kiowas found Jesse after some searching and begged him to resume trading with them.[26] He traded for what little they brought with them and promised he would make a trading trip to the prairie the next spring.

In early April 1865, he was in the territory and saw the wretched conditions that abounded all over. He was shocked to find once proud and affluent Cherokee neighbors begging for food in order to survive.

Suddenly, Jesse was reminded of his friend Sam Houston and his prophetic words: "Some of you laugh to scorn the idea of bloodshed as the result of secession. But let me tell you what is coming . . . your fathers and husbands, your sons and brothers will be herded at the point of the bayonet . . ."[27] Houston, great statesman and patriot, was dead before his prophecy was fulfilled, but his warning served as a gauge by which his mind might be measured.

In their midst, Indians found human jackals. Predictably, Jesse reacted by helping those he could. So widespread was the suffering, he could do but little; but again he set about doing his all. With each one he helped he demanded a promise to try to help some neighbor in need.

He knew instinctively that concern for others often pushed a man further than he could be moved for his own afflictions. If for no other reason, Chisholm could be remembered for teaching these Indians to rekindle the lights in their own lives, so that others might have light.

Ironically, the bully and despot gave him wide berth — whether from fear of him or sure retaliation from his legion of friends is unknown. He did cast a big shadow of influence, but he chose to shade his friends rather than intimidate with his power. As was the custom in his environment, Jesse carried large sums of gold, not to mention valuables including guns, ammunition, food, clothes, and the like. There is no record of anyone trying to rob him. What is even more amazing is that he was able to live in the violent surroundings in which he found himself.

It was at this point in his life, as he neared sixty years, that Chisholm's role of friend took on messianic proportions with Indians. For more than forty years he had been their steadfast friend. Finally, in the twilight of his illustrious career, Indians began to embrace him as their own.

The war was now history. The full measure of death and destruction could now be tallied. After-shock from this war would be felt for decades, but the initial shock came from the realization that Indians were still fighting. Two months after Lee surrendered to Grant, Confederate General Stand Watie was still running amok.[28]

Again it was Jesse who drew the tough assignment to inform Watie his services were no longer needed. Chisholm caught up with Watie at Fort Towson and tried to communicate the news he knew Watie would try to reject. Both of these old friends stood silently, trying to regain some composure, as tears streamed down their cheeks.

General Watie took his leave to inform his loyal troops of Chisholm's news of the South's surrender. To his credit, Watie accepted the bitter news and declared a cessation of warfare, then tried to resume his shattered life in peace.

Those Indians who had been left on reservations to starve, then forced to wander afar in search of food, were now pushed back onto the reservation grounds with no provisions for their care.

To get these Indians to listen to lies of white men now would be a bigger task than when they were first inveigled to settle on a reservation. It was little consolation to Jesse that he had predicted this very thing when whites were trying to draw Indians into their dispute. The coming years would try man's spirit, not to mention his patience. Only this time there were no color barriers for the suffering.

12

Reconstruction: Aftermath of War

his day dawned clear and hot. The old storyteller pointed across Trinity Bay and commented, "Popa took us to live over there at Point Houston, after . . . ." His voice faded away and he paused just long enough for me to interject, "After what, Colonel Houston?"

There was a noticeable delay before he again addressed the subject. "Popa settled us at Point Houston after he . . . retired as governor in 1861." The word he had been groping for was "retired."

On this clarion day we could see across the bay, all the way to Morgan's Point to the north and to the Houston Yacht Club at Shoreacres to the south. A large freighter inched inland up the Houston ship channel.

By now the colonel had warmed to his subject. He continued, "Jesse Chisholm came to visit us over there." Flicking his hand in the general direction of some imaginary dot on the horizon, he designated Point Houston. Then he added, "He also visited us at Huntsville and again at Independence, Texas, after Popa died in '63."

With the advent of peace in the United States came a new set of problems. Reconstruction was a household word, but it didn't apply to Indians on reservations in the territory. There was neither money available nor inclination to worry over these tragic victims caught in the crossfire of whites.

For the victors, if indeed there was a victor, spoils were pretty spoiled before they got to them. The smell of burnt powder and open wounds was too present to allow one to forget the war just declared done. Forgiveness was equally slow in coming for those who bore scars of direct combat.

Those Indians who cast their lot with the vanquished South, for whatever reason, now faced a greater hate and rejection than they had ever known. There simply could be no forgiveness for "dirty savages" who fought with the South. The terrible pall these unfortunate people cast over all Indians was unbelievable.

Indians who served in ranks of the North fared little better. So long as they remained in uniform they had food and clothes like their black counterparts; but once they opted to return home and resume a normal life, they looked like any other "dirty savage."

On Jesse's first trading trip among Comanches in North Texas, he sensed a cocky air that prevailed throughout the tribe. Even his old friend, Chief Ten Bears, gloated about his new prestige.[1] He gave Jesse the news he was now a friend of the Great White Father, Lincoln, whom he had visited in Washington the season before.

Now Jesse had some news for him: Lincoln was dead and a new president was in power. The news had a sobering effect on the old Yamparika warrior, but not for long. Ten Bears hooted at news of the North's military victory over the South. For his part he wasn't conquered, and if he had been he did not believe his captors could contain him. This same feeling best expressed sentiment of all Indians Jesse met on this trip. Back home, reflecting on what he had heard and seen on his trip to trade with Comanches, he sensed an ever widening circle of death and destruction rather than the peace for which he had hoped.

He discussed this ill omen with John Drew, a Cherokee soldier who served with the South. From Drews he learned of the fierce power struggle within Rebel ranks between Gen. Samuel Bell Maxey and Gen. Douglas H. Cooper. The problem that set Maxey and Cooper apart involved Indians. Specifically, General Maxey's ruling stated that Indians with a higher rank than whites should and would command respect and privileges that went with any other ranking officer or enlisted man.[2] General Cooper challenged this order, taking his complaint to the commanding general, John Bankhead Magruder, who ruled in Maxey's favor.[3]

Exercising his Rebel spirit as well as his disregard for rules, General Cooper made a personal visit to his old friend President Jeff Davis to air his complaint.[4] To his discredit, Davis solved the problem by removing Maxey from authority.[5]

The war ended soon thereafter and Cooper returned from whence he had come — oblivion. On the other hand, Maxey served twelve years as United States senator from Texas, after the state was reconstructed following the war.

In another area, Indians were again the cause of fierce infighting among Union officers. Col. John M. Chivington had ambushed and ultimately slaughtered Cheyenne Indians at Sand Creek, Colorado. The peaceful Cheyenne had allowed Union forces unlimited access to their land, and head chief Yellow Wolf had been most helpful in promoting peace among Arapaho and Apache tribes. This senseless and brutal slaughter caused old Indian fighter Kit Carson to brand Chivington's act as the "deed of a coward" and denounced the leader of this vicious act as a man unfit to lead any respectable group.[6]

Accumulating these and countless other affronts, to all Indians, made for bad news. The general temper of wild tribes was so bad that their agents feared to meet with them. Buffalo hunters in Kansas were up to their old habits, slaughtering buffalo for the hide and an occasional tongue. Kiowas threatened to take a hunter for every dead buffalo they found. The Kiowa under Chief Little Mountain, with help from some Comanches, stood off an attack led by Gen. Kit Carson and some 300 soldiers at Bent's Fort.[7] In recounting the incident, Carson said he was fortunate to come out alive.

The largest source of trouble, as Jesse and his friends viewed the Indians' problems, was military personnel of the U.S. Army. With the exception of hunters who were slaughtering buffalo, nearly every recent action against Indians was perpetrated by military people on active duty. A long, documented record compiled by Montfort Stokes, Pierce M. Butler, Sam Houston, Robert S. Neighbors, and other respected men indicted the military for improper handling and mistreatment of Indians. However, few effective steps were undertaken to stop the abuses.

Two new names were added to the list of critics of the U.S. military in 1865: Edward W. Wynkoop and Col. Jesse H. Leavenworth. In the case of Leavenworth, a military man all his life and son of Gen. Henry Leavenworth (who gave his life serving his country), criticism of the military opened some eyes. Leavenworth's contention — that the military was not looking for peace with Indians but rather preferred war — drew loud opposition from his fellow officers as well as the Indian department who supervised his duties. He never backed away from his damning criticism.

Military top brass tried to silence Colonel Leavenworth, but his friend Senator J. R. Doolittle was effective in getting the army called off while peaceful solutions were sought to resolve differences with Indians.[8] Top-ranking officers' viewpoints had become so polarized that no solution was open other than complete eradication of all Indians. There is little evidence to refute the claim of a large segment of the civilian body politic being sided with the military viewpoint.

Two opposing views existed on the subject of why Indians should be dealt with peacefully where possible. On one hand, some reasoned killing of all Indians was not proper for religious or humane reasons. Another view opposing the eradication process was based on cost. The argument regarding cost touched a wider spectrum of the nation than either military or religious views. So far, doing things the military way resulted in monumental monetary expenditures. These costs became too large to absorb when coupled with payments made with human lives — white lives, that is.

The public was no longer clamoring for the gory but rather longed to bask in the glory. It was this message President Andrew Johnson and Congress received, and they then began trying to find an alternate plan for the one being implemented by the army.

Colonel Leavenworth was given rope to either hang himself or tie up a workable peace plan. He immediately called a peace conference to be held on Little Arkansas River near Wichita, Kansas.[9] Jesse was one of the first negotiators he called upon to assist him.

Timing, as far as Jesse was concerned, couldn't have been worse. He told Leavenworth he was still recuperating from the pneumonia attack which felled him earlier, and his business losses and family's needs made it impossible for him to assist the colonel. At this juncture of their talks, Leavenworth agreed to schedule the treaty try and make it conform with Jesse's availability. Leavenworth expressed the belief that without Jesse's help there would be no successful treaty session. To his credit, it seems Colonel Leavenworth tried to be realistic.

The situation was so tense and unfriendly between Leavenworth and the military that they were forced to communicate by intermediary. Jesse discussed Leavenworth's problems with General Harney, but he said the solution was beyond his scope of influence. Powers within the army threatened to boycott the treaty conference on the pretense of fear for safety of their troops. To which Leavenworth retorted, "It would be better for all concerned if the army did stay away." He made this charge with some authority.

Some months earlier, Leavenworth had received assurance from Secretary of War H. W. Halleck that Gen. G. M. Dodge had been instructed to cease war on Indians and give Indian Agent Leavenworth a chance to effect a peace treaty. With this assurance, Leavenworth proceeded to assemble Indians. During this time General Dodge, trying to live with the order while restraining his troops, wrote Secretary Halleck in protest.[10] His letter was so convincing, in regards to dangers of such an attempt at peace, that he got the restraining order lifted and immediately set out to destroy Kiowas and Comanches wherever he found them.

This unwarranted change of orders should not have happened but did. Colonel Leavenworth had already promised Indians there would be no more attacks on them if they would stop marauding. The unprovoked attack by General Dodge left Leavenworth to face crazy-mad Indians who believed he had set them up for an ambush.[11] Comanches tried to kill him but succeeded only in stealing his gear and pack mules. Sadistic army officers who found humor in Leavenworth's plight only heightened bad feelings toward the military by people possessed of honorable intent and purpose.

For all practical purposes, Leavenworth was finished as an instrument of peace. He had been successfully discredited to Indians. By all rights he should have crawled into a hole and pulled dirt in after him. Instead, the gutsy Colonel Leavenworth called Jesse Chisholm and William Shirley and pleaded the Indians' cause with these two reluctant participants.

Jesse had been through this questionable stance of the military so often that he refused to believe they could act honorably when dealing with Indians. He readily acknowledged Indians were not blameless, but he did expect more ethical conduct from top military men of the United States. The horrible position in which the army's action put Leavenworth, and his resultant brush with death, made Jesse sick. But, from his vantage point, he could not understand why he should be subjected to the same fate. Only the desperate circumstance that now existed, in which many innocent whites and Indians would die, convinced Jesse to cast his lot with the brave and dauntless Leavenworth. He and Shirley set out to encourage Indians to listen to peace talks, a task no less difficult than making molasses out of mud.

Jesse found Kiowa Chief Little Mountain and told him the story as he knew it, then waited for his reaction. The old chief seemed almost relieved of a heavy onus. He didn't want to believe Colonel Leavenworth had double-crossed him, but the action taken by General Dodge influenced him to believe otherwise. Little Mountain would go with Jesse to tell their story to Ten Bears of the Comanche Yamparika and Drinking Eagle of the Comanche Nokoni, who were camped nearby. Out of this gathering was arranged a meeting in which Leavenworth would preside and discuss future plans.

On the designated day, Comanches, Kiowas, and Kiowa-Apaches met with Jesse and Leavenworth to work on some possible solution to their mutual purpose — a meaningful peace effort. The group met on Little Arkansas River, and the long awaited "Little Arkansas Treaty Council" was about to begin. On this balmy October 10, 1865, there was a happy but guarded tension all around as five tribes of hostile Indians met for a stab at peace.[12]

The army was represented by none other than Gen. Christopher Carson, the illustrious "Kit," and another of Jesse's army buddies, Gen. William S. Harney, along with Gen. John B. Sanborn. Other commissioners were Thomas Murphy and James Steele. Old William W. Bent had come along as Carson's guest after he persuaded "his Indians" to come in.

Bill Bent's job was to get Cheyenne and Arapaho Indians to attend. This was no easy undertaking, since he found them still gun-shy after their experience at the Sand Creek massacre outside Fort Lyon, Colorado, where Colonel Chivington pulled off his ambush. Although present, they were very subdued and wary.

Bill Shirley and Jesse interpreted for the commission. Six of the nine identifiable units or divisions of Comanches attended and eventually signed a peace pact. This was the best representation Comanches ever recorded at a peace talk to that time. The powerful Kiowa were fully represented with the following chiefs present: Little Mountain, Big Bow, Satank, Satanta, and Kicking Bird.[13]

Probably out of commiseration with Colonel Leavenworth, Indians seemed almost too willing to agree to peace conditions offered by the commission in behalf of the United States. Some Indians even seemed shocked to learn this meant that Texas, too, was included in the peace agreement.

On this point they almost balked. Indians believed, with good reason, that Texans had no intention of remaining peaceful with them — if indeed they ever had been peaceful. They also felt the ledger was

lopsided in Texas' favor on past atrocities, and they wanted to try to seek a balance before agreeing to peace.

One commissioner, Jim Steele, a saucy old trader and trapper, offered a possible solution. He suggested that Texas be given back to Mexico so that they could solve the problem.

Assembled chiefs finally accepted Texas as a part of the package and went about business at hand. During a recess of the council, Carson was relating his experience at Bent's Fort, where he attacked Kiowas led by Little Mountain. Carson remembered his two howitzer guns got him through this engagement but then complained of *Comancheros* who sold these Indians the same quality guns his troops were using.[14] Jesse felt the complaint was directed at him and he challenged Carson: "Why shouldn't they be on equal terms when defending their homes?" The two legendary frontiersmen, at last, openly addressed their personal difference of opinion.

The argument that ensued was hot and heavy, with the tunnel-vision viewpoint of the army on one side and the reasoned views of balanced men taking exception to Carson's viewpoint. At times General Harney let reason pervade his thinking and seemed to be saying Jesse's contention was worthy of study. Nevertheless, neither viewpoint changed one iota, as far as observers could tell. The same question still draws a difference of opinion today.

When the various treaties were prepared by W. R. Irwin, the commission's secretary, all interested parties assembled for signing. The business with Cheyennes and Arapahos was disposed of quickly on October 14. Then the Kiowa-Apache pact was completed October 17. These Indians were released after signing and getting their presents. However, they seemed averse to leaving, like spectators waiting for the main event.

On October 18 Comanche and Kiowa representatives were called forward to sign. Lone Wolf and Satanta stayed back, refusing to participate in the signing ceremony. Bill Shirley questioned the two balky chiefs and reported they objected to boundaries imposed by the U.S. Satanta claimed buffalo were too limited to meet their needs within the proposed boundaries. To prevent this issue from killing the peace attempt, commissioners verbally agreed to let them go a little over defined lines in their search for food and hides. Now Jesse was upset.

Jesse told commissioners there were no limitations left if they allowed Indians to define their boundaries.[15] He maintained Indians had to be disciplined like children and could not be left to their own judgment.

He was overruled by the commission. They reasoned some agreement was better than none. Jesse said they really had none, since Kiowas and Comanches would bend the entire treaty as they pleased. Besides, the Indians probably anticipated breaches of the treaty pact on the part of civilian poachers as well as the military.

As it turned out, Gen. G. M. Mitchell was burning off the prairie from Nebraska to Colorado to drive Indians from this area, and destroying great herds of buffalo, while this meeting was in progress.[16] What had been a very optimistic and pleasant company that convened to search for peaceful solutions to most complex problems was disbanding under a cloud of uncertainty and doubt.

As Jesse was leaving for home he confided to General Harney his own frustrations and rationalized he had become so cynical and cranky he couldn't stand himself at times. He liked Harney and didn't want anything that was said to mar their friendship. Harney expressed the same sentiment.

The doubts Jesse expressed concerning validity of the Little Arkansas Treaty were challenged before ink was dry on the pact. On their way to hunt buffalo, Comanches and Kiowas came upon a party of railroad workers in the act of killing buffalo (a treaty violation).[17] A fight ensued and the treaty was in shreds.

The behavior of the Kiowa and Comanche was little improved. Gen. W. S. Hancock was preparing an all-out war on Indians when his superior, Gen. William T. Sherman, ordered him to give the peace effort a chance to work. Hancock was furious and chafing to pounce on his adversary. Instead he called Kiowas into his office to reprimand them.[18] The innocent showed up and took Hancock's rebuke, but did tell him Satanta was the guilty party.

In May 1866, General Hancock caught up with Satanta and angrily rebuked the cocky chief. This confrontation resulted in Satanta leaving Kansas — for a while. This Indian, as much as any single man could, represented the worst of his people. The image he cast was one that hurt all Indians. He was big, bully-like, mean, deceitful, cruel, and totally unreliable. Satanta's word was as useless as "warts on a hog." Even his own tribal family despised and feared Satanta, the great "White Bear," but none of his tribe had the stomach required to deal with him.

Around Jesse and Bill Bent, Satanta was like a pup. There was a reason he was so docile around these two men. Jesse broke his arm while wrestling, when they were young men, and Bent had beat him to a bloody pulp when the rude Indian started a fight at Bent's Fort. Brute force was the only language Satanta understood or obeyed. He could be handled, but not along conventional lines. Now an old, undisciplined fool, Satanta was killing and pillaging at his will and pleasure.

Shortly after Hancock rebuked Satanta, he was in Texas on a raid. The innocent family of James Box crossed his path and for this sin, Box paid with his life.[19] Satanta brazenly took Mrs. Box and her four children and hurried back to Kansas to cash them in at the army post. He had tried to ransom them to Jesse, who had refused the offer. However, Jesse rode with Satanta to Fort Larned, Kansas, to protect the woman and her children. When Colonel Leavenworth met them at the fort, he too refused to ransom the family and at the same time criticized the cocky Indian.

Satanta continued on to Fort Dodge, where he got an even greater price for the Box family than he had asked of Jesse or Leavenworth. Compassion moved the commanding officer to ransom widow Box and her pitiful children from Satanta and his Kiowas.[20]

This experience convinced Jesse that some men were beyond reach of peaceful persuasion. In the matter of how to deal with Satanta, it was out of his scope of influence, but he did decide Satanta was a man who could not be trusted or tolerated any longer.

To the surprise of no one, the feud between Leavenworth and the military erupted again. Indian agent Leavenworth was requesting rifles for Kiowas and Comanches to hunt the vanishing buffalo (one of the treaty stipulations of Little Arkansas Treaty Council, a month earlier). General Sherman issued an order forbidding sale of firearms to Indians.[21] Leavenworth didn't get rifles he requisitioned, but neither did Sherman's order stop the sale of guns to Indians.

The last giant intellect among Indians, Chief John Ross, died in Washington in July 1865 after signing a treaty with the United States.[22] This Cherokee statesman did more to elevate public understanding and esteem for Indians than any man before or since. He was unrelenting in his zeal for fair treatment of his and other Indian tribes. Every Indian lost an unyielding friend when the little warrior died. While Ross and Jesse differed in methods and tactics, they still maintained a strong bond of friendship and mutual admiration. Jesse mourned the passing of "the smartest man I ever met."

The death of another Indian, Chief Little Mountain or Dohasen, in 1866 would have an even greater initial impact on stability of society than the death of Chief Ross.[23] With Kiowas now leaderless, the tribe split into uncontrollable splinter groups, with no one strong enough to hold them together. In name Lone Wolf was head chief, but he had no illusions that he could manage or direct Satanta.

Two other Kiowa warriors, Chief Big Bow and White Horse, were killers and sadistic men in whom trust was futile or fatal in some instances. On the whole frontier there were no worse despots than Satanta, Big Bow, and White Horse. What made the treacherous White Horse the more dangerous was a boyish, innocent countenance with a beguiling, even friendly, focused smile. It was said he maintained this smile even as he scalped and mutilated his quarry.

When pompous little Gen. Phillip Sheridan publicly called for the hanging of Satanta and Lone Wolf,[24] Sheridan's lackey, Col. George Custer, joined him in condemnation of the Kiowa badmen and all other troublesome Indians. What was so ludicrous about Sheridan and Custer calling for punishment of Indians was their own record as killers. Neither of these men cared a whit for their own lives nor those of others; they had the questionable distinction of being two of the most prolific killers in the army. This was a prime example of Satan complaining about the heat, as it were.

The entire South was under martial law.[25] In some areas, like New Orleans, Birmingham, and Charleston, curfews and their enforcement were very rigid. Some restraint was called for in parts of Texas and Kansas where Indian raids were worse than ever.

The ban on citizens owning firearms in Texas had to be cautiously applied, because marauding Indians soon found there were no troops to repel them and neither were citizens able to fight them off with sticks and rocks.

Most U.S. troop personnel in Texas during this period were blacks, with a few white officers. These particular soldiers of the army of occupation preferred to let Texans have guns rather than fight Indians themselves. This unreasonable and illogical situation did little to alleviate mounting Indian raids in Texas.

A new occupation was just manifesting itself in Texas. The starving, war-weary "Rebs" found a way to eat off the land. They were rounding up maverick, or stray, cattle and selling them for food to hungry buyers, first in the South and then in short order to markets in the North. Jesse had been bartering these range cattle for some thirty years. Now he would be joined by new entries in the cattle business.

Range cattle covered the southern and eastern part of Texas, rummaging wild.

Some enterprising men drove some of these cattle all the way to Sedalia, Missouri, where they found a ready market for all they could bring at three to four dollars a head.[26] By the end of 1866, more than a quarter million head of cattle were sold in Missouri.

Part of the money from these sales went to buy guns. Texans were enterprising in more areas than just the cattle market. Guns brought a tremendous bonus on the "black market" back home. With every returning cowman came as many guns as he could carry or afford. Now Indians would be dealt with in a manner characteristic of Texans. By now the bloody ledger that Indians once claimed to be tilted heavily in favor of Texans was now running red on the Texans' side. No safety was guaranteed any Texan on the outskirts of large cities or outlying settlements from depredations inflicted by Comanche and Kiowa raiders. This would all change if the cattle market held up. Every able-bodied Texan would soon be armed to challenge rampaging Indians.

The territory was split in half by Congress when they granted the Missouri Pacific Railroad an easement through Cherokee-held lands. The last treaty Cherokees signed with the U.S. in effect traded this land (or so it was interpreted) for total amnesty of those Cherokees who sided with the South during the Civil War. Now this last haven of Indian solidarity was stripped away. No longer could Indians expect to control any part of their own destiny.

For Jesse, the coming of the railroads signaled a new set of problems for Indians *and* whites.[27] The influx of construction crews, followed by the inevitable crush of saloons, prostitutes and gamblers that were consistently associated with the rough-and-tumble railroad crews, bode bigger headaches ahead for everyone. But despite all the chaos around him, his own trading houses were prospering once again.

No matter how far he moved from the hub of activity, Jesse ended up on a busy thoroughfare and his business grew faster than he could handle it. His trading house near Council Grove had been on the westward routes to both California and Colorado when gold was discovered. Now the northern route of Texas cattlemen was again bringing him a surge of trade activity which filled his pockets with profit.[28] His salt works also became a money maker. Old "Prairie Jesse" had not lost his "Midas touch," but neither had he lost his compassion for those not so fortunate. He was still feeding and caring for needy Indians, Mexicans, blacks, and whites who passed his way.

On a trading trip into Texas, he looked up his old friend, John W. Durant, at Centerville. When he arrived he learned Durant had been incarcerated, charged with assault on a Union officer.[29] He visited Durant in jail and learned his imprisonment was more politically motivated than felonious. As a lawyer, Durant got carried away in his zeal to defend his client and had accused the black judge and other court officials of rank bias. He was charged with contempt of court and then physically resisted efforts by the court's officers to jail him. His bond was set at $1,000 cash — not horses, not land or any other exchange, just cash. Jesse made up the cash required and posted Durant's bond pending his trial.

Once out, Durant insisted on settling the account with Jesse then and there. After the two men worked out their business, Durant told him he planned to "jump bail" and would disappear from sight, never to be seen in Leon County again. The last time Jesse saw his friend Durant, he was headed for Brazoria County to hide out at his daughter's home at Alvin, Texas. He died of old age there in 1889.

Every place Jesse traveled in Texas, he heard about new raids by Comanches and Kiowas. So complete was a wall of resistance being shaped that no Indians were seen except on raiding excursions. This situation upset Jesse because he knew this marauding could not go unchallenged. A bloody showdown was inevitable, and in fact was already in progress.

General Sherman reacted to Indian raids decisively.[30] He retaliated by cutting off all subsistence for Cheyennes, Kiowas, Arapahos, and Comanches. Only a small segment of these tribes were involved, but they all drew heat from Sherman's edict.

Colonel Leavenworth protested what he believed to be overreaction on the part of the military. Right or wrong, Sherman had to make some positive move. The public was demanding attention to the growing cancer of physical attrition by raiding Indians.

On his way home from Texas, in the spring of 1867, Jesse overtook some Texas cowmen moving a herd of 2,000 Longhorn cattle to the north toward Missouri. He joined them at Spanish Fort Crossing on Red River, where they had camped overnight. He rode with them across the territory to where the trail "forked," and followed the northwest trail to his home-trading post in the southeast corner of present-day Cleveland County, Oklahoma. The other herders continued on the trail north toward Missouri in search of cattle buyers. This brief encounter with Texas traildrivers heading up the "Chisholm Trail" probably was his only direct contact with a trail drive on this historic land-mark that bears his name.

On reaching his trading post, formerly Chouteau's old redan, P. A. Smith, Jesse's bookkeeper, surprised him with the volume he had managed during Jesse's absence. Business was brisk, but money was rarely used. The still unreconstructed South had little to barter but used specie in lieu of money, which was still scarce to nonexistent.

Jesse also had two urgent summons for his services — one from General Harney, the other from Colonel Leavenworth. Both men needed his services to help arrange a treaty council. He silently wished them "good luck" and went about his business. It was good to be home again. He didn't plan to leave in the foreseeable future.

13

The Chisholm Trail

oday offered promise of a time for fun. Colonel Houston chuckled easily as he probed my knowledge of the "world's most famous cattle trail." He feigned shock when I admitted I didn't have the slightest idea where it was located or how it got its name.

The colonel offered this consolation: "For a name that is as widely known as the Chisholm Trail, it's hard to believe so little is known about the trail or the man for whom it was named." He added, "It is a rotten shame no one has ever recorded this story for all America's schoolchildren . . . Jesse Chisholm should be remembered as one of our great national treasures."

The long awaited time was at hand for me to learn about the other "Chisholms" in Texan and Southwestern lore. Spelling of the name varied, but the notoriety of each was parallel.

The old colonel seemed to revel in the plot he was about to unfold. His blue eyes danced and took on a special sparkle as he attempted to wipe away my veil of ignorance about the famous cattle trail's name. Houston, of course, had no doubt it was named for his friend, Jesse Chisholm.

A number of books deal historically with this famous trail, but these same books afford a wide assortment of opinions as to where the Chisholm Trail was situated. At least three men are pretenders to credit for blazing the trail. Obviously, all three claimants didn't open

177

the same trail, so the reason for confusion must lie in the question of which "trail" is under discussion.

A landmark of the magnitude of the Chisholm Trail in the growth and development of the Southwest deserves better coverage than it has received to date. The man responsible for opening this "avenue of industry" should also be accorded his proper recognition. Making this declaration is easy. Carrying out the assignment takes the historian into many unexpected crevices of Pandora's box, with resulting "finds" serving as balm for diligent searchers. Truly remarkable is the wealth of unpublished information still available for students of Chisholm Trail history.

Some confusion swirling around the trail can be traced to a book by Louise and Fullen Artrip, *Memoirs of Daniel Fore (Jim) Chisholm and the Chisholm Trail,* published in 1949. The authors state, "The first cattle trail Northward out of Texas — established by Thornton Chisholm in 1866, is not to be confused with the several trails established by Jesse Chisholm: nor is it to be confused with the 'extreme Western Trail' established by John Chism [Chisum]."

In this brief statement the authors have been careful not to dispute claims of either Jesse Chisholm or John Chisum, but in a very significant point — the date — they have tried to eliminate the other two claims. Unfortunately, this late arriving claim for Thornton Chisholm is the only shred of information available that would tend to substantiate his claim.

With the other two men mentioned, both have a wealth of documented, though widely scattered, material which establishes their proper position beyond any reasonable doubt. In a capsule, Jesse Chisholm "marked" the "Chisholm Trail" in 1865. John Simpson Chisum, one of the biggest cattle owners of all time, established many trails between Texas and New Mexico. Because of his fame and a name that was pronounced the same as the blazer of the trail, it is easy to classify who did what, and where and when and why. But relating the other accomplishments and history attached to these two giants would fill several books.

Jesse's original trail, known as Chisholm's trail,[1] was only 220 miles long, extending southward from the present site on Wichita, Kansas, to Council Grove, Oklahoma, near Yukon, Oklahoma, about twelve miles west of Oklahoma City. It was not a cattle trail in the inception but was turned into one thanks to the promotional genius of Joseph G. McCoy of Abilene, Kansas.

In an unprecedented action, McCoy single-handedly set in motion his dream of moving Texas cattle across country in trail drives to his railhead at Abilene, Kansas.[2] McCoy was branded as crazy by bankers and railroad management, but his irresistible momentum was already in motion. He hired a civil engineer, Tim F. Hersey, and a crew to help him mark off a trail from Abilene to Wichita and then south across Oklahoma into North Texas cattle country. It is, in fact, Hersey, at McCoy's direction, who marked the trail over which Texas cattle were driven to McCoy's railhead in Abilene.

There is and always will be some conjecture about how Hersey was steered to, or inadvertently stumbled onto, the old wagon trail near a settlement named for an Indian tribe, Wichita. There is no doubt Hersey and his crew followed the trail without any trouble, leaving their marks at reasonable intervals, blazing trees and using colored cotton cloth where marking was deemed necessary.

From the start, Hersey heard settlers refer to the path he was following as old Jesse Chisholm's trail, or more usually Chisholm's trail.[3] There are any number of reasons for the name "Chisholm" to be associated with this particular trail, but with no more reason than would Black Beaver's name or that of Col. W. H. Emory be logical choices.[4] Like it or not, it was the name "Chisholm" that Hersey heard. In turn, he directed Texas cattlemen to "pickup Chisholm's trail North of the Red River, about 80 miles due North."[5] Hersey couldn't have cared less what name the trail was called. He took an obvious route, one easy to identify, and his biggest job was "selling" cattlemen to hit the trail. The easier Hersey made the trip sound, along a well-known and well-marked trail, the better chance he stood to get cattle headed for Abilene.

In truth, the trail wasn't all that well known. Certainly, it was no household word in either Kansas or Oklahoma. Nor was the trail marked off that well. But Hersey did his best to make it sound like the Texas Road or Santa Fe Trail.

The first cattle drive moved over this trail in 1868, but there is no record of any person named Chisholm or Chisum being connected with this first drive or subsequent drives for the next two years. Detailed records kept by McCoy of cattle movements into Abilene furnish the best, and in many instances only, records of what was transpiring within the cattle industry during the 1860s.

When big cattle drives began moving from Texas, they were rounded up from many areas to be moved over the "Chisholm Trail."

Consequently, there became many "fingers" or subtrails that were to become a part of the prime trail.

The casual student is frequently drawn into the swirling controversy surrounding the trail before he realizes this subject is controversy itself. The illustrious Walter Prescott Webb, historian and author, plunged into this controversy in the early stages of his career.[6] Webb's leap into the fray was occasioned by a storm of protest raised over a fictional novel, *North of 36,* by Emerson Hough. The book purportedly dealt rather harshly and untruthfully with real life characters of the Chisholm Trail, especially Joseph G. McCoy, the man most responsible for this overland cattle trail. Webb, armed only with his newly acquired title, professor of history at the University of Texas, wrote in defense of the fictional novel as to its historical accuracy. Where the young history professor lacked facts, he allowed his educated imagination to take over and easily spanned the "fact gap." By no means was Webb the only one to be trapped in the Chisholm Trail enigma, but he is probably the most famous author to become ensnarled in the tangle of legend that still enshrouds the historically significant cattle trail.

In numerous books and articles about the trail, there is a difference of opinion as to where the trail was located. Some have it laid out north to south, while others have it situated east to west. There are at least three different men who are credited with "marking" the trail, depending, of course, on which trail is being advanced as the trail in question. To add to the general confusion, there are also at least three different dates in history on which the trail was marked.

The task seems to be to research each of the well-documented claims and eliminate two that do not qualify. A small, contiguous, and thoroughly conscientious group of historians — Grant Foreman, Joseph B. Thoburn, T. U. Taylor, Wayne Gard, Henry B. Jameson, and Stuart Henry — all agree that the Chisholm Trail was named for Jesse Chisholm and was located within bounds of a stretch between a point near Wichita, Kansas, and another 220 miles south, at Council Grove, Oklahoma. The date is "conceded" to be 1865, with no attempt to pinpoint exact day and month.

What is so remarkable about claims for John S. Chisum and Thornton Chisholm is the coincidence of their respective proximity to the famous trail at the precise time it came into being.

It seems appropriate to give a brief resume of the other two pretenders. Both were most respected and unusually deserving men in their own right. For one, John Simpson Chisum, fame of a certain nature was assured when his life was depicted, but not documented, by actor John Wayne in the movie *Chisum*. That John Chisum "blazed" trails is indisputable. As one of the biggest cattle dealers of all time, Chisum moved most of his herds in either eastward or westward directions. During the War Between the States, he supplied a great number of cattle to the Confederacy, delivering them to Shreveport, Louisiana, or Fort Smith, Arkansas. Since moving cattle from Chisum's ranch in Texas to Louisiana and Arkansas was new to the area, trails he established could easily be distinguished and were called "Chisum's" trail. After the war, in 1865, Chisum moved his cattle from his ranch in Concho County, Texas, to his new ranch at Bosque Grande, New Mexico, and the route he followed was a first. So this trail could have been known, and with justification, as Chisum's trail.

The venerable and sagacious John Chisum was a big factor in the Southwest during the time that the Chisholm Trail was getting its name. But what was generally conceded to be a trail from Red River northward to Abilene, Kansas, eliminated him as the "blazer" of the south-to-north trail. At the zenith of cattle drives from Texas to Kansas between 1868 and 1872, there is no record extant of a "Chisum" having made a trip to Abilene, Kansas, with a cattle drive.[7]

Thornton Chisholm, a cattleman and native of DeWitt County, Texas, third claimant, was opening new trails in the 1860s along with Jesse Chisholm and John Chisum. His claim, though, is tarnished by the lateness of its appearance. The only ties now available in the way of documentation were sworn affidavits from men who either made this trip with him or remembered him making the trip.

Thornton's heirs state in the book *Chisholm Trail,* published in 1949, that his claim is not to be confused with trails claimed for either Jesse or John. Instead, they use the south-to-north segment of the trail through Texas from Caldwell Flats in DeWitt County to Red River and a junction with the trail across Indian Territory (Oklahoma), Kansas, and finally to St. Joseph, Missouri, as the "Chisholm Trail" claimed for Thornton Chisholm. Their contention is that Thornton blazed the entire trail on a drive he made in 1866.

The whole case for Thornton Chisholm is a tragic commentary of times in which he lived. His death in 1868, as reported in the book written by his granddaughter, Louise Artrip, adds another dimension of mystery to his story. The death was recorded as having taken place in a remote area near Burnet, Texas, after being crushed beneath wheels of his own wagon. His burial place is unmarked, and no evi-

OREGON TERR.
(WYOMING)
(COLOR
"Stony Mts."
SAN FRANSICO
CALIFORNIA
Great American Desert
NEW MEXICO TERR.
SANTA FE
ALBU.
SAN DIEGO
APACHES
RIO GRAN
MEXICO
TO CALIF
MATZALA

CHISHOLM'S TRAILS

① & ② LOOKING FOR HIS FATHER

③ COMANCHE & KIOWA TRADE RTS.
ALSO LEAVENWORTH DODGE EXP.

dence of his final resting place exists. Regardless of the lack of documents to corroborate his claim, old-timers who knew and rode with Thornton Chisholm will always believe "their trail" was the real Chisholm Trail. Nevertheless, McCoy's log lists no Chisholm.

McCoy should be the best authority on this subject, assuming his records and recollections were accurately reported. It was the promotional genius of McCoy who gave birth to the idea of a trail to move cattle from Texas to Kansas. McCoy or one of his men dubbed his trail south as the Chisholm.

At the conclusion of the Civil War, the North was hungry for beef while the South, with an abundance of beef, was hungry — period. McCoy planned to satisfy hungers of North and South with his colossal scheme. There were no railroads, in usable condition, extending farther south than Abilene, Kansas. McCoy conceived an idea of transporting cattle in large numbers by means of overland drives from Texas to Abilene, where he would buy them and transport them by rail to principal markets in the North and East, Chicago being his biggest and most accessible market.

His idea was an instant success from the standpoint of Texas cattlemen and McCoy. Both quickly became wealthy as cattle entrepreneurs. McCoy bought all cattle he could get at eight dollars a head and needed cattle faster than he could buy them. In 1868, McCoy's agents were actively promoting his cattle highway, but his best advertising source was the noise made by McCoy's money jingling in Texas cattlemen's pockets.

Soon after early traildrivers got home from their first trip, business began to pick up in epidemic proportions. Now in the heyday of the trail's existence, word spread in letters, conversation, newspapers, and songs, telling the world about the Chisholm Trail.

As the result of McCoy's highly successful innovations and the accompanying media blitz, many things happened along the trail that had a tremendous impact on the entire nation. Where destitution abounded in Texas before the trail was opened, cattle money changed everything to wealth and plenty — plenty, that is, of crime, hustlers, gamblers, prostitutes, murderers, and about every other plague imaginable from Kansas to Texas.

Old Jesse Chisholm was living less than twenty miles west of the trail that bore his name, but as a cattleman he didn't use it and in fact died suddenly only months after the trail opened for cattle movements.

Years later, McCoy acknowledged he was not acquainted with

Jesse Chisholm or John Chisum and could shed no light on how the trail got the name of Chisholm. He just remembered that was the name by which his trade route was called.[8]

As each new finger or branch of the trail was added, cowboys knew only one basic fact: to wit, they were "hitting the Chisholm Trail." This grand avenue, over which more than a million cattle moved to Abilene, was abandoned with completion of a railroad line, which obviated need for long drives.

Toward the last days of the trail's use, it extended all the way to the Rio Grande Valley in Texas. There were literally hundreds of paths leading to the primary trail.

Some historians readily admit Jesse's path from Wichita to Council Grove is the path in question, but they steadfastly maintain he did not mark it in the beginning. Their conclusions, with some merit, are based on their contention that Jesse merely followed four-year-old ruts made by wagons, horses, and men of the Union Army as they beat a hasty retreat from Confederate troops.

When the War Between the States began in 1861, Col. William H. Emory, commanding First U.S. Cavalry, tried to get Jesse to guide him to Fort Leavenworth in Kansas. All normal escape routes by both water and land were blockaded by soldiers of the Confederacy. Jesse told Colonel Emory he had to stay with his family but recommended his friend Black Beaver, a Delaware Indian scout and guide, to lead his troops out of Indian Territory.

Black Beaver did lead Colonel Emory and his entire command to the safe confines of Fort Leavenworth in 1861. For his efforts, Black Beaver is named by some as "blazer" of the trail named for Chisholm. Whether Jesse actually opened the same route taken by Colonel Emory, Black Beaver, and the fleeing Union forces is a question to be locked in the abyss of time.

It is highly probable that Jesse directed Black Beaver to follow some path he had previously traversed while trading with Kiowas in that area. In any event, the trail Chisholm marked or followed from Wichita to Oklahoma was the trail that was destined to be Jesse Chisholm's main link with posterity.

One significant clue persists regarding Jesse's relation to the "boulevard grande" that bears his name. His very presence in the area of Wichita bears some importance with relation to this account.

After the Civil War began, Jesse not unexpectedly elected to remain neutral, as did many Indian tribes and segments of tribes. In order to maintain their neutrality it was necessary to move to an area remote enough to hide them from both factions. Apparently, Chisholm already knew the beauty and remoteness of an area on the Arkansas River near the present site of Wichita; he is known to have guided Chief Opothleyohola and his Creek tribe to this area during the war. For years, Jesse had traded with the Kiowas in the region around what is now Wichita, Kansas.

En route to their home in exile, Creeks took a rather circuitous route, because of harassment and attacks by Creek and Cherokee soldiers who were aligned with the Confederacy. This remote rendezvous selected by Jesse afforded neutral Indians, who eventually reached the "promised land," a chance to live in peace. There was ample game, good water, and arable soil for growing crops. In fact, this area proved so idyllic for some Indians that they elected to remain there for the rest of their lives.

It was from this quiet spot that Jesse moved, after the ugly war ended, to reestablish his trading post in Indian Territory to the south. Although Wichita was sparsely settled during the period when big cattle drives were passing, it became one of the better grazing and watering stops along this trail. To some degree, the city of Wichita owes a debt of thanks to Jesse for his efforts in getting things started.

Some controversy that embroiled the trail has undoubtedly enabled historians to quickly spot those who knew as opposed to those who thought they knew. Old Texas traildrivers of the era in question most frequently erred in their facts.

The tough old president of Trail Drivers of Texas, George W. Saunders of San Antonio, told great tales for campfires, but they were lacking in fact when exposed to daylight. He was quick to jump on any person who dared dispute his "novel approach" with differing facts. In one of Saunders' many gaffs, appearing in an article in *Frontier Times,* October 1926, he stated that "Joe McCoy of Abilene, who built the stockyards there, hired Jesse Chisholm, a half breed Indian who was a trader and a scout, to blaze a trail from Abilene, Kansas to Red River, to guide Texas cattle to that Market." As reported earlier, McCoy said he wasn't acquainted with any Chisholm.

In another version appearing in *Frontier Times,* Donald F. McCarthy of Montrose, California, derided Saunders for his errors concerning the Chisholm Trail's origin and other things. McCarthy once and for all gave us the final word: "The origin of the Chisholm Trail, over which were driven the greatest herds of cattle known to history and the first and most famous ever blazed in this or any other country, was always more or less a mystery and a source of much dispute among early cattlemen, until cleared up some years ago by the late Captain Henry Spekes, of Bryon County, Oklahoma, then passed eighty, who took the first herd of cattle ever driven over it, to Kansas City in the Spring of 1866."

He continued, "Jesse Chisholm, for whom the trail took its name, was an Indian trader and trapper, and had an extensive ranch, and a trading post at Council Grove on the north bank of the North Canadian River, a few miles west of the site of Oklahoma City. The winter preceding the arrival of Captain Spekes at the North Canadian had been an unusually profitable season for trapping and hunting, and as a result, Chisholm had collected great piles of fur pelts, beaver and otter, deer elk and wolf skins and many buffalo hides, which he hauled to Kansas City the following Spring . . . arriving at the crossing of the North Canadian a few days after the Chisholm wagon train had departed from Council Grove, Captain Spekes, in view of the plain wagon trail that now lay ahead of him, cut deep into the soft prairie soil, followed it up to its junction with the Santa Fe Trail, and thence over the latter to the Missouri River. It was thus that the historic Chisholm Trail came into existence."

It made a great story but it just wasn't possible if dates McCarthy used are correct. The fact is, the Civil War ended for Grant and Lee in April 1865 but was dragged to a conclusion in the territory by Gen. Stand Watie's determined holdout until June 1865.

Jesse, then living near Wichita, Kansas, was planning his return trip to his old home in Cleveland County, Oklahoma, when Generals "Kit" Carson and Bill Harney enlisted Chisholm's aid in July 1865. They needed his help in rounding up nomadic Kiowa and Comanche Indians for a treaty session on Little Arkansas River in Kansas during October and early November 1865.

This effort on his part consumed all of Jesse's time until treaty sessions began in October. Jesse also acted as interpreter during the confab.

Since the season was into winter, he stayed with Creeks near Wichita, Kansas. Jesse would have been surprised to learn he had a profitable winter in 1865–66. On paper, his 1865 profit record was bad. Spekes undoubtedly followed some tracks because he said he did, but it is virtually impossible that Jesse accompanied wagons that made the tracks Spekes followed.

Some historians have mistakenly reported that Jesse Chisholm never dealt in cattle.[9] It is common knowledge he did, dating back to the 1830s. True, his main source of income was horses and, for a while, buffalo hides, but he did traffic in cattle for more than thirty years. The only reason he didn't do more business in cattle was due to lack of demand.

Before McCoy's ingenious breakthrough, the problem with cattle business in Texas was an overabundance of these animals. They roamed wild like horses. Owning a herd was as easy as harvesting wild pecans; holding a herd together after they were captured was the secret few had. Keeping these lean, mean, and keen-horned brutes called "Longhorns" took a brave man, with plenty of roping and horseback riding skills. Trying to milk one of these cows was like wrestling an alligator in a ditch, possible but seldom successful. Meat of sinewy Longhorn was tough as a frozen cup of coffee and twice as hard to down. Given a choice between buffalo or even dog as opposed to Longhorn steaks, there was no choice.

In short, the cattle business didn't come into its own until cross-breeding made range cattle more palatable, even though range animals were shipped north in great numbers. They were kept in feeder pens to be fattened and theoretically tenderized before they were slaughtered.

One fact seems obvious: if raising cattle was a profitable business, Jesse would have been up to his ears in Longhorns. He was very successful in all of his business ventures and undoubtedly would have joined King, Pierce, Goodnight, Littlefield, Slaughter, Chisum, and other cattle barons around him if the beef market had opened sooner.

From 1861 until his death early in 1868, his business activities never regained the volume and dimensions he enjoyed before the Civil War. But Jesse Chisholm was as worthy as any man to have a trail, or anything else for that matter, named for him.

For controversy to swirl around his name is most lamentable. He would have laughed at a suggestion that anything bear his name. A modest man, he surely never imagined he was doing anything special as he ambled through life's maze of trails while helping others.

He probably couldn't have cared less if they called this disputed trail by any of a hundred options available. Jesse Chisholm, the man for whom this famous trail was named, was as logical a choice as one could find.

14

Grand
Finale

*fter three summers, taken up for the most part by daily ses-
sions of storytelling, Colonel Houston said abruptly that this would be his last
story. During these meetings, which averaged about three hours a day, Houston
used the occasions to bring the memory of his friend Jesse Chisholm to life,
through his personal recollections.*

*This unique character in the lore of the Southwest may have been slighted
by chroniclers of this particular history, but Houston never missed a chance to
tout Chisholm and his accomplishments. When he could have been lionizing the
Houston name, he chose instead to bandy old Jesse's star.*

The coming of the Iron Horse to the Indians' homeland, more
than any other occurrence, divided Indians and at the same time set in
motion the means for their systematic destruction.[1] Long before he saw
steam-driven locomotives, Jesse had been instrumental in leading survey crews about their business of opening rail routes.

Even before the epic struggle between North and South ended in
1865, U.S. industrialists on both east and west coasts were gearing up
to lay new track. Without exception, acts of various speculators set off
wide resentment wherever they operated.

Congress gave railway builders eminent domain of all they surveyed. As war ground to a halt, some railroaders began laying track in

every direction — some parallel, some to nowhere, but all operating with a free hand to speculate with investors' money wherever they pleased.

Cherokee Chief John Ross had forced railroad companies to operate within prescribed zones and plans, while keeping them out of the territory. But since his death, no Indian had stepped forward to assume his role of leadership; in fact, few if any could have filled his shoes. For years, Jesse translated the wild Indians' complaints to U.S. Indian peace commissioners about railroad encroachment on their hunting grounds. But with each encroachment came some unwilling concession on the part of Indians.

Almost simultaneously, in 1865, Indians revolted against unlawful encroachment by whites. It is known that Jesse counseled Indians against hostile acts, but when challenged by his friends he admitted they had been provoked.

Kiowa, Comanche, Cheyenne, Arapaho, and Apache Indians were killing railbuilders and tearing up freshly built roadbeds. The mighty Sioux under Chief Red Cloud and Chief Joseph's Nez Perce now joined the Plains Indians in all-out warfare.[2] So formidable was the aggregate pressure of the various tribes, the United States was forced to close Bozeman Trail into Montana as well as several others in the Southwest.

President Johnson and Congress were deluged with complaints from angry citizens demanding "some" action on the part of government. Some wanted a stepped-up war on Indians, while others favored seeking peaceful relations with the Indians and another faction recommended the government stay out of the Indians' territory. There was unanimity of opinion that something must be done, but from there on few could agree on what to do.

A hastily called peace meeting at Fort Laramie in 1866 was typical of the poor planning and absence of purpose that prevailed. Peace commissioners were trying to convince Sioux attending a peace conclave that the government would keep trespassers off their land. Col. H. B. Carrington interrupted the Laramie peace try to announce the War Department's orders to build forts along Bozeman Trail, through Sioux land, and use American troops to maintain peace.[3]

Those unfortunate U.S. agents trying to work out a peaceful solution with Chief Red Cloud and his Sioux followers were demolished by the War Department's action.[4] The box score on this misfire: three hundred dead and hundreds more wounded — all white — before the year ended. Indians had their dead, too, but their casualties mattered little. Only the dead count of whites raised tempers in Washington.

Jesse, a participant at the ill-fated Little Arkansas Treaty agreement of 1865, remembered it didn't last much longer than the Laramie peace talks. Rail crews cutting across Kiowa hunting ground, illegally, were intercepted by bands of Indian hunters. Whites paid with their lives for this trespass.

Both the military and railroaders turned to the architect of Indian removal for help. Andrew Jackson's plan book directed: "Set off harrassing incidents to accomplish what you can not do directly."

Since railroaders couldn't legally go into Indian Territory, they circumvented this estoppel with the ingenious act of circulating rumors of gold discoveries on whichever boundary they were trying to encroach. This was a proven successful ploy everywhere it was utilized. Invariably, there followed a horde of treasure-seekers "escorted" by the military — not to protect the Indians but to protect poachers![5] Railway jackals feasted off the land while gold-seekers died trying to steal Indian land or Indians perished trying to keep it from being stolen.

In addition to Indian uprisings, there were other attacks on reconstruction of the South. Obstructionists in the form of radical merchants of hate in the North dominated Congress and did little to bring the nation back together. President Andrew Johnson, never a very forceful leader, was trying to fill in for the assassinated President Lincoln. This postwar Congress would have presented a problem to Lincoln or for that matter any other humane person. For Southern-born Andrew Johnson, ex-Tennessee senator, Congress paid special attention to "put him in his place." A powerful segment of Congress demanded a "show-them-no-mercy" policy toward all Southerners. This rationale was safe in the halls of Congress, but implementing such a hate-filled policy in the South was difficult to perform and very dangerous for the enforcer.

To deal with the harsh enforcers of the Federal army, Southerners, masquerading as Indians, destroyed oppressive Union occupation troops.[6] This ploy was used widely until Indians were driven from the area.

When he was asked to help, Jesse advised Indians to leave the infected region. Indians, instead of leaving, chose a revenge-filled guerrilla counterattack.

The acts of these two different guerrilla resistance movements, Indians and "Rebs," finally prompted Congress to yield to pressure for another peace try. Neither President Johnson nor Congress had found any grounds for mutual admiration, but public pressure was so great that they couldn't ignore the outcry of citizens any longer.

In one of the few instances where Congress acknowledged President Johnson as head of state, they met with him to work out a plan to try to seek peace with the raging Indians. From this meeting came the appointment of a peace commission headed by Rev. Nathaniel G. Taylor and three members appointed by Congress and three by President Johnson.[7] The president was voted full authority to implement the program along with $150,000 to pay expenses incurred.[8] Besides Taylor, those appointed were Senator John B. Henderson, chairman of the Senate Committee for Indian Affairs; S. F. Tappan, former Colorado militia officer; Gen. John B. Sanborn; Gen. William S. Harney; Gen. Christopher "Kit" Carson, who became ill and had to be replaced by Gen. C. C. Auger; and Gen. A. H. Terry.[9]

A carnival atmosphere surrounded every meeting of this "blue ribbon task force." The public clamored for daily progress reports. Countless volunteers wanted to sit in and advise commissioners on how best to deal with Indians. More for their own peace, commissioners voted to move their operation to Fort Larned, in the wilds of Kansas, where they could meet quietly to discuss their problems.

Seasoned treaty agents for the U.S. including Generals Harney and Sanborn, both of whom officiated at the ill-fated Little Arkansas session in 1865, were expecting help from Edward W. Wynkoop, Cheyenne agent, Col. Jesse H. Leavenworth, Comanche agent, Capt. Black Beaver, Delaware Indian scout, D. A. Butterfield, trader, and John Shirley, trader — all of whom were regularly in contact with the rampaging Indians. Jesse's participation was considered "a must." But he declined to serve, reasoning the whole idea was an exercise in futility.

After months of diligent effort on the part of these dedicated peace-seekers working without Chisholm, they had little good news to report. The Indians simply were not receptive. An explanation follows: "When the autumn season was at hand, the Indians were generally ready to attend a peace council. Solicitude for their hungry families and the desire for warm clothing for winter generally quickened an interest in the reestablishment of peace.

"In autumn of 1867, it was different; Indians were not disposed to sue for peace. It was, therefore, necessary to send them to men in whom they had confidence — such men as Chisholm, Black Beaver and

Wynkoop — for the purpose of persuading them to attend a peace council." [10]

For Colonel Leavenworth, who was trying to coordinate efforts of all emissaries dealing with the Indians, the results were disheartening. Jesse's refusal to help typified his troubles. He knew first-hand the ill temper prevailing among the savages. They had tried to kill him earlier after becoming convinced he had led them into an ambush.

Leavenworth insisted the Indians' natural habitat was the only place they might consider. Medicine Lodge, Kansas, hunting ground of these Indians, was selected for this reason, and it was just seventy miles from the army post at Fort Larned. One nagging problem persisted: no Indians were going to appear.

Colonel Leavenworth in his report to a joint committee described Chisholm as his guide and interpreter and that he had helped "to keep the Indians quiet." He added that "[Chisholm] had been the guide and interpreter of his father, General Henry Leavenworth on his expedition to the Comanches in 1834 and that Chisom [Chisholm] had been with these Indians ever since; that he spoke their language perfectly." [11]

Through army channels, Jesse was contacted again at his Council Grove trading post in the Creek Nation. The call was urgent. His summoner was General Harney, chief spokesman for President Johnson's peace commission. To emphasize the importance of this summons, Harney arranged for a military escort to accompany him to Fort Larned. Jesse declined the escort but agreed to meet with Harney and other commissioners as soon as he could get his business in order.

When Jesse arrived at Fort Larned for his audience with commissioners, he was greeted warmly by several members; the majority had despaired waiting for him and had returned home. [12] He listened as one after another told of Indians' refusal to negotiate. First Harney, then Leavenworth, and finally Sanborn gave negative reports. It was Chairman Taylor's job to sum up their failures, then entreat with Jesse to help them. One negative report had Cheyenne Indian Agent Wynkoop being attacked by his charges.

Jesse wouldn't give in to their pressure. They were still trying to get him to change his mind when nightfall interrupted talks. Next morning, U.S. agents were again pleading with him to try to get Indians in for a peace try. Chisholm remained unmoved.

It was General Harney who finally hit the nerve which would make Jesse relent and agree to act as their agent. When Harney implied total eradication of Indians was the option if they did not agree to peace terms, he got Jesse's agreement to help bring Indians in for a peace try.

So many lives hung in the balance that failure was unthinkable. Taylor implied that Jesse represented the only reasonable hope remaining to span the vast chasm of hatred and mutual distrust, to reopen channels of communication between two dedicated adversaries.

Two years earlier, Harney and Kit Carson had used this same ploy to enlist his help getting the Little Arkansas Treaty off the plan board.[13] Jesse was being asked for an encore. Based on his past experiences, he held little hope that his efforts would bring different results from those in the past.

He deliberately set out alone in search of the Plains tribes. He wanted time to prepare his thoughts. Chisholm recalled he was full of apprehension about his undertaking. He expected to find Chief Ten Bears and his tribe in North Texas, and he planned to "test the water" with the Comanche chief.[14]

Yamparika Comanches were camped near Wichita Falls when Jesse called on them. But before he located his friends, he learned there were others also looking for these Comanches. Near Ten Bears' camp, Jesse came upon two other groups also seeking them but for different reasons: a detachment of Texas Rangers and a company of U.S. Second Cavalry. For concern over being followed, Jesse didn't mention the reason for his presence in the area.

Tension was at fever pitch wherever he traveled, with both Indian and white leery of every bush that moved. Particularly in Texas, the internecine strife was claiming new victims daily. Those weary of killing found themselves in a maelstrom with no place to go.

This mood prevailed when Jesse met his friend, Ten Bears. The two old friends, now well into the twilight of their respective careers, had nothing but respect for each other. The old Comanche sensed that something special surrounded the circumstances of this visit.

Jesse, usually a nerveless one, was tense as "frog legs in a hot fry pan" as he blurted out the purpose of his call. The great responsibility the old chief shouldered for his tribe caused him to stiffen as he listened to Chisholm's story. After a reflective interval, the wise old pair agreed that another peace try was their only alternative. But both knew that convincing other Indians was no small order.

In quick succession Ten Bears called his tribe to council and gave Jesse to understand he was on his own. Assembled chiefs gave him a subdued, if reserved, ear. Contrary to his earlier declaration, and two days and nights of boisterous debating, Ten Bears "shook the ship off the rocks" with his suggestion they all go with their friend and see what new proposals the United States had. Just to listen was his only commitment.[15] The rest of the Indians, in response to Ten Bears' move, followed his lead. Later the Kiowas, Cheyennes, and Arapahos agreed to join Comanches at Medicine Lodge — to listen.

When it was apparent Indians were coming in, Jesse had misgivings whether he had done the right thing, considering the belligerent mood of the savages. It was too late for him to back off now, but he resolved to watch those wild leaders of the Kiowas — Satanta and Lone Wolf, in particular.

Chisholm took Satanta to Fort Larned in advance of the main event at Medicine Lodge to give the peace effort a fair try.[16] As Satanta and Jesse arrived at the fort, a large body of soldiers was leaving for the treaty site at the home of the Cheyennes' annual Sun Dance to set up facilities to feed the horde that would descend there.

This move by Jesse gave Seventh Cavalry commandant Maj. Joel Elliot a strategic advantage over Satanta. Elliot was leading the Seventh Cavalry while its regular commander, Col. George Custer, was temporarily suspended.[17] Literally, Major Elliot now had Satanta in his gunsights, and could maintain order should the chief get too obstreperous.

From the reception Jesse received from General Harney and other commissioners, he felt his efforts just might bear fruit at last. It was a festive atmosphere in which past pain and agony seemed to give way to rampant optimism. Even the military seemed happy about the forthcoming event.

When he passed through Osage country, en route to Fort Larned, Chisholm inadvertently invited these Indians to the conclave. When Osages arrived they were informed their presence was not wanted or needed. After being fed, "the tame Indians," as Harney described the Osage, were dismissed. Old soldiers, Harney in particular, had an aversion to "civilized" Indians like the Osage.[18]

At last, there would be a peace council meeting at Medicine Lodge in which all leading characters were present. Medicine Lodge was not a "lodge." In fact, there was not even so much as a tepee gracing the site of the nation's biggest Indian peace council. Instead, the grounds consisted of about ten acres of semi-barren land surrounded on three sides by a grove of cottonwood, spruce, and gum trees. Autumn leaves spread a riot of color over trees already busily loosing their fall foliage of earthly ornaments. The idyllic cascade across nature's easel was nearly barren of wildlife. Only an occasional bluejay's scream or a crow's caw disturbed the quiet veiling this solitary shrine of the Cheyenne. Nature's stage was set for a monstrous drama about to be unfolded.

Now Chisholm's headiest dream was rendezvousing with stark reality. Old memories poured over his mind like an avalanche. Nearly half a century earlier, he had brought his new bride to this exact spot for a week of loving and leisure. But today, dreams had to be placed in the background.

After a month in his sweat-soaked, cracked-leather saddle, his lips burned raw from briny sweat and dust sympathized with his bloodshot eyes, long tormented by wind and dirt. The long trip had consumed two of his finest horses as well as his own patience and stamina. The stamina was gone, probably beyond recall. But the patience had to be restored quickly if he was to deal with those men, ever questioning his way, men who couldn't find the sun if left to their resources. Jesse knew his greatest trial lay ahead, and he tried to prepare his thoughts for the certain challenges he and other peace-seekers would encounter.

At Medicine Lodge, he mingled with newsmen from all over the nation, but few were attracted to this modest hero. He was interviewed by both Henry M. Stanley of the *Missouri-Democrat*[19] and Milton Reynolds, editor of the *Lawrence State Journal*,[20] but neither found his humble mien very newsworthy. Even with Chairman Taylor regularly alluding to Chisholm's outstanding job in getting the meeting transformed from wishful thinking to one of reality, Jesse still didn't inspire any feature articles. With at least thirty writers and illustrators who turned out reams of tripe and human interest copy, little mention was made of Jesse. This was to his liking since he hated to be the center of attention.

Jesse watched with amusement as writers, artists, and photographers followed flamboyant Satanta's every move, and for good reason — he gave them "copy." The great "Orator of the Plains" never disappointed his audience. In fact, Satanta so up-staged all other actors it is no small wonder that others received little press.

Before the second day of meetings was done, Jesse spotted one of the sacred icons of Kiowas in the possession of a newsman.[21] It had been taken from the Kiowas' camp area while the tribe was in council.

The icon was an essential part of their tribal ritual, and its loss could provoke hostilities. To guard against such a situation, the commission had declared Indian quarters "off limits" to all but the occupants.

Without calculating the risk involved, Jesse forcibly took the offending newsman before the startled commissioners and demanded his arrest. Although he was warned there might be repercussions from the press, Jesse continued his demands without prejudice to protect the peace effort.[22] The souvenir-seeking reporter's thoughtless act had endangered the lives of everyone present.

Jesse assumed the task of returning the sacred piece to the Kiowas' temple before it was missed. Had the Kiowas found any unauthorized person in possession of their sacred icon — including Chisholm — it probably would have meant death.

To fully appreciate the task of dealing with the rampaging Indians at this peace table, one must examine the various egos involved. There were four major tribal categories: Comanche, Cheyenne, Kiowa, and Arapaho, within which were numerous subtribes or branches off the main stem. Comanches had four head chiefs; six by some counts. Ten Bears was spokesman for Comanches, representing the powerful Yamparikas.[23] Horses' Back was head man of the Nokoni branch of Comanche.[24] The Penateka branch, now diluted in power and pride from living on a reservation, were also represented.[25] The Kwahadis were not present,[26] and there was only token representation from the Kotsoteka.[27]

Kiowas came with a full representation. Their chief, Lone Wolf,[28] was completely overshadowed by the noisy White Bear, better known as Satanta. Black Kettle headed the once powerful but now badly split Cheyenne tribe.[29] And finally there was Little Raven, pompous head chief of the Arapaho.[30] Within each main tribe, as many as ten subchiefs demanded some attention.

In all, the Indians had at least forty different personalities clamoring for the spotlight. With each new violation by whites, the minor chiefs among various tribes demanded retaliation by their main chiefs.

Everyone wanted to be heard. Besides Indians, members of the commission, high-ranking military personnel, guests of the government, and the "Third Estate," in the form of working newsmen, were added to the VIP list. Since Jesse was the most fluent and widely educated interpreter, he was called on constantly by members of the commission to create meaning out of "mumbo-jumbo." (The Kiowa language was especially difficult to master; few whites ever mastered this strange tongue.) Newsmen also sought special interpretations as well as background material about various Indians.

Satanta, Kiowa chief, was the first to speak.[31] A mob scene grew around Jesse as he relayed the savage's words. As Satanta railed on, it became apparent why he was called "Orator of the Plains." When the old Indian became repetitious and unnecessarily vulgar, Jesse translated only a brief synopsis.

Satanta captivated the audience a few hours with his audacity. When his unbridled lust for action became apparent, it dawned on all who watched him that he wasn't putting on an act. He was as relentless as a horsefly and twice as repulsive.

It was apparent Satanta was going to be a mountain-sized headache. He tried to occupy center stage at all times. The cantankerous chief dressed in a U.S. trooper's jacket, and the small U.S. Army cap he wore on his monstrous head seemed "ridiculously small." Fresh scalps hung from his waist band (they had been taken in Texas a month earlier).[32]

His manners were atrocious and he seemed to revel in the uproar he caused, especially when he would interrupt negotiations periodically with loud blasts on a U.S.-issue bugle.[33] He did this when he was bored, which was anytime he wasn't the focus of attention.

Satanta's presence threatened to stall peace negotiations. Commissioner Taylor, in desperation, appealed to Jesse to "do something."

In language only Satanta understood, Jesse silenced the surly savage. While his words were lost on commissioners, the impact was not missed.

When the exchange became heated between negotiators, Jesse's head revolved like a pendulum as he tried to keep the debaters informed. Each tribe had its own interpreters, but Phillip McCusker and Black Beaver helped Chisholm more than all the rest.[34]

Almost simultaneously, another crisis was threatening peace. The biggest challenge for "women's rights" ever mounted was unfolding in this Kansas wilderness.[35] Little Raven, head chief of Arapahos, brought a white woman, Mrs. Margaret Adams, with him and announced she would act as his interpreter and advisor. At the same time Black Kettle, head chief of Cheyennes, introduced Julia Bent, daughter of William Bent, famous scout and trader, and informed U.S. agents that she would represent him. In the case of Julia, her position could be justified because her mother was a Cheyenne. But in the case of Mrs. Adams, commissioners[36] ruled she had no authority and therefore could not serve in any official capacity. Chief Little Raven was outraged. He refused to participate unless Mrs. Adams was allowed to serve. Little Raven was not bluffing, and an ugly confrontation seemed imminent.

Jesse reacted instinctively.[37] After some preliminary idle chatter, he suddenly proceeded to publicly chide the fat little Arapaho chief for his stand — wondering aloud why Little Raven couldn't speak for himself. His bait was taken. The stinging insinuation provoked Little Raven to tell one and all he *could* speak for himself. Chisholm dutifully translated the irate chief's torrent of angry words for commissioners. But the translation problems evaporated as Jesse helped his friend Little Raven with his language barrier. Without realizing he had been tricked, Little Raven used Jesse to make himself understood.

It was an unorthodox solution to a complex problem. Jesse pulled off the ruse without a hitch. Peace negotiations began again, with Mrs. Adams now occupying a coveted front-row "spectator" seat.

Chisholm was stretching to reach the acme of his influence. Time and again, military men representing the United States had their vanity chafed and the ultrasensitive Indians had their pride and integrity abused to the breaking point. These two monumental egos had to be protected while at the same time bent constantly toward attainment of peace.

On occasion, Chisholm held up proceedings to poll both sides to learn what they understood of the question being debated. Too many times one faction or the other came away from these treaty conclaves claiming to not understand what was said or written. It was Jesse's purpose to try to eliminate this excuse when Medicine Lodge Treaty was history.

He controlled the tempo at the bargaining table because only he knew all actors on both sides. It became a challenge of gigantic dimensions when many voices rang out at the same time, demanding to be heard. On more than one instance the chaos moved the troops close to taking over the meeting to restore order. As wild as these outbursts were, Jesse remained calm. When he restored order, he guided deliberations back to the subject under discussion when bedlam erupted.

Several newsmen crowded around Chisholm to ask him about what he knew about Satanta. He tried to avoid their questions. When they persisted, Jesse sent them to General Harney, telling them Harney was fully acquainted with the "star" of the peace conclave.

After all the reporters, save one, left Jesse to find General Har-

ney, the lone newsman asked Chisholm who he worked for. He answered his duty was to serve both factions, but he wouldn't receive any pay for his work there. Then the reporter deluged Jesse with a spate of questions: Who is the boss of the Indians? Who supervises the Indians after they leave the treaty council? Why does the U.S. have to feed and care for these lazy Redskins? What makes you think they can be trusted? There seemed no end to the dizzying flood of mundane probing. He dispatched each question as best he could and departed quickly when the opportunity presented itself. He, too, was still hunting for some answers.

The dedicated endeavor by Jesse removed one obstacle to peace — misunderstanding. But for all his efforts he couldn't supply the resolve required to make it work. As it turned out, understanding was not the missing ingredient here; rather, innate honesty was the commodity both sides failed to supply.

Throughout negotiations, Jesse was called on to restore order in addition to his task of interpreting. In some unexplainable manner, Indians detected the position of U.S. commissioners as one of "peace at any price."

Neither side seemed able to behave honestly. Even before this council was agreed to by Indians, Gen. W. S. Hancock launched attacks on peace-abiding Cheyennes.[38] Hancock's act breached a promise of peace that United States agents made to Indians in exchange for their return to a reservation. Bad publicity following the slaughter of these Indians caused Hancock to take his frustration out on Colonel Custer, charging him with being AWOL from his post.[39] It was not unusual for Custer to be in trouble with superiors, but for his friend and carousing partner, General Hancock, to blow the whistle, surprised everyone.

Major Elliot, substitute commander while Colonel Custer served his suspension, was not a friend of the peace parley concept. He found much fault. He publicly accused commissioners of a defeatist attitude. He quoted one commissioner as saying Indians were justified when they retaliated and was sorry they didn't kill more whites.[40]

If there was to be any hope for reaching agreement on a peace plan, someone was going to have to instill some reason into Indians' demands or the party was destined for sudden death. Selling this idea to the Indians would be a problem.

Indians, particularly Kiowa Chief Satanta, were enjoying their new role immensely. Telling them to back off and let their enemy bring up reinforcements when they sensed whites had lost their enthusiasm for war didn't square with their wishes or logic.

Emotions and tempers were at the breaking point. One Cheyenne warrior, Roman Nose, was furious.[41] When General Hancock attacked the Cheyennes in March, Roman Nose had taken a near fatal wound in his chest from a .50-caliber Spencer repeating carbine. Six months later, at Medicine Lodge, Roman Nose, instead of being grateful for being alive, was mad. He was so outraged he had to be subdued to keep him from taking revenge on General Hancock and his troops.

Chisholm had to convince Indians when they went for whites' jugular veins that they were in truth pulling the spring latch on their own hanging. His was a delicate presentation even in quiet surroundings but nigh impossible in the stress-filled treaty council. Those who witnessed his messianic power over Indians marveled at his reasoned restraint.

A Kansas editor, Reynolds, of the *Lawrence State Journal,* fueled the confusion at Medicine Lodge by writing that Kansas Governor Samuel Crawford was a liar and a thief who had armed white squatters to help drive Osages from their homesteads.[42] Stanley, a reporter covering the parley for the *Missouri Democrat,* also attacked Governor Crawford. Stanley's stories seemed to corroborate Reynolds' charges that Governor Crawford was a major factor in causing unrest and inciting strife against Indians.[43] Stanley would become world-famous later when he tracked down Dr. Livingston in Africa. For now, he busied himself chronicling exploits of General Hancock, whom he had accompanied on the ill-fated Cheyenne attack a month earlier. He reported details of this raid as well as an in-depth report of Colonel Custer's court-martial.[44]

Kicking Bird, a Kiowa subchief, made a strong bid for prominence by currying approval of whites. He turned on his chief, Satanta,[45] his superior in more ways than rank. Kicking Bird informed commissioners that Satanta had a white girl, whom he had captured in Texas, in his tent at the council. He also charged that Kiowas were being intimidated by Satanta and wanted protection from reprisals he was sure Satanta would heap on "loyal Indians" such as he.

A thorough search of the Kiowa campground yielded no white hostage. Instead, there were many wagers on how long Kicking Bird would kick after Satanta caught him. During the monthlong conclave, reports were made of thefts, mayhem, wife stealing, and other minor distractions.[46]

Treaty sessions dragged. A stench from animal and human dung, exposed to blistering Kansas sun for weeks, intensified tempers of men and beasts. Under these trying conditions it was hard to imagine that anything of historical significance was within reach. Rapidly deteriorating conditions in this hellhole, where the only things predictable were flies and heat, began to test nerve and sinew.[47]

Years of fruitless efforts to get representatives with sufficient authority to sign treaty agreements that would be working guidelines for future conduct now seemed to be paying off. That some treaty agreement was reached was a miracle, as well as a testimony to Chisholm's dedication, in view of the improbable circumstances.

It is of no great import that Jesse got Satanta to "sign" with his "X" even reluctantly, since he had little, if any, intention of learning what he signed and even less thought of complying with the compact. But he did sign.

No one suggested the peace pact from Medicine Lodge was perfect, or even a good treaty, but it offered hope. Two old friends, Chisholm and Chief Ten Bears, could add to the stature they gained there. It could be a lifeline for all.

Various tribes signed a new agreement of peace, which in reality shrunk their previous land holdings and at the same time authorized railroads to divide their hunting ground with rails. General Sherman said years later while discussing Medicine Lodge Treaty, "Still the Indian peace commission of 1867 did prepare the way for the great Pacific Railroads, which, for better or worse, have settled the fate of the buffalo and the Indian forever." [48]

This candid view expressed by the highest ranking officer in the military at the time was in a capsule the intent of white negotiators from the beginning of treaty conclaves with Indians. Chisholm recognized the intent of white negotiators from the inception. He also warned that the duplicity practiced by both sides would bring one or the other to complete serfdom. Both Indian and white operated on the premise, "Might makes right."

When all the treaty business had been finished, Jesse was approached by Senator Henderson with a request for a rerun of the Comanches' opening day display of horsemanship. He conveyed this request to Chief Ten Bears, who readily accepted the challenge.

When the old chief bellowed his riding orders, hundreds of bored braves made a wild scramble for their horses. Like a thunderclap, the wild, screaming warriors engulfed the environs. Riders from other tribes quickly joined the festivities. For more than two hours, these unsurpassed horsemen continued their pompous pageant as the president's peace contingent looked on. Indians loosed all restraint as they tried to outdo all prior performances. They changed horses in midstride; rode under their ponies; shot at targets from under their streaking mustangs; picked up fallen mates while running at full tilt; and engaged in impromptu races within the inner periphery of their spectacular show. Some of the spectators sagged from the tensions these wild antics evoked, but to a man they agreed it was a memorable show.

Jesse, with all his being, wanted to believe the two sides were dealing in good faith. It did not happen.

To say Chisholm failed, even though he felt he had, is not true. The failure belonged to those combatants who turned loose of the lifeline he had given them.

Jesse scarcely got home before Chief Ten Bears was calling on him. The Comanche chief complained about pressure from settlers in Texas. Chief Ten Bears was still ranting when Chisholm interrupted him to ask what he and his braves were doing in Texas since they were supposed to be settling on their home reservation in the territory. Between angry outbursts, Chief Ten Bears told Jesse the land assigned to Comanches was occupied by the Wichita Indians when they reached the reservation. A fierce dispute had erupted.[49] Henry Shanklin, Wichita agent, intervened and asked Chief Ten Bears, as a favor to him, to get his tribe off the land in dispute, until he could get a ruling to settle the issue. Shanklin also told Chief Ten Bears there were no provisions for his braves since he wasn't expecting them.

From here on Jesse could easily figure what had happened. Facing his tired, hungry and angry warriors, Chief Ten Bears told them they would go to Texas and look for food and shelter. The rest is history.

Turbulent Texas was unreceptive to the homecoming of the Comanches. Once again, Indians with good intentions were placed in an untenable position, one in which retaliatory acts seemed to offer the only solution.

The era of peace was over before it really began. The Commission for Indian Affairs erred gravely when they sent Indians to the reservation before any preparations had been made to accommodate these people. The Indians should have exercised more patience; Chief Ten Bears should have controlled his tribe; and President Johnson should have had super powers.

For all the excuses and alibis, the one constant to haunt all participants was the return of war. Perhaps, as some rationalize, they had to defend themselves. Chisholm wanted to share his ability to live peacefully with all mankind, but players in this arena gambled on their own resources — their unbridled egos. And they lost.

In quick succession, Special Agent Phillip McCusker reported that "Comanches and Kiowas are going to Texas to steal horses continually, and if they get them without any trouble, they do so, but if in order to get them it is necessary to kill a family or two, they do so." [50]

Simultaneously, United States troops set upon any and all Indians they could find. These confrontations set off the deadliest winter of war the Southwest had yet experienced. Neither side was the least bit interested in even a truce, much less peace, so no measures could be undertaken to right the wrongs. The die was irrevocably cast. War was the mandate of perennial intransigents. Jesse wept for his friends on both sides, locked in mortal combat.

15

Immemorial

las, the ravages of time forced old Colonel Houston to
abandon his dedicated effort to make the whole world aware of his friend Chisholm and his accomplishments. However, he challenged me to carry the torch
and never let the light of this patriot be dimmed. He concluded, "Where Jesse
Chisholm was concerned, I feel sure Popa would have stood with me and I'm sure
he would have done a more colorful story."

The epic struggle of Indians versus whites would rage on until
one would grind the other into the dust. Jesse realized that regardless
of which side prevailed, the ongoing conflict would ultimately determine who would go and who would stay.

Never again would these two confirmed enemies sit down as
equals to try to resolve differences. The last opportunity for such an
agreement came and went with their colossal try at Medicine Lodge,
Kansas.

In this sylvan retreat, far from congested cities, decisions were
formulated which sounded a death knell for the Indians' old way of
life. When Chisholm was called upon to help bring Indians in for
peace talks at Medicine Lodge, the military was "sure" of two things:
He would not accept the challenge; and if he did, he would not succeed
at bringing in the fighting mad savages again, as he had done before.

207

They were wrong on both scores. But since they held advantages in numbers and firepower, they could tolerate some delay in their dedicated goal — eradication of Indians.

Back at his home, Jesse tried to occupy his time, busying himself with his trading post duties where he worked with his clerk, P. A. Smith, and helped his teamster Richard Cuttle sort and bale hides.[1] He even found time to visit with his family. Though he smiled and seemed at ease, his facade masked a broken heart and a crushed spirit. The fire of hope was extinguished.

He decided to rest a few days and hunt with his friend and business associate, Jim Meade. They killed a large black bear and two deer before making camp at Johnny Lefthand Springs on the northern bank of Canadian River. While camped there, Chisholm became ill from food poisoning and died in violent convulsions. Meade reported later he believed bear grease in a brass pot caused the poison attack. He was away hunting when Jesse became ill and learned from others at camp about his death. A few Indians on hand when Chisholm was stricken fled in terror.

The date was March 4, 1868, at a place so remote it is still hard to find. He was buried in an unmarked grave near where he died, some thirty miles northwest of El Reno, Oklahoma, on the southern border of Blaine County.

News of Jesse's death affected many people. Outpouring of grief in the territory exceeded any death prior to his or since, until his world-famous nephew, Will Rogers, died in 1936. Men in all walks of life who knew and revered Chisholm's memory came to pay homage to this unusual man.

No person in modern times surpassed Chisholm for peaceful endeavors. In an atmosphere of violence and bloodshed, he stood out like a priest in a pool hall. His word was as reliable as man's ability to measure it. In short, he was the man that other men turned to when manhood was measured.

For more than a century, a small group of knowledgeable historians have tried to get this giant of peace some recognition, preferably in the U.S. Hall of Honor in Washington, D.C. There he would stand beside many of the men he guided, like Houston, Austin, Sequoyah, and a later arrival, his nephew, Will Rogers. No more worthy man exists.

One group, at least, has acted to honor Jesse Chisholm. His grave marker was purchased by schoolchildren of Oklahoma, and its inscription tells the whole story: "No man ever left his home cold or hungry." [2]

Notes

Introduction

1. Washington Irving, *A Tour of the Prairies*, vol. 7.
2. House Executive Document 97, 40th Congress, 2nd Session.
3. *Chronicles of Oklahoma*, 2:98. (Hereafter cited as *Chron. Okla.*)
4. J. B. Thoburn and M. H. Wright, *Oklahoma — A History, Its State and Its People*, 13:25.
5. *Cincinnati Daily Gazette*, October 29, 1867.
6. *Chron. Okla.*, 2:98.
7. *Ibid.*
8. *Ibid.*, 2:113.
9. *Ibid.*
10. *Ibid.*, 2:99.
11. A. J. Houston letter to Grant Foreman.
12. *Ibid.*
13. Fischer, *Civil War Era in the Indian Territory*, 119.

1. *Early Life*

1. T. U. Taylor, *Life of Jesse Chisholm*, 6.
2. *Ibid.*, 5.
3. *Ibid.*, 6.
4. *Ibid.*, 15.
5. *Ibid.*, 8.
6. *Ibid.*
7. *Ibid.*, 12.
8. *Ibid.*
9. *Chron. Okla.*, 8:239.
10. *Ibid.*
11. *Ibid.*
12. 5th Annual Report, Bureau of Ethnology 1883–84, 191.
13. *Ibid.*, 195.
14. *Ibid.*, 193.
15. *Ibid.*, 203.
16. Wm. C. Crane, *Life and Literary Remains of Sam Houston of Texas*, 39.
17. *Ibid.*

18. *Ibid.*, 19.
19. Taylor, *Life of Chisholm*, 12.
20. *Ibid.*, 5.
21. A. J. Houston Papers.
22. *Ibid.*
23. *Ibid.*
24. Taylor, *Life of Chisholm*, 8.
25. Thoburn and Wright, *Oklahoma — A History*, 1:102.
26. Office of Indian Affairs, Commission Report, 1865.
27. *Chron. Okla.*, 3:103–104.
28. Josiah Gregg, *Commerce of the Prairie*, 231–232.
29. *Chron. Okla.*, 13:25.
30. *A Tour of the Prairie*, vol. 12.
31. *Chron. Okla.*, 13:25.
32. *Ibid.*, 103.
33. *Handbook of Texas*, 1:44.
34. Grant Foreman, *Pioneer Days in the Early Southwest*, 212.
35. *Ibid.*
36. Crane, *Life of Houston*, 30.
37. *Ibid.*
38. A. J. Houston Papers.
39. *Ibid.*
40. *Ibid.*
41. *Ibid.*
42. Vinson Lackey, *The Chouteaus and the Founding of Salina*, 1–30.

2. *Chance*

1. A. J. Houston Papers.
2. Office of Indian Affairs, Commission Report, 1820.
3. Mathew Lyon biography, Library of Congress.
4. *Ibid.*
5. *Ibid.*
6. *Ibid.*
7. *Ibid.*
8. *Ibid.*
9. Lackey, *The Chouteaus*, 1–30; Foreman, *Pioneer Days*, 25.
10. Foreman, *Pioneer Days*, 23.
11. *Ibid.*
12. Thomas Nuttall, *A Journal of Travels Into the Arkansas Territory*, 136.
13. *Ibid.*, 135.
14. *Chron. Okla.*, 8:157.
15. *Ibid.*, 157–158.
16. *Ibid.*, 158.
17. *Arkansas Gazette*, October 27, 1821.
18. Foreman, *Advancing the Frontier*, 35.
19. Office of Indian Affairs, Commission Report, 1833.
20. A. J. Houston Papers.

21. Foreman, *Advancing the Frontier,* 26.
22. *Ibid.,* 27–28.
23. A. J. Houston Papers.
24. R. N. Richardson, *Comanche Barrier,* 312.
25. A. J. Houston Papers.
26. *Ibid.*
27. A. M. Williams, *Sam Houston and the War of Independence,* 83.
28. *Ibid.*
29. Crane, *Life of Houston,* 101.
30. A. J. Houston Papers.
31. Crane, *Life of Houston,* 101.
32. 5th Annual Report, Bureau of Ethnology, 26.
33. Williams, *Sam Houston,* 33.
34. *Chron. Okla.,* 2:98.
35. A. J. Houston Papers.
36. *Chron. Okla.,* 2:61.
37. *Ibid.*
38. Thoburn and Wright, *Oklahoma — A History,* 1:65.
39. *Ibid.*
40. Messages and Papers of the President.
41. *Handbook of Texas,* 1:82.
42. *Ibid.*
43. *Ibid.,* 83.
44. *Ibid.,* 82–84.
45. Foreman, *Advancing the Frontier,* 37.
46. Charles J. Kappler, *Law and Treaties,* 2:214–215.
47. Thoburn and Wright, *Oklahoma — A History,* 1:116.
48. Taylor, *Life of Chisholm,* 12.
49. *Ibid.*
50. 5th Annual Report, Bureau of Ethnology, 241.
51. *Ibid.*
52. Foreman, *Five Civilized Tribes,* 299.
53. John H. Brown, *Indian Wars and Pioneers of Texas,* 11.
54. *Ibid.*
55. Foreman, *Advancing the Frontier,* 147.
56. A. J. Houston Papers.
57. *Ibid.*
58. *Ibid.*
59. *Ibid.*

3. Indian Woes

1. Foreman, *Advancing the Frontier,* 221.
2. Foreman, *Pioneer Days,* 122.
3. Crane, *Life of Houston,* 36.
4. *Ibid.*
5. 5th Annual Report, Bureau of Ethnology, 241–290.
6. *Ibid.,* 266.
7. *Ibid.,* 133–378.

8. Crane, *Life of Houston*, 37.
9. *Ibid.*, 25.
10. Marquis James, *The Raven*, 30.
11. 5th Annual Report, Bureau of Ethnology, 233.
12. *Ibid.*, 266.
13. *Ibid.*, 264–266.
14. A. M. Williams, *Sam Houston*, 33.
15. Crane, *Life of Houston*, 37.
16. 5th Annual Report, Bureau of Ethnology, 231.
17. Foreman, *Five Civilized Tribes*, 148.
18. *Ibid.*, 252–253.
19. Foreman, *Five Civilized Tribes*, 384.
20. Foreman, *Advancing the Frontier*, 322.
21. T. U. Taylor, *Life of Chisholm*, 9.
22. Crane, *Life of Houston*, 39.
23. *Ibid.*, 41.
24. A. J. Houston Papers.
25. Foreman, *Advancing the Frontier*, 38.
26. Crane, *Life of Houston*, 42.
27. Eaton Papers, Library of Congress.
28. *Ibid.*
29. Thoburn and Wright, *Oklahoma — A History*, 1:150.
30. *Chron. Okla.*, vols. 8 and 13.
31. Foreman, *Advancing the Frontier*, 38.
32. *Chron. Okla.*, 8:43.
33. Foreman, *Advancing the Frontier*, 38.
34. Foreman, *Five Civilized Tribes*, 289.
35. A. J. Houston Papers.
36. *The South Central States*, 60.
37. Foreman, *Advancing the Frontier*, 24.
38. Crane, *Life of Houston*, 42.
39. *Chron. Okla.*, 43.
40. Crane, *Life of Houston*, 44.
41. *Ibid.*
42. A. J. Houston Papers.
43. Foreman, *Advancing the Frontier*, 40.
44. A. J. Houston Papers.
45. T. U. Taylor, *Life of Chisholm*, 10.
46. *Ibid.*
47. Crane, *Life of Houston*, 46.
48. Foreman, *Five Civilized Tribes*, 291.
49. *Ibid.*, 374.
50. 5th Annual Report, Bureau of Ethnology, 301.
51. *Ibid.*, 291–292.
52. *Arkansas Gazette*, June 10, 1833.
53. A. J. Houston Papers.
54. *Ibid.*
55. Foreman, *Advancing the Frontier*, 218–246.

56. A. J. Houston Papers.
57. *Chron. Okla.*, 8:417.
58. *Ibid.*
59. Office of Indian Affairs, Commissioners Report, 1833.
60. 5th Annual Report, Bureau of Ethnology, 251.
61. *Ibid.*, 243.
62. *Ibid.*, 218–219.

4. *Two Titans Square Off*

1. John Ross Papers, Oklahoma Historical Society.
2. Foreman, *Five Civilized Tribes*, 291–295.
3. Foreman, *Advancing the Frontier*, 49.
4. *Ibid.*, 47.
5. *Ibid.*, 36.
6. *Ibid.*, 41.
7. A. M. Williams, *Sam Houston*, 83.
8. *Ibid.*
9. A. J. Houston Papers.
10. R. N. Richardson, *Comanche Barrier*, 42–43.
11. A. J. Houston Papers.
12. R. N. Richardson, *Comanche Barrier*, 126.
13. *Ibid.*
14. *Ibid.*, 129.
15. A. J. Houston Papers.
16. R. N. Richardson, *Comanche Barrier*, 126.
17. Foreman, *Advancing the Frontier*, 118.
18. A. J. Houston Papers.
19. *Chron. Okla.*, 13:25.
20. Foreman, *Advancing the Frontier*, 17.
21. *Ibid.*
22. John Ross Papers, Oklahoma Historical Society.
23. *Ibid.*
24. 5th Annual Report, Bureau of Ethnology.
25. *Arkansas Gazette*, 1833.
26. Crane, *Life of Houston*, 25.
27. Thoburn and Wright, *Oklahoma — A History*, 1:180.
28. Foreman, *Advancing the Frontier*, 27.
29. John Ross Papers, Gilcrease Museum.
30. *Ibid.*
31. Crane, *Life of Houston*, 46.
32. *Handbook of Texas*, 1:84.
33. *Ibid.*
34. A. J. Houston Papers.
35. Thoburn and Wright, *Oklahoma — A History*, 1:25.

5. *Jackson's Extravaganza*

1. Thoburn and Wright, *Oklahoma — A History*, 1:180.
2. American State Papers, vol. 5.
3. *Chron. Okla.*, 3:28.
4. *Ibid.*
5. Foreman, *Advancing the Frontier*, 129.
6. *Ibid.*, 44.
7. West Point Academy Officers Biography.
8. Papers of John H. Eaton, Secretary of War.
9. *Ibid.*
10. *Chron. Okla.*, 13:25–30.
11. Thoburn and Wright, *Oklahoma — A History*, 1:180.
12. *Chron. Okla.*, 8:30.
13. Thoburn and Wright, *Oklahoma — A History*, 1:180.
14. *Ibid.*
15. *Ibid.*
16. Foreman, *Advancing the Frontier*, 130–131.
17. Thoburn and Wright, *Oklahoma — A History*, 1:184.
18. *Chron. Okla.*, 13:28.
19. *Ibid.*, 13:30.
20. George Catlin, *Letters and Notes on the North American Indians*, 2:44–56.
21. A. J. Houston Papers.
22. Thoburn and Wright, *Oklahoma — A History*, 1:180.
23. *Ibid.*
24. Journal of Lt. T. B. Wheelock, American State Papers, 5:373.
25. *Ibid.*
26. *Ibid.*
27. Thoburn and Wright, *Oklahoma — A History*, 1:181.
28. *Chron. Okla.*, 3:195.
29. Thoburn and Wright, *Oklahoma — A History*, 1:182.
30. A. J. Houston Papers.
31. Thoburn and Wright, *Oklahoma — A History*, 1:182.
32. *Chron. Okla.*, 3:180.
33. *Ibid.*, 3:180–190.
34. *Ibid.*, 185–190.
35. Foreman, *Advancing the Frontier*, 131.
36. Thoburn and Wright, *Oklahoma — A History*, 1:184.
37. A. J. Houston Papers.
38. *Chron. Okla.*, 3:178.
39. Thoburn and Wright, *Oklahoma — A History*, 1:182.
40. *Ibid.*
41. *Chron. Okla.*, 3:184.
42. Thoburn and Wright, *Oklahoma — A History*, 1:182.
43. *Ibid.*
44. *Ibid.*
45. Journal of Lt. T. B. Wheelock.
46. Thoburn and Wright, *Oklahoma — A History*, 1:182.

47. George Catlin, *North American Indians,* vol. 2.
48. Thoburn and Wright, *Oklahoma — A History,* 1:182.
49. *Ibid.,* 183.
50. *Ibid.*
51. *Ibid.*
52. *Ibid.*
53. *Ibid.,* 184.
54. *Ibid.*
55. *Ibid.*
56. *Ibid.*
57. *Ibid.*
58. *Ibid.;* Journal of T. B. Wheelock, vol. 2.
59. Thoburn and Wright, *Oklahoma — A History,* 1:185.
60. *Ibid.,* 47–48.
61. *Ibid.,* 185.

6. *Jesse Rescues Houston*

1. A. J. Houston Papers.
2. Thoburn and Wright, *Oklahoma — A History,* 1:186.
3. Foreman, *Pioneer Days,* 122.
4. Thoburn and Wright, *Oklahoma — A History,* 1:186; Journal of Lt. T. B. Wheelock, 1–25.
5. Journal of Lt. T. B. Wheelock, 1–25.
6. *Ibid.*
7. *Ibid.*
8. *Ibid.*
9. Foreman, *Pioneer Days,* 223.
10. *Ibid.*
11. Thoburn and Wright, *Oklahoma — A History,* 1:186.
12. *Ibid.*
13. Foreman, *Advancing the Frontier,* 143–144.
14. *Ibid.,* 144.
15. Washington Irving, *Tour of the Prairies,* 8:32.
16. The Chouteaus, appendix.
17. Thoburn and Wright, *Oklahoma — A History,* 1:178.
18. A. J. Houston Papers.
19. *Ibid.*
20. *Ibid.*
21. *Ibid.*
22. *Ibid.*
23. Thoburn and Wright, *Oklahoma — A History,* 1:47–48.
24. *Ibid.*
25. T. U. Taylor, *Life of Chisholm,* 21.
26. Crane, *Life of Houston,* 63.
27. *Ibid.*
28. A. J. Houston Papers.
29. *Ibid.*
30. *Ibid.*

31. Crane, *Life of Houston*, 84.
32. 5th Annual Report, Bureau of Ethnology, 281–282.
33. Foreman, *Advancing the Frontier*, 55.
34. *Ibid.*
35. Crane, *Life of Houston*, 116.
36. Thoburn and Wright, *Oklahoma — A History*, 1:234.
37. A. J. Houston Papers.
38. Thoburn and Wright, *Oklahoma — A History*, 1:234.
39. A. M. Williams, *Sam Houston*, 245.
40. Crane, *Life of Houston*, 117.
41. A. M. Williams, *Sam Houston*, 244.
42. T. U. Taylor, *Life of Chisholm*, 32.
43. *Chron. Okla.*, 3:103–104.
44. *Ibid.*
45. *Ibid.*
46. *Ibid.*
47. *Niles Register*, July 15, 1837.
48. A. J. Houston Papers.
49. Foreman, *Five Civilized Tribes*, 256.
50. Crane, *Life of Houston*, 24–30.
51. A. J. Houston Papers.
52. Foreman, *Advancing the Frontier*, 218.
53. *Chron. Okla.*, 3:104.
54. T. U. Taylor, *Life of Chisholm*, 18.
55. Foreman, *Five Civilized Tribes*, 157.
56. *Ibid.*, 156–157.
57. *Ibid.*, 157.
58. *Ibid.*, 158.
59. Houston Papers, Library of Congress.
60. *Ibid.*
61. Foreman, *Advancing the Frontier*, 50.
62. *Ibid.*, 66.
63. *Ibid.*, 232.
64. Houston Papers, Texas State Library.
65. *Ibid.*
66. *Ibid.*
67. R. N. Richardson, *Comanche Barrier*, 92.
68. A. J. Houston Papers.
69. *Ibid.*
70. Crane, *Life of Houston*, 131.
71. Houston Papers, Texas State Library.
72. Foreman, *Advancing the Frontier*, 164–166.
73. Crane, *Life of Houston*, 138.
74. R. N. Richardson, *Comanche Barrier*, 285.
75. Foreman, *Advancing the Frontier*, 165.
76. A. J. Houston Papers.
77. *Ibid.*
78. Foreman, *Five Civilized Tribes*, 155.

79. A. J. Houston Papers.
80. 5th Annual Report, Bureau of Ethnology, 291.
81. Foreman, *Five Civilized Tribes,* 284.
82. American State Papers, Indian Affairs, vol. 4.
83. *Encyclopedia Britannica,* 851.
84. *Ibid.*
85. Thoburn and Wright, *Oklahoma — A History,* 1:65; Office of Indian Affairs, Commission Report, 1858, 141, and 1859, 159.
86. Foreman, *Advancing the Frontier,* 55.
87. *Ibid.,* 53.
88. John P. Brown, *Old Frontiers,* 511.
89. A. J. Houston Papers.
90. *Ibid.*
91. *Ibid.*
92. Thoburn and Wright, *Oklahoma — A History,* 1:87.
93. *Ibid.*

7. *Cherokee Civil War*

1. Foreman, *Five Civilized Tribes,* 321–324.
2. John Rogers Papers, Gilcrease Museum.
3. 5th Annual Report, Bureau of Ethnology, 297.
4. *Ibid.,* 160–161.
5. T. U. Taylor, *Life of Chisholm,* 6.
6. 5th Annual Report, Bureau of Ethnology, 280–282.
7. *Ibid.,* 193.
8. Thomas V. Parker, *The Cherokees,* 170.
9. Thoburn and Wright, *Oklahoma — A History,* 4:257.
10. *Ibid.,* 258.
11. *Ibid.*
12. 5th Annual Report, Bureau of Ethnology, 301.
13. A. J. Houston Papers.
14. *Ibid.*
15. *Ibid.*
16. John Ross Papers, Gilcrease Museum.
17. Foreman, *Advancing the Frontier,* 301.
18. Foreman, *Five Civilized Tribes,* 308.
19. 5th Annual Report, Bureau of Ethnology, 326–327.
20. Foreman, *Advancing the Frontier,* 301.
21. A. J. Houston Papers.
22. Foreman, *Five Civilized Tribes,* 153.
23. 5th Annual Report, Bureau of Ethnology, 321.
24. Josiah Gregg, *Commerce of the Prairies,* 231–232.
25. A. J. Houston Papers.
26. *Ibid.*
27. Gregg, *Commerce of the Prairies,* 232.
28. Foreman, *Advancing the Frontier,* 218.
29. Gregg, *Commerce of the Prairies,* 231.
30. *Ibid.,* 232.

31. Foreman, *Advancing the Frontier*, 219.
32. Indian Archives, Oklahoma Historical Society.
33. A. J. Houston Papers.
34. *Ibid.*
35. *Ibid.*
36. Foreman, *Advancing the Frontier*, 218.
37. A. J. Houston Papers.
38. Foreman, *Five Civilized Tribes*, 79.
39. Indian Archives, Oklahoma Historical Society; *Arkansas Gazette*, August 21, 1839.
40. Foreman, *Five Civilized Tribes*, 136.
41. *Chron. Okla.*, 8:417.
42. R. N. Richardson, *Comanche Barrier*, 109–111.
43. *Ibid.*, 113.
44. A. J. Houston Papers.
45. Gregg, *Commerce of the Prairies*, 396.
46. *National Intelligencer*, December 1840.
47. 5th Annual Report, Bureau of Ethnology, 297.
48. Foreman, *Advancing the Frontier*, 97–98.
49. *Ibid.*, 100; Thoburn and Wright, *Oklahoma — A History*, 1:63.
50. *Ibid.*
51. *Ibid.*
52. *Ibid.*
53. Foreman, *Five Civilized Tribes*, 324.
54. *Ibid.*
55. Crane, *Life of Houston*, 349–359.
56. *Telegraph and Texas Register*, December 1842.
57. A. J. Houston Papers.

8. *Sam Houston's Trouble-shooter*

1. Foreman, *Advancing the Frontier*, 203.
2. *Ibid.*
3. *The Northern Standard*, 1842.
4. Crane, *Life of Houston*, 140.
5. *Ibid.*, 334.
6. *Ibid.*, 362–364.
7. Walter Prescott Webb, *The Great Plains*, 172–173.
8. *Washington Texian* and *Brazos Farmer*, April 15, 1843.
9. Indian Papers, Texas State Library, vol. 8.
10. Crane, *Life of Houston*, 344; *Handbook of Texas*, 2:551.
11. *Ibid.*
12. A. J. Houston Papers.
13. *Handbook of Texas*, 2:790.
14. Foreman, *Advancing the Frontier*, 102.
15. A. J. Houston Papers.
16. Office of Indian Affairs, Annual Report.
17. R. N. Richardson, *Comanche Barrier*, 123.
18. Foreman, *Advancing the Frontier*, 171–172.

19. R. N. Richardson, *Comanche Barrier*, 125.
20. Indian Papers, Texas State Library, vol. 8.
21. *Telegraph and Texas Register*, October 26, 1844.
22. Indian Papers, Texas State Library.
23. Foreman, *Five Civilized Tribes*, 371–374.
24. *Chron. Okla.*, 8:176.
25. Foreman, *Five Civilized Tribes*, 374.
26. T. U. Taylor, *Life of Chisholm*, 8.
27. R. N. Richardson, *Comanche Barrier*, 141; Thoburn and Wright, *Oklahoma — A History*, 1:80.
28. Journal of Elijah Hicks; R. N. Richardson, *Comanche Barrier*, 141.
29. A. J. Houston Papers.
30. Thoburn and Wright, *Oklahoma — A History*, 1:80.
31. T. U. Taylor, *Life of Chisholm*, 18.
32. Messages and Papers of the President, Polk's Administration.
33. A. J. Houston Papers.

9. *Gold Rush Mania*

1. Foreman, *Five Civilized Tribes*, 264.
2. Thoburn and Wright, *Oklahoma — A History*, 13:88.
3. Foreman, *Advancing the Frontier*, 246.
4. *Ibid.*
5. R. N. Richardson, *Comanche Barrier*, 161.
6. Foreman, *Advancing the Frontier*, 246.
7. *Ibid.*
8. Biography of Thomas Hart Benton, Library of Congress.
9. *Chron. Okla.*, 12:76.
10. R. N. Richardson, *Comanche Barrier*, 210.
11. A. J. Houston Papers.
12. R. N. Richardson, *Comanche Barrier*, 163.
13. Crane, *Life of Houston*, 375–393.
14. *Ibid.*
15. A. J. Houston Papers.
16. *Ibid.*
17. Foreman, *Advancing the Frontier*, 246; Thoburn and Wright, *Oklahoma — A History*, 1:88.
18. A. J. Houston Papers.
19. *Chron. Okla.*, 62, #5.
20. A. J. Houston Papers.
21. *Ibid.*
22. Exec. Doc. 78, Sen. 33rd Congress, 2d session; Pacific Railway Survey Report.
23. Thoburn and Wright, *Oklahoma — A History*, 13:282.
24. Office of Indian Affairs, Commission Report, 1854, 238, #25.
25. John W. Whitefield, Agent. OIA Report, 2:600.
26. A. J. Houston Papers.

10. *Texas Trails and Trials*

1. Crane, *Life of Houston*, 413.
2. Thrall, *History of Texas*, 2:188.
3. Foreman, *Five Civilized Tribes*, 265.
4. A. J. Houston Papers.
5. *Leon Pioneer*, August 16, 1854.
6. *Arkansas Gazette*, June 21, 1854.
7. Sen. Ex. Doc. 134th Cong., 1st Sess., Part I: 502.
8. Crane, *Life of Houston*, 433–434.
9. *Ibid.*, 313 and 433.
10. *Chron. Okla.*, 3:103.
11. Foreman, *Advancing the Frontier*, 280.
12. *Northern Standard*, November 26, 1856; *American Military History*, 180; War Department Files, Camels.
13. R. N. Richardson, *Comanche Barrier*, 159.
14. A. J. Houston Papers.
15. *Dallas Herald*, April 7, 1857; *Northern Standard*, March 25, 1857.
16. R. N. Richardson, *Comanche Barrier*, 191.
17. A. J. Houston Papers.
18. Thoburn and Wright, *Oklahoma — A History*, 21:282.
19. *Chron. Okla.*, 12:75–83.
20. Thoburn and Wright, *Oklahoma — A History*, 21:290; Foreman, *Advancing the Frontier*, 286–288.
21. R. N. Richardson, *Comanche Barrier*, 238–245.
22. Foreman, *Five Civilized Tribes*.
23. Indian Papers, Texas State Library.
24. A. J. Houston Papers.
25. Foreman, *Five Civilized Tribes*, 144.
26. Crane, *Life of Houston*, 231.

11. *Jesse Chisholm: Bigger Than War*

1. Crane, *Life of Houston*, 219–220, 233.
2. *Epic Century*, (Naylor: February 1938), 12.
3. Crane, *Life of Houston*, 234.
4. 5th Annual Report, Bureau of Ethnology, 328.
5. *Ibid.*, 328–329.
6. Thoburn and Wright, *Oklahoma — A History*, 1:311.
7. Albert Pike Papers, Arkansas Historical Society.
8. Fischer, *Civil War Era in Indian Territory*, 118.
9. *Ibid.*, 114–118.
10. *Ibid.*
11. 5th Annual Report, Bureau of Ethnology, 328.
12. *Ibid.*
13. *Ibid.*, 329.
14. *Ibid.*, 328.
15. Fischer, *Civil War Era in Indian Territory*, 89, 104.
16. *Ibid.*, 104.

17. *Ibid.*, 89, 104.
18. *Ibid.*, 102.
19. *Ibid.*, 329.
20. Thoburn and Wright, 1:327.
21. R. N. Richardson, *Comanche Barrier*, 284–285.
22. Thoburn and Wright, *Oklahoma — A History*, 2:325–329.
23. *Ibid.*, 279.
24. A. J. Houston Papers.
25. *Ibid.*
26. T. U. Taylor, *Life of Chisholm*, 16.
27. A. M. Williams, *Sam Houston*, 354.
28. Fischer, *Civil War Era in Indian Territory*, 119.

12. *Reconstruction: Aftermath of War*

1. Office of Indian Affairs, Commission Report, 1867, 302.
2. Fischer, *Civil War Era in Indian Territory*, 104.
3. *Ibid.*, 105.
4. *Ibid.*
5. *Ibid.*, 107.
6. *American Military History*, 309.
7. R. N. Richardson, *Comanche Barrier*, 296.
8. *Ibid.*, 288.
9. *Ibid.;* Thoburn and Wright, *Oklahoma — A History*, 1:384.
10. Mildred P. Mayhall, *The Kiowas*, 205.
11. *Ibid.*, 250.
12. Thoburn and Wright, *Oklahoma — A History*, 1:384; R. N. Richardson, *Comanche Barrier*, 288–289.
13. Thoburn and Wright, *Oklahoma — A History*, 1:384; Mayhall, *The Kiowas*, 204.
14. R. N. Richardson, *Comanche Barrier*, 287.
15. Mayhall, *The Kiowas*, 206.
16. Office of Indian Affairs, Commission Report, 1867.
17. R. N. Richardson, *Comanche Barrier*, 292–293.
18. Office of Indian Affairs, Commission Report, 1868.
19. *Ibid.;* Mayhall, *The Kiowas*, 206.
20. Mayhall, *The Kiowas*, 207.
21. *Ibid.*, 249.
22. 5th Annual Report, Bureau of Ethnology, 348.
23. Mayhall, *The Kiowas*, 307.
24. Oklahoma Historical Society, Indian Affairs, 1954 Report.
25. Thrall, *History of Texas*.
26. Wayne Gard, *The Chisholm Trail*, 50–51.
27. *Chron. Okla.*, 9:300.
28. A. J. Houston Papers.
29. *Ibid.*
30. R. N. Richardson, *Comanche Barrier*, 297.

13. The Chisholm Trail

1. Wayne Gard, *The Chisholm Trail*, 72.
2. *Historic Sketches of the Cattle Trade*, 70–78.
3. *Ibid.*, 24.
4. *Chron. Okla.*, 24:279.
5. *Historic Sketches of the Cattle Trade*, 70–78.
6. Henry Stuart, *Conquering Our Great American Plains*, 366.
7. *Historic Sketches of the Cattle Trade*, 70–78.
8. *Ibid.*
9. *Chron. Okla.*, 8:417.

14. Grand Finale

1. *Chron. Okla.*, 2:116.
2. *American Military History*, 306–307.
3. *Ibid.*
4. *Ibid.*
5. Thoburn and Wright, *Oklahoma — A History*, 2:857–858, appendix.
6. A. J. Houston Papers.
7. R. N. Richardson, *Comanche Barrier*, 298; Thoburn and Wright, *Oklahoma — A History*, 2:858, appendix.
8. R. N. Richardson, *Comanche Barrier*, 297; Thoburn and Wright, *Oklahoma — A History*, 2:857–858, appendix.
9. R. N. Richardson, *Comanche Barrier*, 298.
10. Thoburn and Wright, *Oklahoma — A History*, 2:858, appendix.
11. *Ibid.*, 13:328.
12. A. J. Houston Papers.
13. *Ibid.*
14. *Ibid.*
15. *Ibid.*
16. *Ibid.*
17. *Missouri Democrat*, October 14, 1867.
18. *Chron. Okla.*, 13:25–26.
19. *Lawrence Journal*, October 12, 1867.
20. *Ibid.*
21. A. J. Houston Papers.
22. *Ibid.*
23. *Ibid.*
24. R. N. Richardson, *Comanche Barrier*, 298, 302.
25. *Ibid.*
26. *Ibid.*
27. *Ibid.*
28. *Ibid.*
29. *Ibid.*
30. *Ibid.*
31. Thoburn and Wright, *Oklahoma — A History*, 2:857, appendix.
32. *Ibid.*
33. *Ibid.*

34. R. N. Richardson, *Comanche Barrier*, 302.
35. *Chron. Okla.*, 2:98–103.
36. *Ibid.*
37. A. J. Houston Papers.
38. *Missouri Democrat*, July 22, 1867.
39. *Ibid.*
40. *Ibid.*
41. *Ibid.*
42. *Lawrence Journal*, October 12, 1867.
43. *Ibid.*
44. *Missouri Democrat*, October 18, 1867.
45. Office of Indian Affairs, Commission Report, Medicine Lodge, 1867.
46. *Chron. Okla.*, 2:117.
47. A. J. Houston Papers.
48. *Chron. Okla.*, 2:116.
49. R. N. Richardson, *Comanche Barrier*, 312.
50. *Ibid.*

15. *Immemorial*

1. A. J. Houston Papers.
2. T. U. Taylor, *Life of Chisholm*, 8–10.

Bibliography

In addition to the following sources, the author consulted various and extensive files from these archival collections:

Arkansas Historical Association.
Clayton Library, Houston, Texas.
Eugene C. Barker Texas History Center, University of Texas at Austin.
Gilcrease Institute, Reference Library, Tulsa, Oklahoma.
Houston Public Library.
Kansas Historical Society.
Lawson–McGhee Library, Knoxville, Tennessee.
Library of Congress, Manuscript Division, Washington, D.C.
Louisiana State Historical Society, New Orleans, Louisiana.
National Archives, Washington, D.C.
Oklahoma University Library, Phillips Collection.
Rosenberg Library, Galveston, Texas.
Sam Houston State University Library, Huntsville, Texas.
Tennessee State Library, Indian Archives, Nashville, Tennessee.
Texas State Library, Texas Governors' Papers, Indian Papers, Austin, Texas.
U.S. Adjutant General's Records.
U.S. Office of Indian Affairs.

Abel, Annie Heloise. *James S. Calhoun, Official Correspondence at Santa Fe.* Washington, D.C.: 1915.
Andreas, A. T. *History of Kansas.* Wichita, Kansas: 1883.
Artrip, Louise, and Fullen Artrip. *Memoirs of Daniel Fore (Jim) Chisholm and the Chisholm Trail.* 1949.
Atkinson, M. Jourdan. *Indians of the Southwest.* San Antonio: Naylor Co., 1958.
Austin City Gazette. Austin, Texas. 1839.
Bancroft, H. H. *History of the North Mexican States and Texas.* 2 vols. San Francisco: 1883 and 1889.
Barker, Eugene C. *The Life of Stephen F. Austin, Founder of Texas.* Nashville and Dallas: 1925.

————, ed. *The Austin Papers*. 3 vols. Austin: University of Texas Press, 1927.

Bieber, Ralph P., ed. *The Southwestern Trails to California, 1849*. Glendale, California: 1931.

————. *Journal of a Santa Fe Trader*. Glendale, California: 1931.

Brown, John H. *Indian Wars and Pioneers of Texas*. Austin: L. E. Daniell, 1896.

————. *A History of Texas*. 2 vols. St. Louis: 1892.

Brown, John P. *Old Frontiers*. Kingsport, Tennessee: 1938.

Bruce, Henry. *Life of General Houston*. New York: Dodd, Mead & Co., 1891.

Bureau of Ethnology, *Annual Reports*. Vols. 1–17.

Catlin, George. *Letters and Notes on the Manners, Customs, and Condition of the North American Indians*. 2 vols. Philadelphia: 1857.

Chronicles of Oklahoma. Oklahoma City, Oklahoma.

Crane, William C. *The Life and Select Literary Remains of Sam Houston of Texas*. Philadelphia: 1884.

Creel, George. *Sam Houston: Colossus in Buckskin*. New York: 1928.

Crockett, David. *Exploits and Adventures in Texas*. New York: 1845.

Cullum, George W. *Biographical Register of the Officers and Graduates of the U.S. Military Academy*. Vol. 1. New York: 1868.

Cushman, H. B. *History of the Choctaw, Chickasaw, and Natches Indians*. Greenville, Texas: 1899.

Dale, Edward Everett. *Cherokee Cavaliers*. Norman, Oklahoma: 1939.

Dallas Herald. August 21, 1858; April 27, 1872; July 22, 1872; and November 11, 1876.

Davis, John B. "The Life and Work of Sequoyah." *Chronicles of Oklahoma*. Vol. 8 (June 1930).

de Cordova, Jacob. *Texas: Her Resources and Her Public Men*. Philadelphia: 1858.

Derby, J. C. *The Life of Sam Houston*. New York: 1855.

Drago, Harry Sinclair. *The Great American Cattle Trails*. New York: Dodd, Mead & Co., 1965.

————. *The Steamboaters*. New York: Bramhall House.

Durant, John Wesley. Personal papers, owned by Birdie Durant.

Duval, John C. *Early Times in Texas*. Austin: H. P. N. Gammel & Co., 1892.

Edward, D. B. *History of Texas*. Cincinnati: J. A. James & Co., 1836.

Elliot, Sarah Barnwell. *Sam Houston*. Boston: 1900.

Featherstonehaugh, G. W. *Excursion Through the Slave States*. New York: 1844.

Fischer, Leroy H. *The Civil War Era in the Indian Territory*. Journal of the West: 1973.

Foote, Henry Stuart. *Texas and Texans*. 2 vols. Philadelphia: Thomas, Cowperthwait & Co., 1841.

Foreman, Grant. *Advancing the Frontier*. Norman, Oklahoma: 1933.

————. *The Five Civilized Tribes.* Norman, Oklahoma: 1934.
————. *Pioneer Days in the Early Southwest.* Cedar Rapids: 1926.
————. *Indian Removal.* Norman, Oklahoma: 1932.
————. *Indians and Pioneers.* New Haven: 1930.
————. *A Traveler in Indian Territory.* Cedar Rapids: 1930.
————. Files with Oklahoma Historical Society.
Fort Smith Herald. Fort Smith, Arkansas. 1839 issues.
Friend, Llerena B. *Sam Houston: The Great Designer.* Austin: University of Texas Press, 1954.
Frontier Times. Published by J. Marvin Hunter. Bandera, Texas.
Gard, Wayne. *The Chisholm Trail.* Norman: University of Oklahoma Press, 1954.
Gerson, Noel B. *Kit Carson: Folk Hero and Man.* New York: Doubleday, 1964.
Gregg, Josiah. *Commerce of the Prairies.* Cleveland: 1904–08.
Hall, Ted Byron. *Oklahoma Indian Territory.* Fort Worth.
Harper's New Monthly Magazine.
Henry, Stuart. *Conquering Our Great American Plains.* New York: E. P. Dutton Co.
Hogan, William Ransom. *The Texas Republic: A Social and Economic History.* Norman: University of Oklahoma Press, 1946.
Holley, Mary Austin. *Texas.* Lexington, Kentucky: J. Clarke & Co., 1836.
Houston, Andrew Jackson. *Texas Independence.* Anson Jones Press, 1938.
————. Private manuscripts and papers.
Hunt, Lenoir. *My Master.* Dallas: 1940.
Irving, Washington. *A Tour of the Prairies.* Annotated by J. B. Thoburn and G. C. Wells. Oklahoma City, Oklahoma: 1955.
James, Marquis. *The Raven: A Biography of Sam Houston.* Indianapolis: The Bobbs-Merrill Co., 1929.
Jameson, Henry B. *Miracle of the Chisholm Trail.* 1967.
Jones, Anson. *Memoranda and Official Correspondence Relating to the Republic of Texas.* New York: D. Appleton & Co., 1859.
————. Papers. Texas State Historical Association.
Jones, Douglas C. *The Treaty of Medicine Lodge.* Oklahoma Press.
Kansas: A Guide to the Sunflower State. New York: 1939.
Kappler, Charles J. *Indian Affairs, Laws and Treaties.* 3 vols. Washington, D.C.: Government Printing Office, 1903.
Kemp, L. W. Papers. San Jacinto Museum.
Kendall, George W. *Narrative of the Texan Santa Fe Expedition.* 2 vols. London: Henry Washbourne, 1847.
Lackey, Vinson. *The Chouteaus and the Founding of Salina.*
Lamar, Mirabeau B. *The Papers of Mirabeau Buonaparte Lamar.* 6 vols. Austin: 1921–1927.
Leon Pioneer. Published by William D. Wood. 1854.

Lester, Charles Edwards. *Sam Houston and His Republic.* New York: Burgess, Stringer & Co., 1846.

Lowe, P. G. *Five Years a Dragoon.* Kansas City: 1906.

Lumpkin, Governor Wilson. *The Removal of the Cherokees From Georgia, 1827–1838.* 2 Vols. New York: 1907.

McAllister, J. Gilbert. "Kiowa-Apache Social Organization." *Social Anthropology of North American Tribes.* 1937.

McCaleb, W.·F. *Memoirs of John H. Reagan.* New York: Neale Publishing Co., 1906.

McCall, Gen. Albert A. *Letters From the Frontier.* Oklahoma Historical Society.

McReynolds, Edwin C. *Oklahoma — A History of the Sooner State.*

Magruder, John Bankhead. Papers. Rosenberg Library, Galveston, Texas.

Marcy, Randolph B. *Thirty Years of Army Life on the Border.* New York: 1866.

Missouri Democrat. 1867.

Niles Register. Baltimore and Washington, D.C.

Northern Standard. Published at Clarksville, Texas. 1842–62. (Copies in Eugene C. Barker Texas History Center, University of Texas at Austin.)

Nuttall, Thomas. *A Journal of Travels Into the Arkansas Territory.* Originally published 1821. Reprint. Norman: University of Oklahoma Press, 1980.

Olmsted, F. L. *A Journey Through Texas.* New York: Dix, Edwards & Co., 1857.

Pacific Railroad Survey Reports. 13 vols. Washington: 1855–60.

Parker, Thomas V. *The Cherokee Indians.* New York: 1907.

Pennybacker, Mrs. Anna J. H. *A New History of Texas for Schools.* Tyler, Texas: 1888.

Perrine, Fred S., and Grant Foreman. *The Journal of Hugh Evans — Dragoon, 1834–35.*

Phelan, James. *American Commonwealths: Tennessee.* Boston: 1887.

Pike, Albert. Papers. Arkansas Historical Association, 1917.

Ramsdell, Charles Wm. *Texas in the Confederacy, 1861–65.*

Reagan, John H., "The Expulsion of the Cherokees From East Texas." *Quarterly of the Texas State Historical Association,* vol. 1 (1897).

Red, George Plunkett. *The Medicine Men of Texas.* Houston: 1930.

Richardson, R. N. *The Comanche Barrier to South Plains Settlement.* Glendale, California: 1933.

Richardson, T. C. "Chisholm Trail." *Handbook of Texas.* Vol. 1. Austin: Texas State Historical Association, 1954.

Ridings, Sam P. *The Chisholm Trail.* Guthrie, Oklahoma: Co-operative Pub. Co., 1936.

Roosevelt, Theodore. *Thomas H. Benton — American Statesman.*

Russell, I. C. *Rivers of North America.* 1898.

St. Louis Republican. July 25, 1858.

Smith, Ashbel. *Reminiscences of the Texas Republic.* Galveston: 1876.

Smithwick, Noah. *The Evolution of a State.* Austin: Gammel Book Co., 1900.
Southern Historical Publication Society. *The South in the Building of a Nation.* 12 vols. Richmond: 1909.
Southwestern Historical Quarterly. 1927–1928.
Starr, Emmet. *History of the Cherokee Indians.* Oklahoma City, Oklahoma: 1921.
Taylor, Alfred. *Medicine Lodge Peace Council.* Chronicles of Oklahoma: 1924.
Taylor, T. U. *Life of Jesse Chisholm.* Bandera, Texas: 1939.
————. *The Chisholm Trail and Other Routes.* 1936.
Telegraph and Texas Register. Houston, Texas. 1835–1849.
Terrell, A. W. *Recollections of General Sam Houston.* Published by Southwestern Historical Quarterly: 1912.
Texas Almanac. Galveston: 1856–1857.
Texas Republican. Marshall, Texas. 1849–1869.
Texas State Gazette. Austin, Texas. 1849–1855.
Thoburn, J. B., and M. H. Wright. *Oklahoma — A History of the State and Its People.* 4 vols. New York: 1929.
Thoburn, J. B. *Standard History of Oklahoma.* 1916.
Thomas, David Y., ed. *Arkansas and Its People.* 4 vols. 1931.
Thrall, H. S. *History of Texas.* 1885.
U.S. Official Records of the Union and Confederate Armies. Series I-IV.
Ward, H. G. *Mexico.* London: 1829.
Washington Texian. 1843.
Webb, Walter P. *The Great Plains.* New York: 1931.
West Texas Historical Association Yearbook. Vols. I–IV (1928).
Whipple, Lt. A. W. *Report of Explorations for a Railway Route Near the Thirty-fifth Parallel of North Latitude.* Washington: 1853–54.
Wilbarger, John W. *Indian Depredations in Texas.* Austin: 1889.
Williams, Alfred M. *Sam Houston and the War of Independence in Texas.* Boston: 1893.
Wood, William D. *Life and Times of John Wesley Durant.* Leon County, Texas: 1866.
Yoakum, Henderson. *History of Texas.* 2 vols. New York: 1855.

JESSE CHISHOLM
BORN   1805
DIED MAR 4 1868
—
NO ONE LEFT HIS HOME
COLD OR HUNGRY

Inscription on Chisholm's tombstone at Johnny Lefthand Springs, Oklahoma. The grave marker was donated by schoolchildren of Oklahoma as an expression of their esteem for this much loved patriot.

IN HONOR OF
JESSE CHISHOLM
1806–1868

PIONEER
PATRIOT
PEACEMAKER
PATHFINDER
PROPHET
PROTECTOR

T. U. Taylor beside the plaque he helped to erect in 1938 to commemorate the life of Jesse Chisholm. The scene was the J. Marvin Hunter's Museum and offices of his Frontier Times *magazine at Bandera, Texas.*

— Eugene C. Barker Texas History Center

Chisholm Tavern, Knoxville, Tennessee, built 1792 by John Chisholm, grandfather of Jesse Chisholm.

— Eugene C. Barker Texas History Center

Gravestone of Talahina Rogers, aunt of Jesse Chisholm and wife of Gen. Sam Houston, Fort Gibson, Oklahoma.

— Eugene C. Barker Texas History Center

Julia Chisholm Davenport, granddaughter of Jesse Chisholm, at ceremonies honoring Chisholm at Bandera, Texas, May 1938.

— Eugene C. Barker Texas History Center

Dignitaries assembled to pay homage to Jesse Chisholm at Bandera, Texas, in May 1938. Left to right, T. U. Taylor, organizer of the tribute, Dave Dillingham, Julia Chisholm Davenport, granddaughter of Chisholm, Governor James V. Allred, and J. Marvin Hunter, whose publication, Frontier Times, *devoted much space to Chisholm fact and fantasy.*

— Eugene C. Barker Texas History Center

Back porch of Andrew Jackson Houston's bayshore home at LaPorte, Texas, overlooking Trinity Bay. From 1935 to 1941, the author, Ralph Cushman, spent many hours on the porch with Colonel Houston listening as the old storyteller brought history to life.

— Eugene C. Barker Texas History Center

The occasion of Andrew Jackson Houston being announced as the appointed successor to U.S. Senator Morris Sheppard, who died earlier, by Governor W. Lee O'Daniel at La Porte, Texas, in 1941. Left to right: Mrs. W. Lee O'Daniel, Margaret Houston, A. J. Houston, Ariadne Houston, and O'Daniel. Houston was sworn in at Washington, D.C. and served three weeks before he died in June 1941.

— Eugene C. Barker Texas History Center

Col. Andrew Jackson Houston, last surviving son of Sam Houston, at his La Porte, Texas, home in 1941, with Governor W. Lee O'Daniel. The governor was at La Porte to announce the appointment of Houston to fill the unexpired term of Morris Sheppard as U.S. senator from Texas. Houston would occupy the same desk as his illustrious father had used nearly a century earlier.

— Eugene C. Barker Texas History Center

Ten Years Ago at San Jacinto Battleground

1937 SAN JACINTO BATTLEGROUND CORNERSTONE CEREMONY
In April 1937, at San Jacinto Battleground, Jesse H. Jones applied the first trowel of
mortar on the cornerstone of the San Jacinto Memorial shaft, for which he had done so
much to make a reality as a lasting monument to freedom for the people of Texas. Left
to right: Mr. Jones, Andrew Jackson Houston, Ralph B. Cushman (the author), and
Walter H. Woodul, then lieutenant governor of Texas.

— Houston Chronicle

Index